C000295808

Celebrity Worship

Celebrity Worship provides an introduction to the fascinating study of celebrity culture and religion. The book argues for celebrity as a foundational component for any consideration of the relationship between Religion, Media and Culture. Celebrity worship is seen as a vibrant and interactive discourse of the sacred self in contemporary society.

Topics discussed include:

- Celebrity culture.
- Celebrity worship and project of the self as the new sacred.
- Social media and the democratisation of celebrity.
- Reactions to celebrity death.
- Celebrities as theologians of the self.
- Christian celebrity.

Using contemporary case studies, such as lifestyle television, the religious vision of Oprah Winfrey and the death of David Bowie, this book is a gripping read for those with an interest in celebrity culture, cultural studies, media studies, religion in the media and the role of religion in society.

Pete Ward is Professor of Practical Theology at Durham University, UK; NLA University College, Bergen, Norway; and MF The Norwegian School of Theology, Oslo, Norway.

Media, Religion and Culture

Series Editors:
Stewart Hoover, *University of Colorado, Boulder, USA*
Jolyon Mitchell, *University of Edinburgh, UK*
Jenna Supp-Montgomerie, *University of Iowa, USA*

For more information about this series, please visit: https://www.routledge.com/Media-Religion-and-Culture/book-series/MRC

Celebrity Worship

Pete Ward

Routledge
Taylor & Francis Group

LONDON AND NEW YORK

First published 2020
by Routledge
2 Park Square, Milton Park, Abingdon, Oxon OX14 4RN

and by Routledge
52 Vanderbilt Avenue, New York, NY 10017

Routledge is an imprint of the Taylor & Francis Group, an informa business

© 2020 Pete Ward

British Library Cataloguing in Publication Data
A catalogue record for this book is available from the British Library

Library of Congress Cataloging-in-Publication Data
A catalog record has been requested for this book

ISBN: 978-1-138-58708-3 (hbk)
ISBN: 978-1-138-58709-0 (pbk)
ISBN: 978-0-429-50378-8 (ebk)

Typeset in Bembo
by Taylor & Francis Books

Printed and bound by CPI Group (UK) Ltd, Croydon, CR0 4YY

Contents

Boxes

Introduction

Celebrities are all pervasive, one might even say omnipresent. They are the people that feature in every aspect of media representation. A celebrity is then a person who is mediated. Mediation describes the complex ways in which, through technology, media industries and social relationships, individuals are actively engaged in processes of production, representation and consumption. The explosion in media platforms and new technologies of communication has had one constant. Whatever the format or device, the vast majority of coverage will centre around people. When we consume media, we consume people, and these people are celebrities, or rather they are transformed into celebrities as they participate in processes of production, representation and consumption. People are metamorphosed into celebrities by their presence in the media, and by the way that each of us participate in developing relationships with them as a result. The celebrity phenomenon is one of the defining characteristics of our time.

Celebrity has ceased to be the preserve of the famous or of an elite. With the mobile phone, the selfie and social media, celebrity has been democratised. The mediation of the self means that each of us share in celebrity culture. Daily life is interwoven with media technologies, and identity is something that is performed both online and offline. Through our various feeds and posts, we participate in what might be called the 'celebrification of everyday life.' The 'self' is performed daily on media platforms such as: Instagram, dating websites, Facebook, Snapchat or Twitter. Each of us, as a result, has become as attentive to likes, shares, comments and various emoji, as much as we are to smiles and hellos. Paying attention to how our lives are presented through social media has become a preoccupation that is moderated and adjusted through the pervading sense that we have an audience who are watching us. As they are watching us, we are also watching them. The flow of stories, pictures and posts that we swipe across the phone are welcomed because they are a means to make sense of ourselves and others. All of this taken together means that the mediation of the self and hence celebrity has become a central aspect of all our lives.

Making sense of Celebrity Worship: David Attenborough

The idea that celebrity has somehow taken the place of religion has become commonplace. Celebrities are routinely described as divine or semi-divine figures, and fans are said to be worshipping their idols. Celebrity is spoken of as a cult. Celebrity Worship, it seems, is a widespread phenomenon that many see as having its roots in the decline of formal, or traditional, kinds of religion. In considering the extent to which celebrity might, or might not, be religious in nature, it is useful to focus on a particular individual. David Attenborough is probably not someone who immediately comes to mind when the word celebrity is used. He seems to be a million miles away from the reality television stars, pop singers, YouTube influencers, and game show contestants, that feature in the celebrity magazines and on Instagram. Thinking about Celebrity Worship through someone like David Attenborough is helpful precisely because he is not seen as part of the celebrity world. It is hard to dismiss him as inconsequential, fabricated or shallow. At the same time, he is deeply influential, and his media output has had an amazing impact on both individuals, and on society as a whole. Nowhere is this more evident than with his remarkable television series *Blue Planet II*.

In 2017, the BBC nature documentary *Blue Planet II* was broadcast in the UK, and across Europe. By the end of 2018, the programme had been shown in almost every region of the world, including both the USA and China. *Blue Planet II* was quite simply a game changer in the global awareness of the catastrophic impact that the use of plastic is having on our natural environment. Episode 7 was entitled, *Our Blue Planet*, and it was a hard-hitting account of the pollution of the oceans, and the harmful effects of microplastics on the fish, mammals and birds. Viewers were shown the tragic effects of ingesting plastic on all kinds of animals, and, in particular, the terrible effects that discarded plastic bags were having. The images of dolphins playing with plastic in the sea, and an albatross feeding a plastic bag to her chicks, did more for the environmental cause than any number of scientific reports. The effect that these images had was immediate. Companies, supermarkets and politicians began to respond to an upsurge of pressure from the public to change policies around plastic bags, food wrapping and single use plastic bottles. Imogen Calderwood, writing in the *Global Citizen*, reported that, 88 per cent of those people who had seen the programme had changed their behaviour.[1]

It would be impossible to understand the importance of *Blue Planet II* without taking into account its presenter David Attenborough. It is 'Sir David' that is our guide to the amazing creatures of the sea. His voice takes us to places of wonder, and lays before us things that have never been seen before. Through his presence, close to the animals and the birds, we are also drawn close to them and we actively embrace this experience. The audience is shown the harmful effects of plastics, but we are reassured and convinced, because we have developed a relationship with David Attenborough over the years. His is a voice from our childhood, present on the television before most of us can remember. The phrase, 'national treasure,' seems to have been made for him. He is someone who has given his life to bringing to us the marvellous beauty of the natural world, and it is because of his authenticity built up over decades on the television, that millions of people were motivated to adjust their life-styles, and to campaign to try to rid the world of harmful plastics. However, Sir David is who he is because of the ways in which his audience over decades have chosen to engage with his message. A 'national treasure' is not simply made by the media but by the nation.

There are many aspects of David Attenborough's work as a broadcaster that might be considered similar to religion. He is a guide that leads his viewers into knowledge. His acceptance as an authoritative figure is similar to that of a minister, or a religious teacher. In his programmes, the natural world is por-trayed as something that is not only beautiful, but full of wonder. Humans are located as both a part of this overarching natural environment, but also as a threat to the planet. As a consequence, there is a strong ethical dimension to his nature programming that emphasises the responsibility of individuals. Despite these parallels, it is a stretch to argue that what is taking place in *Blue Planet II* is a new kind of religion or a cult. The active participation of his audience in consuming the programmes is deeply significant but it does not constitute a religious community. Nevertheless, David Attenborough and the shows he presents, do serve as a helpful guide to understanding the key dynamics within Celebrity Worship.

Blue Planet II is an example of one of the central elements of celebrity culture, i.e. that the primary content of media is people. Although the programme is about the sea and the creatures within it, the package works because of the presenter. David Attenborough is the beating heart of the programme. He is the one who we embrace and welcome as someone who draws us in and takes us out, to see things we have never seen before. Although the programmes are about the natural world, it is the person of the presenter that provides the emotional connection to what is being shown. David Attenborough, as the wise teacher, is central to the persua-siveness of this message, but his presence is more important than this. He does not just present a message, he invites the audience into the experience of what is being shown. The engagement of the audience and their decision to participate in the show comes from how he functions as a representative of the viewer. Quite simply, because he is there, we are there. Who he is, and how we relate to him, undergo a transformation and this is what is meant by Celebrity Worship. This is a relationship in which the representation of the television programme must be matched by the different ways that audience members chose to share in the experience. There are then two sides to the process of mediation in Celebrity Worship. There is the pre-sence of an individual, such as David Attenborough, in media representation and there are the varied ways in which, through identification and participation, mem-bers of the audience choose to make meaning out of what they are viewing. The metamorphosis implied in Celebrity Worship brings about a transformation in the dynamics of relationship that is not unique to *Blue Planet II*, it is a characteristic of media and the ways in which audiences are actively engaged in generating their own meanings. One of the reasons for this is that whatever media platform we engage with, at root we are taken up with individuals. People form the primary content of every kind of media and the people that we relate to through the media are celebrities.

It's not about them, it's about us: celebrity and the self

Celebrity Worship is fundamentally about the self. It does not describe a religion that is concerned with the worship of celebrities as semi-divine beings. No one worships David Attenborough, and yet he represents something that is deeply moving and meaningful. Viewers have a relationship with him, such that when he issues an ethical and environmental challenge, they chose to participate and as a result motivate themselves to act. This relationship is entirely generated by his presence in the media. He is a mediated person. Through the media his presence has been magnified, and millions of people around the world know who he is, and as they actively consume media in some way, they make him a part of their lives. It is this connection that I want to argue is the first and primary meaning of the term, Celebrity Worship. The meaning of David Attenborough, then, is not about who he is, but about who he is to us or rather what we make him into as a part of our lives. Media processes generate an association between audiences and celebrities that are charged with an energy. This energy does not simply come from the processes of production and representation, it is also generated by the different ways in which individuals and groups choose to make sense of themselves in relation to celebrities. Media processes are therefore not determinative or uniquely powerful. They gather their charge from the active participation and creativity of individuals as they construct their sense of self in and through the narratives and images that form the primary content of media representation. The religious analogy that is implied in the term Celebrity Worship expresses this energy metaphorically. It is akin to, or like, religion.

Celebrity Worship has another significant reference point; this is again concerned primarily with the self. David Attenborough is significant, not simply because he is present in the media and famous, he is significant because of what he represents. This meaning is not something that he carries within himself; it is what individuals generate in relation to his media persona. In Celebrity Worship, someone like David Attenborough is regarded as a resource for the processing of identity and values among viewers. Worship then is not focused on who he is, but on who we might, or might not, be. This dialogue concerning the self, takes place in relation to media representation – it is not simply caused by it. Celebrity should be seen as forming part of a much larger, and widespread, shift in society and culture, towards the self, as the primary concern and central project of life. It is this focus on the self that has become the new sacred. Celebrities are important, because they are one of the primary resources used in processing the project of the self.

The people that we encounter through our consumption of media form a resource to process our own sense of who we are. This is most evident in social media where the flow of images and stories that come into our feed generate a social world. This world involves us in a real time, continuous process of observation and comparison. Who we are, and our place in the world, is increasingly understood in relation to this flow of mediated individuals. Posting pictures and stories about ourselves becomes a means to be present in this flow, and through likes and shares, we can gauge the impact of how we construct ourselves in this media space. The significance of social media is not found solely in the characteristics of any social media platform but in the myriad of ways in which people choose to negotiate who they are and who they might wish to be as they actively share in making sense of themselves by participating in being present to themselves and others through their feeds. Something very similar is taking place through the consumption of every kind of media. Celebrities offer a resource for personal comparison. This might simply be at the level of fashion and lifestyle. It might be around issues of sexuality and the dynamics of personal relationships. Celebrities become the content, for both individual debates about identity, and for more social interaction. Here the social function of gossip is fundamental. Gossip allows the audience to make moral and aesthetic judgements about people featured in the media. Celebrities are the target of gossip precisely because we do not really know them. They are people who we will not directly hurt or injure by expressing our opinions. Celebrity magazines thrive on stimulating and feeding gossip of this kind, again the key dynamic that is at play has very little to do with who the celebrity might be, or what they might or might not have done. The real subject is the watching audience. Celebrity Worship, then, is a means to process the complexities of identity. Celebrity Worship does not describe the admiration of the mass audience for a few people who are in the media. This notion of a cult of enthusiastic followers is a misunderstanding. Celebrity Worship is an active project of the self, where the individual celebrity is simply a means to work on what really counts: the self.

The self as the new sacred

The turn towards the self is one of the most significant changes that has taken place in contemporary religious sensibilities in the West. David Attenborough and *Blue Planet II* exemplify the shift towards the self in culture. At a very basic level, through his physical presence in front of the camera, the presenter signifies how the world is seen through the self. He represents our presence in the world and our relationship to it. This is the function of television personalities. They take us into events and situations, be it a terrorist attack, a sporting event, or a royal wedding. The camera shows them present, and down in the action, and they take us, as the audience, with them. The subtext of these media tropes is that the world is to be read through the individual, and the personal. The self, in the person of the presenter, is placed in the middle of the story not simply for effect. The self becomes the epistemological ground for the story. What is true for a television programme is true for life in general and particularly for religion.

Religion in the developed world has been realigned to become a resource for the project of the self. Fundamental to this change has been the ways in which choice has become a driver in the shaping of religious identity and practice. These changes have been linked in a variety of ways to the effects of media on religion. The Internet, for example, is seen as providing access to varied forms of religious knowledge and practice, and this encourages the construction of religious identities that are less monochrome. Religious hybridity is encouraged by the opportunities provided by new technology. At the same time, it is clear that religious groups and communities are making use of media technologies to spread their message more effectively. As a result, these groups may experience significant changes. An example of this is the way that Evangelical Christians have used technology to grow new kinds of megachurches. These changes, however, are not simply caused by the influence of media, rather they come about as individuals and communities actively share and participate in making meaning in and through representation. The relationship between media and religious change has been explored in some detail, and the link to the 'self' as a key driver has been commonplace in theorising these changes. Paradoxically, the study of celebrity has been, to date, something that has been marginal to the consideration of the relationship between media and religious change. This is something of an oversight. Rather than being a topic within the study of media and religion, I want to suggest that celebrity is a key element in these changes. There are two reasons for bringing celebrity centre stage in the discussion of media and religion. The first is quite simple. If media is about people and these people are celebrities, then it is just not possible to talk about media, without seeing celebrity culture as central. The second reason is that mediated people are a key driver in the deepest aspect of religious change, and this concerns the turn towards the self. How celebrities facilitate this change and how audiences actively participate in the process of change forms the central topic of this book.

The first two chapters are intended to lay the theoretical groundwork for a consideration of celebrity and religion. Chapter 1 surveys the religion, media and culture conversation. The way in which celebrity culture might contribute to this field of study is presented drawing upon the theoretical frameworks generated in British Cultural Studies. Chapter 2 reviews the way in which Celebrity Worship has been likened to religion and argues that, while this analogy has its limitations, the turn towards the self in religion and wider society has generated a new formulation of what is regarded as sacred. Celebrity worship is then linked to these changes. The next three chapters explore the dynamics of celebrity culture. Chapter 3 traces origins of contemporary celebrity culture in previous notions of fame and the background in the economic development of celebrity by the cultural industries. Chapter 4 discusses the way in which celebrity offers a resource for the construction of identity through a series of case studies around lifestyle. Chapter 5 examines the phenomenon of reality television and Internet celebrity, and how these facilitate the democratisation of celebrity. The final chapters deal explicitly with religious themes and how celebrity forms a part of the shift towards the self in contemporary religion. Chapter 6 examines how celebrity facilitates a religion of the sacred self through case studies of Kabbalah, Oprah Winfrey, and the One Love concert in Manchester. Chapter 7 uses music videos to show how the 'self' is merged with religious themes to generate theologies of the self. Chapter 8 looks at ritual forms of mourning and celebrity death. The final chapter deals with the celebritisation of the Evangelical Church in the United States.

Note

1 Imogen Calderwood. '88% of People Who Saw *Blue Planet II* Have Now Changed Their Lifestyle.' *Global Citizen*, 1 November 2018. www.globalcitizen.org/en/con tent/88-blue-planet-2-changed-david-attenborough/

Chapter I

Media, religion and celebrity

Celebrities are a missing piece in the Religion, Media and Culture jigsaw puzzle. That celebrity has been overlooked is curious because understanding it is fundamental to making sense of media as it operates in contemporary society. There is a simple reason for this; people form the fundamental substantive content of media representation and consumption. As a result, whatever form of media is being considered, there will always be people right at the heart of it. Whether thinking about social media, such as Facebook, Instagram or Twitter, or legacy media, such as magazines, film, television, or the music business, or technologies, such as the mobile phone, or Skype, each is primarily oriented towards the representation of people. Not just people, but individuals, or personalities. The vast majority of media representation and consumption boils down to images and stories, that are either narrated by, or focus upon, faces, voices and bodies. The media and the various ways in which individuals choose to participate and actively consume media, first and foremost, mediates people. Media stories always have a personal orientation or predilection, and this means that the study of media should rightly give full consideration to the people that are represented by it. These individuals, I am arguing, are celebrities. My definition of celebrity is quite simple, a celebrity is a mediated individual, or to put it another way, celebrity is what media processes do to individuals. Celebrity is the result of what media does to the representation of individuals, and the kinds of relationships that result between individuals who are represented in media, and those who consume these representations, and, as a result, have relationships with mediated individuals. It is worth stressing at the outset my use of the term mediation includes the active participation of audiences and individuals. I use the term media processes as a shorthand for the dynamic interaction that takes place between audiences and media in the interweaving and complexities of production, representation and consumption. The use of the terms mediation and media processes should not be read as endorsing a view of media as powerful influencers that determine how audiences behave and think, rather, these terms in my view describe complex interactions where audiences are engaged in making meaning in relation to production, representation and consumption. I take media processes and the idea of mediation as an arena in which audiences are actively shaping their own meanings. Celebrity then does not just refer to individuals who appear in the media, it also describes the kinds of relationships that audiences actively construct as they consume the representation of individuals by media technologies. Celebrities do not have to be special or talented necessarily, they simply need to be mediated and consumed. This means that with the advent of the mobile phone and with social media, celebrity has become democratised. The representation of the self online, and the consumption of stories and images of individuals posted online, has become so interwoven with daily life that mediation and the self are increasingly connected.

Celebrity culture is quite simply foundational for understanding media because people are at the heart of media. This observation brings a distinctive perspective to the developing conversation concerning Religion, Media and Culture. Celebrity focuses attention on the central role that mediated individuals play in various layers and complexities of relationship that have been traced between religion and media. Where religion has been represented in media, people are always central, and where religions pick up and use media technologies and forms of communication, the individual is generally the emotional heart of the communication, and these individuals function as a means of identification and connection. These are the dynamics of a Celebrity Worship, i.e. a culture where individuals are mediated and actively consumed by audiences. Religion therefore cannot be understood in relation to mediation without a thorough consideration of Celebrity Worship. Celebrity Studies and the study of Religion, Media and Culture, have a further connection. They both inhabit a sensibility that finds its origin in the wider field of Cultural Studies. This shared sensibility suggests that there is a common theoretical conversation that has influenced the way celebrity is studied, and the developing academic conversation concerning the relationship between religion and media. This common thread comes specifically from what has become known as British Cultural Studies, and in particular from the work of Raymond Williams and Stuart Hall.[1] This British tradition in Cultural Studies provides a basic family resemblance that enables an exploration of how religion and media and academic work on Celebrity Culture interact in their basic theoretical construction. They are, in short, related and parallel academic conversations. Understanding this commonality, however, also serves to suggest ways that each area might act to inform and nuance the other. This shared theoretical point of origin serves to structure a more extensive argument concerning the rightful place of the consideration of celebrity within academic work in Religion, Media and Culture.

Raymond Williams: a common sensibility

British Cultural Studies traces its roots to the work of two key figures, Raymond Williams and Stuart Hall. Both Hall and Williams generated their theoretical frameworks because of what they saw as the inadequacies of Marxist cultural theory. Marxist criticism had advocated a cultural determinism where art and media are regarded as inevitably following the material conditions of economic relations. This approach can be briefly illustrated by reference to the Frankfurt School and the work of Theodore Adorno. For Adorno, what he called 'mass culture' was an extension of the forms of manipulation and propaganda that he had witnessed in Nazi Germany during the 1930s. Industrial processes and commercial interests, he argued, operated in very similar ways to that of the Nazi regime, in that they sought to co-opt, pacify and dupe the 'masses'. The Culture Industry achieves this, Adorno argues, because workers seek an effortless form of sensation. This is delivered in the 'standardisation' that is a characteristic of the then fast emerging popular culture.[2] Mass Culture, or media, thus serve to reproduce and maintain social relationships that are determined by economics. This is what is often referred to as the base/superstructure argument, where culture is seen as the superstructure that derives its basic shape from the economic relations.

Raymond Williams is critical of the determinism inherent in Marxist critical theory. He makes two key moves as he develops his approach to culture. The first relates to mediation and the power of economic relations. The second formulates a complex interaction between the materiality of cultural and artistic forms and their place in society. In doing so he effectively fired the discursive starting gun for what became known as British Cultural Studies. Mediation as a term, Williams says, carries within it the notion of intercession or reconciliation, or interpretation, between opposing parties.[3] This dualism is problematic in that it restricts the action of media to an indirect action that passes between two separate entities, e.g. Art and Society.[4] In the discussion of popular culture this distinction lends itself to debates around the influence that media, such as film, or popular music, might have on society. Mediation suggests a relationship that is artificial, or an influence on social reality that comes via an alien or disconnected media.[5] Here concern is focused on the effects and influence of media.[6] In contrast to this dualism, Williams argues for mediation as a process that generates meaning and values. Mediation then is a 'necessary form of the general social process of signification and communication.'[7] Making this argument, Williams signals a crucial shift in cultural theory that places cultural processes of communication, rather than economics, at the centre of any understanding of society.

With the emphasis upon communicative processes and meaning making, Williams is then able to build a connection between the notion of mediation, and the ordinary and everyday lives of individuals and communities. He calls this a social definition of culture. For Williams, 'the social definition of culture is descriptive of a particular way of life, which expresses certain meanings and values not only in art and learning but also in institutions and ordinary behaviour.'[8] His emphasis on the 'ordinary' is developed as a refutation of the high culture/low culture distinction that had dominated cultural theory. Culture was not to be read as the communication of the best that had been thought and said, as Matthew Arnold had argued in the nineteenth century.[9] Culture is concerned with values and meaning, but it is fundamentally ordinary and located in the everyday. This lived cultural reality, Williams describes as, a 'structure of feeling.' Williams adopts the notion of feeling as a retreat from more formal notions of ideology or worldview. Feeling denotes 'meanings and values as they are actively lived.'[10] It is an alternative to the determining nature of systematic, or formal 'belief,' but cultural analysis should attempt to trace the relationships between the formal, and the less defined affective dimensions of the everyday. At the same time, structure indicates notions of power, institutions and social class.

There is a key element that runs alongside, and through, Williams' reframing of notions of mediation, the social process of meaning making in the lived, and the idea of culture as a structure of feeling, i.e. the signifying function of art. Williams was a literary critic, and also a novelist, and understanding the connections between society and art lay at the centre of his project. He therefore argued that there was a convergence that takes place between his anthropological notion of a whole way of life, and the more widespread acceptance that culture was concerned with artistic and intellectual activities. This convergence is practical, or part of a process and it is connected to what he calls 'signifying practices.'[11] The material forms of art, or we might broaden this to media, form part of the processes of symbolic communication and meaning making. Understanding culture as a particular way of life necessarily involves understanding the relationship between the material forms of artistic (or media) expression and the signifying practices that make up ordinary life. These relationships, however, are not marginal or trivial, but necessary and essential to meaningful ways of life; they make up a 'whole way of life.'[12]

The key sensibilities that shape Raymond Williams' approach to culture, have been formative for both Celebrity Studies and scholarly work on religion and media. While the dialogue with Marxist cultural theory has ceased to be central to debates in these fields the remnants of the perspectives generated as a response to economic determinism and the high culture/low culture perspective remain. The Culture Industry argument, for example, continues to play a significant role in conversations. This translates into debates concerning how Celebrity Culture erodes news output, or how it trivialises political discourse. Similar concerns arise in relation to the impact that the media has on religious life and communities. In both disciplines, debate has developed around the way that cultural forms interact with the lived. High culture/low culture frameworks have been replaced by a focus on the ordinary, and this shift in focus is carried in the term, popular culture. Related to these ideas, there is the continuing interest, in both areas of academic work, in the processes of signification, and the interaction between representation in material, artistic, or media forms, and meaning making in the everyday. It is this aspect of Williams' work that is taken up and developed by the other key figure in British Cultural Studies, Stuart Hall.

Stuart Hall: representation and meaning

In his seminal article 'Encoding and Decoding', Stuart Hall develops notions of mediation and the social definition of culture, first seen in Raymond Williams' work.[13] His starting point is a critique of a linear conception of communication theory as characterised by a sender/message/receiver paradigm. The problem with this conceptualisation of communication is that it focuses on the transmission of messages. Hall is concerned to emphasise the significance of the different moments, in what he sees as a circle, or loop, of communication. These moments are 'articulated', or joined together, but they also remain distinct moments of production, circulation, distribution/consumption, reproduction. Processes of production, Hall argues, generate media products, in discursive form. This is what he terms, encoding. Media products then, in this encoded form, are symbolic vehicles that are able to be circulated. Circulation takes place, through the action of various media, each carrying their own logic and ways of operating. Symbols circulate, subject to the various rules and conditions that shape transmission. These products, however, need to be transformed again into social practices. This is what Hall speaks of as decoding. Decoding generates meaning in relation to practices. Cultural products are only significant as, and when, they are articulated in practice, if they are to be read as meaningful.[14]

The pattern of cultural description and analysis that Hall described as encoding and decoding, is developed into what he terms the 'circuit of culture.'[15] In the circuit there are five interconnected moments: representation, identity, production, consumption and regulation. Each of these is distinct, and yet a full consideration of any area will involve a treatment of the others. In an academic context, it is possible to separate out the moments in the circuit, but the authors make clear that, 'in the real world they continually overlap and intertwine in complex and contingent ways.' Taken together, however, they constitute a, 'cultural study of an artefact or a product.'[16] The cultural circuit structures the discipline of Cultural Studies and the way that cultural analysis takes place. It rests, however, on Stuart Hall's particular understanding of how representation and identity are 'articulated.'[17] Articulation is Hall's way of speaking about the way in which new meanings are produced in popular culture. Articulation has a dual point of reference. First, it relates to expression or speech. New cultural forms 'articulate,' i.e. bring into communication. Articulation, however, also is seen, by Hall, as a means of speaking about the ways in which different 'bits' of cultural symbolism are joined together. The linking of these symbolic bits is a way of expressing new approaches to seeing and living life. Fundamental to these connections is the creation of meaning. Culture is then, for Hall, primarily about shared meanings.[18] The emphasis upon shared meanings does not, however, mean that he sees culture as, in any way, unitary or cohesive. Meanings are in flux and disputed. Cultural products, or as Hall calls them, 'things,' rarely have a single, fixed or unchanging meaning.[19]

Culture consists of systems of representation, he argues, and these work like a language. The significance of facial gesture, media image, an item of clothing, or a piece of recorded music does not lie in the things themselves but how they operate in a system of communicating meaning, i.e. through media discourses.[20] The circuit of culture then is a way of describing the key aspects of how discourses are produced and circulated. Alongside productive processes of representation, identity and subjectivity are also seen as being generated within the set of relations, or articulations, set out in the circuit of culture.[21] Hall therefore argues that media and representation form a decisive element in how the sense of self is generated and sustained. As he puts it, 'Identities are thus points of temporary attachment to the subject positions which discursive practices construct for us. They are the result of a successful articulation or "chaining" of the subject in the flow of discourse.'[22] The pattern of analysis developed in Williams' theory of culture and Hall's notion of the circuit of culture represent a common point of departure for Celebrity Studies and Religion, Media and Culture. Academic work in both fields generally assume the understanding of how culture works that Williams and Hall developed. Academic work, be it on celebrity, or on media and religion, to a large extent echoes these fundamental categories of the signification of representation and how this relates to the everyday and the ordinary, often structured as the relationship between production, representation and identity/consumption. This shared framework of analysis, however, also structures the debates and conversations that take place in these two areas of work, as scholars locate their work in relation to aspects of the circuit of culture, and prioritise one of the moments over the others.

The religion and media conversation

The Religion, Media and Culture conversation has its origins in the late 1990s, with the realisation that the study of media, and of religion, had taken place with little reference to each other. Within the field of cultural and media studies, religion had been largely overlooked, and scholars, in the sociology of religion and religious studies, had paid very little attention to media.[23] In the groundbreaking volume that they edited, *Rethinking Media Religion and Culture*, Stuart Hoover and Knut Lundby argued for the central importance of religion to debates concerning media. They made a similar argument in relation to the study of religion. A consideration of media should be central to the discussion of the changing nature of religion in Western society. The religious aspects of media, they suggested, were more than simply a consideration of how media discourses represent religion, it was also the case that aspects of media consumption and representation appear to carry religious significance in themselves. In relation to religious institutions and communities, they argued that a consideration of media was fundamental to the communicative practices of institutions, and the experience of individuals living within religious communities. This meant that media and mediation are connected to many of the changes that are evident in religious life and institutions.[24]

In the beginning of the discussion concerning religion and media, the relationship was primarily conceptualised as the relationship between two distinct institutions.[25] Attention has focused on the ways in which the media may work to influence or change religious beliefs and practices.[26] At a theoretical level these perspectives form an aspect of what has been called 'technological determinism' but they might also be seen as operating in parallel to Adorno's Culture Industry theory, where the power of productive processes predominate over the meaning making of individuals and communities. The classic account of technological determinism is found in the work of Marshall McLuhan. McLuhan argued that media are 'extensions of the self' that generate both social and personal consequences. The result is that in operational and practical terms, 'the medium is the message.' Technology for McLuhan inevitably brings about changes in society.[27] A similar approach to media and their influence on society is developed by Neil Postman in *Amusing Ourselves to Death*.[28] Postman's key argument is that media forms, by their nature, limit public discourse. The effect on a culture that is continually fed on a diet of these truncated forms of media expression, is a widespread 'dumbing down' of politics, and of cultural life in general. Religious concerns over the effects of media have led to two different approaches. The first deals with an analysis of the different ways in which the treatment of religious practice, and belief, in media discourses, brings about change. The determinist perspective has often led to critical or pessimistic readings of the role that media can play, in relation to religion, but alongside the more pessimistic readings, there has been considerable work generated on the ways that religion, when it is represented in media discourses, is creatively and constructively transformed in various ways.[29] The second dynamic, is that a determinist approach to debates, concerning relationship between religion and media, arises from the effects that are generated as religious communities adopt aspects of contemporary media. Here again, the focus is often upon the various ways in which the technologies associated with new media reshape, or bring about, change in religious life.[30] These approaches to religion and media, map on to the Cultural Studies framework of analysis as perspectives that locate cultural power on processes of production.

In Stig Hjarvard's work, similar dynamics between productive media processes, and the changing nature of religion, are shaped into an overarching theory, that he calls 'mediatisation'.[31] Hjarvard's theory of media starts by accepting that media is a distinct institution within society. Media have forms that generate their own ways of operating, and crucially, their own logic. Mediatisation is a theory that speaks of the ways in which media processes effect change in the wider society.[32] 'Mediatisation,' says Hjarvard, 'designates the process through which core elements of a social or cultural activity (for example politics, teaching, religion, and so on) assume media form.'[33] It is a way of speaking about the influences that media forms have, on both society and religion. Religion, says Hjarvard, is not replaced by media, rather it is being subsumed, through mediatisation. There are three interrelated ways in which mediatisation is manifest: conduits, language and environments. Media as conduits, refers to the ways in which media transmit symbols and messages, between sender and receiver. Media languages designate the ways in which messages are shaped and formatted, through communicative processes. Media environments focus attention on the ways that media structure and facilitate, social relationships.[34] The result is a diminishing of religious institutions, as they become, what he calls, 'banal religion.' Hjarvard's theory of mediatisation develops a more complex framing of how media and religion operate than the more deterministic theories. His work, however, situates power, and influence, on the productive and the representational aspects of the cultural circuit.

Mediatisation and technological determinism have been seen as problematic mainly because they fail to account for the complex interaction of media processes. In effect, they reproduce the model of communication theory that Williams and Hall reject. Technology takes the place of Marxist notions of the base and the superstructure, but the sensibilities around determinism remain. Communication is about dualities. There are, then, echoes of Adorno's Culture Industry scepticism that are carried into the discussion of the relationship between religion and media, when it is framed around the determinative duality. At a theoretical level, religion is seen as being influenced in a similar way to how the masses are regarded by Adorno, and it is seen as being similarly shaped and 'duped' by the all-powerful media. Hjarvard's mediatisation avoids the pessimistic overtones of technological determinism, but it reads the effects of media, in a dualistic framework, where power and influence come from media, and religion is inevitably shaped by these ways of operating. Hjarvard's reading of mediatisation is significantly critiqued by Lynn Schofield Clark, who argues that his focus on television and film tips the emphasis towards the influence of media on society.[35] In contrast, she argues, that in a new media environment, agency and influence are diffused and disparate. Building on actor network theory, Schofield Clark argues that mediatisation should be seen as networks of influence, between the material forms that media take and individual agents. Mediatisation is, then, a process of social change, that occurs, 'within the network of humans, technologies and cultural practices.'[36] This dynamic network of interaction is facilitated and made possible by the new interactive communication technologies that have developed since television and film.[37]

Religious identity construction

Technological determinism and mediatisation emphasise the power of production in contemporary culture. There are approaches, however, that prioritise the individual and the lived, as the primary location for the generation of meaning. These perspectives have been influenced by the notion of social construction.[38] Constructivist understandings of the relationship between media and religion prioritise the freedom of individuals to generate a particular religious self. Daniel Stout refers to the choice that is involved in generating a religious self as, 'personalised religion.'[39] Religion, he argues, is no longer 'captured' by fixed definitions. In the new media context, people have access to rituals, advice and almost unlimited religious knowledge, through digital media. Jeffrey Mahan describes the consequences of the rise of social media and digital culture, as the facilitation of a 'vast array of new voices.'[40] This does not simply provide access to new kinds of information or experiences. The rise of new media, Mahan argues, encourages a social constructivist approach to developing knowledge and shaping identities. Religion is put together in very similar ways to the sampling that is a characteristic of hip hop, or the way that information is created by multiple people and from multiple sources in a Wiki text. 'Religion,' says Mahan, 'is not simply a matter of inheritance. Religion is constructed and performed, often with elements sampled from different traditions.'[41]

Central to the constructionist understanding of religion is the notion that individuals are increasingly choosing their religious sources of identity. The self is a project that is performed and chosen.[42] This phenomenon is characterised by the willingness of individuals to select from within a religious tradition what they choose to accept and follow. Selectivity is not, however, confined to how individuals operate within a particular religion. The increased access and awareness of different kinds of religious and non-religious forms of knowledge that comes through new media has accelerated the various ways in which individuals feel empowered and free to develop multiple or hybrid religious selves. Mahan describes these tendencies through two different descriptions: 'hyphening' and 'sampling'. Hyphening arises when different religious traditions, or forms of expression are brought into a connection or are articulated. This enables people to speak of themselves as, for instance Christian-Buddhist, or Hindu-Christian. With these kinds of identities people feel free to move back and forwards between communities and religious practices and ideas. Sampling by contrast is shaped by the ability of individuals to select and appropriate practices or ideas from a range of different religious traditions. Examples of this kind of identity construction might include someone who purchases a statue of the Buddha to decorate their home, even though they may not have any particular inclination to practice meditation; or someone who listens to Gregorian chant but does not believe in a Christian God or attend church. These kinds of spiritual consumption are increasingly common and form part of a fast-changing religious landscape.[43] Sampling is necessarily more fragmented and fragmenting of religious tradition than hyphening, but both have been brought about, and made more common, by access to new forms of media. The representation and circulation of religion through media practices leads to commodification. Religious media products are therefore made available to be consumed in contexts that are often removed from the formal religious environment. This has direct consequences on notions of religious coherence and authority.

As religion is circulated and made available through media practices, identity construction can draw upon a variety of sources. There is what Mahan calls an acceleration that is brought about in the way that individual identities are shaped. The result is that multiple sources of religious knowledge, practice and experience are made available and this serves to encourage religious sampling. People are therefore increasingly generating a religious self from loosely associated pieces or bits of various traditions.[44] The social construction of religion understands the individual as a consumer who is accessing religious knowledge, practice and experiences in a fundamentally different manner to more traditional ways of understanding the self in relation to a religion. An example of this, says Mahan, is the way that Americans, when they move from one part of the country to the other, will seek out a religious community that, 'meets their needs', rather than feeling that they need to maintain a fixed identity, as for instance, a Baptist or a Methodist. Religious identity, in this consumerist form, therefore, becomes more fluid. Authority shifts from the tradition to the individual, who is free to choose. Religious leaders and sacred texts are consulted, but the individual does not regard them as sources that determine or decisively shape religious practice. Religious authority or significance is, therefore, something that is granted by the individual, who will often be situating this voice in a range of different competing sources.[45] Consumers are, therefore, not seen as being passive, in the way that they interact with media, instead, for Mahan, consumption is performative. Individuals are active in relation to media representation, building a sense of self.[46] The constructivist approach to religion and media might be seen as a form of what McGuigan calls cultural populism, i.e. an understanding of culture that is overly optimistic and the creativity and meaning making of individuals.[47] The cultural circuit operates as a corrective to the overemphasis on consumption and identity, by suggesting that production, representation and regulation should be considered; so while it is possible to emphasises construction, attention also needs to be paid to those aspects of media production and representation that limit choice and structure the possibilities for meaning making.

Religious social shaping of technology

The notion of religious social construction, as described by Mahan and others, emphasises the ways in which individuals, through consumption and the circulation of media representation, reshape religious traditions making them more fluid and personal. Heidi Campbell, by contrast, has developed a theoretical framework that focuses on how religious communities are active in negotiating a distinctive and shared approach to technology and media. She calls this theory, 'religious social shaping of technology' (RSST).[48] Campbell develops her approach, by adapting perspectives on media and technology, that emphasise, both the technological and the social factors, that are significant, in the design and use of technology. This theory, which has been termed, 'the social shaping of technology', is a move away from technological determinism, towards a perspective that emphasises how social groups are able to shape technologies to their own ends. This notion of social process has two aspects.[49] The first, focuses on how groups develop a particular form of use, or interaction, with technologies. The second, describes the ways in which these socially produced ways of operating, themselves, act as an influence on how people situate themselves in relation to media practices. It is a central premise of this approach that technology is shaped by choices, and, as a result, it should be seen as the sum of the negotiation that groups of users generate.[50] Technology is regarded as being situated in moral lives, or domesticated in ways that locate it in spaces that are shaped by the values and commitments of individuals and communities. The social shaping of technology offers a significant way to explore how technology interacts with everyday life. For Campbell, it is this aspect of the theory that she sees as having significant potential for dealing with the various ways that religious communities and individuals interact with and shape technology.

The religious social shaping of technology approach does not simply adopt the social shaping of technology theory. Campbell argues that there are a number of factors that are religiously defined and generated, which means that communities interact with technology out of, and in relation to, their different traditions. The theory, therefore, rests on the assumption, that 'a technology is shaped by the setting in which it lives and by the agents who utilize it.'[51] At the same time, in this negotiated arena, communities are themselves also changed, as they use particular media technologies. Religious communities share particular beliefs and practice, such that they are a moral community. These social and religious meanings influence the way that individuals and groups make use of media, and how they construct meaning in relation to it. Religious social shaping of technology sets out to give an account of the specific religious factors that influence and guide the way that communities negotiate their use of technology. How technology operates, and the place that it finds in everyday life is, therefore, not solely determined by the characteristics of the technology itself. Religious factors are highly significant, in that they constrain social groups, through shared belief structures and worldview. Of particular importance, Campbell points out, is the recognition that it is not simply the use of technology that should be considered, but the way that religious beliefs generate ways of perceiving and understanding technology and media. Religious social shaping of technology, therefore, rests on a detailed understanding of religious traditions and communities in themselves, as a starting point for the consideration of how meaning is made in relation to media and technology.[52]

New media technologies represent both opportunities and threats to religious communities. On the one hand, new forms of communication might be seen as offering a new way to evangelise, or to share in community life. On the other hand, particular media forms might be seen as spreading and promoting

content that is offensive or forbidden. As a consequence, individuals and communities can be seen to share in what can often be detailed and protracted
debates on how, and to what extent, it might, or might not, be possible, or
advisable, for members to engage with different forms of media.[53] Campbell
argues that the religious social shaping of technology should examine three key
elements. The first of these relates to the particular community that is being
considered. It is the specifics of individual communities that bear most significantly on how technology might, or might not, be used. Close attention is
therefore required into the detail of how the specific religious community that
is under consideration, might have developed their shared beliefs and practices.
In a religious tradition, there will be a range of common or shared elements,
but there will also be a range of different groups, and ways of articulating the
tradition. It is the distinction between groups, and the various ways in which,
in everyday life, they have of practicing the shared tradition, that will play a
significant part in how media is used.[54]

Secondly, communities have different cultural and social patterns that structure how authority is exercised. Groups develop cultural histories, and particular ways in which they generate authoritative versions of their own tradition.
Understanding how authority is exercised, in relation to social groups, is a
central concern in the religious social shaping of technology perspective. Differences in approaches to authority can be marked. For instance, one group
may prioritise the role that religious figures play in the ordering of communal
life, while other groups may place more emphasis on how sacred texts are
interpreted by the group as whole. Other groups may be shaped around the
traditions that structure ritual, or liturgical practice. Authority may be exercised
in very different ways, and so understanding how the use of technology is
negotiated will require close attention being given to who or what is seen as
most authoritative in a particular religious group.[55] The third most important
element is the different attitudes that a community may have towards its own
sacred text. Here, Campbell draws attention to the older media form of printed
texts and the ways in which these form a part of the everyday ritual and beliefs
of communities. Campbell focuses particularly on Christianity, Judaism and
Islam, where written texts form a central aspect of their religion. Printed texts
in these religions shape particular forms of action and ways of life. Moreover, it
is through a constant interaction with texts over history that these religions are
shaped as communities of interpretation. Habits of interpretation, over time,
generate rules and boundaries around the way that these texts may, or may not
be, interpreted. These factors, of authority and sacred texts, are central to how
these religious communities, and particular groups within the larger traditions,
respond to new forms of media.[56]

The religious social shaping of technology approach has been revised by Tim
Hutchings based on his study of online churches.[57] Hutchings found in his
study that the homogeneity, that lies at the heart of Campbell's theory, was not
accurate. Communities would often disagree about how to engage with

technology. They would argue, not simply about the use of the technology, but also about the core values that the community shared. In his ethnographic work, Hutchings observed that 'theology' in the way it is described by RSST, was often not significant in how these negotiations took place, and that other considerations were often evident. To account for these aspects of his research he argues for what he calls, 'mediated religious design'. This is a hybrid theory that incorporates aspects of mediatisation theory, accepting that there are logics and dynamics, that arise from how media operates, that influence religion. At the same time, there are also elements within religious communities that are at play.[58]

Mediation and the media age

Hoover rejects the idea that media and religion exist as two separate institutions. Scholarship that focuses on the relationship of the effects of media on religion, or on the ways that media transmit religious messages, he argues, have neglected notions of meaning making.[59] Media and religion have converged. 'They occupy the same spaces, serve many of the same purposes, and invigorate the same practices in late modernity.'[60] Media, he suggests, are a resource for values and imagination. Television and film, for instance, are widely regarded as sources for symbols of nationhood or ideas of masculinity, for example. However, this understanding of the way that media carries values has often been read in instrumentalist terms. Hoover suggests, however, that how media interacts with society should be understood in a more layered or nuanced way. He develops this textured, and interactive approach to mediation, through what he calls, a culturalist approach. This is directly influenced by British Cultural Studies.[61]

The culturalist approach to the study of media, focuses on issues of identity and meaning. As a consequence, it adopts more qualitative methods of enquiry that concentrate on the significance of media in daily life.[62] The study of media rituals, for instance, or the values conveyed in media, require a form of analysis that looks at how these might play a part in the everyday activities of people, families and communities. Hoover's approach is therefore directed towards the consumption of media. He advocates going to where people are, and 'looking back' with them at the cultural context in which they live and, along with them, understanding how the various elements – that connect, media, symbols, social relations, identities, meanings, etc. – relate to one another.[63] At the heart of his concern is a desire to understand how individuals create meaningful narratives concerning their lives, and the part that the consumption of media might play in these processes. The method he develops, takes account of the processes of production, representation and circulation through the cultural context, but it is the specific role that media takes in the social processes of meaning making that take priority. In particular, it is religious meanings that come to the centre of his attention and how media as it is consumed plays a role in the everyday.[64] In this enterprise, Hoover uses Raymond Williams' notion of culture, as a 'structure of feeling'. Meaningful knowledge, he therefore argues, is that which connects individuals to their structures of feeling.[65] As individuals seek to make sense of themselves, and the world around them, it is clear that media act as a symbolic resource in these endeavours.[66] There are what he calls, 'affordances', in media texts, and these call, or beckon, individuals into particular ways of acting and practices that are at the same time both 'determining, and empowering'.[67] The effect of these processes brings about a reformulation of religion.

'Mediated commodity culture can be seen today to be supporting the development of new religious and spiritual sensibilities. In addition to the new sources of authority that seem inevitable, the media sphere provides new and reconstituted symbols and values and new contexts and systems for relationships, solidarities, social networks and (perhaps) new social movements.'[68] The effects of media arise from the meaning making of individuals and communities. Hoover then theorises change, not as some form of technological determinism, but as the result of a process of meaning making, that arises from an interaction with media. This what he describes as the 'media age,' i.e. a new context where religious identities are constructed in, and through, engagement with media.

The move away from understanding the relationship between media and religion as primarily concerning two institutions is helpful. The focus on institutional relationships means that the debates concerning religion and media have been structured around questions of influence and power. This plays out as a discussion concerning the extent to which religion is manipulated, or controlled, by media processes. Technological determinism, for instance, would see religion and wider society as being decisively influenced by media. Social constructionism, on the other hand, emphasises the extent to which individuals are free agents in relation to media processes. A similar dynamic can be seen in the differences between mediatisation, which emphasises the effects of media on society and religion, and Campbell's RSST, which situates meaning making as an aspect of the agency of communities and individuals. These debates, in large part, follow along the lines of theoretical conversation that have been followed within Cultural Studies. A simplified approach to the paradigm developed within Cultural Studies is the idea of culture as production, representation and consumption. Using this kind of theoretical framework, it is possible to structure the religion and media conversations in relation to the relative significance of these moments. If the problem of media is approached in this way, then the discussion is shaped around which of these elements is of primary significance. The problem with this is it is not helpful or accurate to, for instance, situate media as an aspect of production. If media and production are made equivalent, then religion takes on the role of consumption. The conversation then becomes a judgement about the relative significance of these moments. This is what is at play in the distinction between technological determinism and social constructivism. The approach to the theoretical frameworks developed in the religion and media conversation, it could be argued, misses key insights from the circuit of culture.

The 'circuit of culture' theory is based on the assumption that a cultural analysis, to be complete, needs pass through each of the moments on the circuit. Cultural analysis, therefore, needs to give due consideration to production, consumption, representation, identity and regulation, to be complete. However, it is possible to situate a study primarily in one of these areas. In other words, while there is a conversation around the relative significance of each of the moments, nevertheless, each has a place in understanding how culture works. When a cultural analysis is located mainly in one of the moments of the cycle, then the others need to be taken into consideration. Introducing celebrity into these theoretical conversations around religion and media emphasises the nuanced functioning of the circuit of culture as part of this field of study. From this Cultural Studies' perspective, while there may be differences between theoretical frameworks, such as technological determinism and social construction, or mediatisation and the religious social shaping of technology, the suggestion might be that these can be treated as useful theoretical perspectives that illustrate and inform aspects of the various moments in the circuit of culture. Theories, then are useful and play a part in developing understanding and knowledge, depending on the particular interests and concerns of the researcher.

Celebrity and the religion and media conversation

Celebrity, and Celebrity Culture, bring a particular dynamic to the religion and media conversation. If all forms of media have the representation and consumption of individuals at their heart, and a celebrity is a 'mediated individual', then it follows that celebrity will play a significant role in every aspect of the way in which media and religion interact. Celebrity should not be seen as a topic within the Religion, Media and Culture discussion, or indeed as primarily a distinct area for study, although it is certainly important as such. Celebrity Worship describes a more fundamental and ubiquitous aspect of media, in a global sense, i.e. celebrity is what media does to people. This means that, however religion and media are understood, Celebrity Worship should be situated as a key consideration. How this kind of consideration might function within the conversation will be complex and multi-faceted. The cultural circuit, I have argued, contributes to the debates around media and religion, by opening spaces to consider the relative significance of different moments in the circuit, while not losing sight of the importance of others. This allows a place for the utilisation of multiple theoretical perspectives, depending upon the interests of the researcher. Celebrity, or the significance of mediated individuals, forms a part in each of these moments of the circuit. Celebrity has arisen, because it is a means for the Culture Industry to promote and sell products. Celebrities offer points of attachment, and association, that draw consumers into a relationship with the individuals represented, and consequently, with the items being sold. These forms of productive relationships arise, both in media industries, and also in religious communities, as the personality of the preacher, or the spiritual guide, becomes the means to develop an emotional connection to what is being taught. At the level of representation, the people whose images, voices and bodies are reproduced, function as a logic, or an order within media processes. Similarly, curating the self, online, has become an aspect of everyday life, and this online self is a means of sharing in a structure that is framed by social media.

Celebrity also plays a role in each of the theoretical perspectives on religion and media. Where religion is changed through media processes, significant individuals are at the heart of these changes. When media begins to function as religion, then the emotional connection that delivers this possibility is to be found in people who are present in and through the media. The representation of religion in media is framed by personal narratives, and facilitated, by the choices and creativity of mediated individuals. When religious communities seek to make use of new forms of media, then what is most often at stake relates to the mediated self, as religious subject in relation to media. When social construction, or the fragmentation and realignment of religious tradition, is discussed, then celebrities become key carriers of culture. Choosing, editing and selecting, in the construction of a religious self, is an aspect of Celebrity Culture. It is both influenced by, and performs, the self, as part of a flow of representation of 'mediated selves,' that is fundamentally shaped by celebrity. The religious self, as it is performed on social media, is shaped by, and generated within, a sensibility that is part of Celebrity Culture. This construction of the self frames religious identities, in the same way as it does those that are not part of religion. At every level, then, mediated individuals are fundamental to the changes and dynamics that are explored in the religion and media conversation. It is, in short, a missing piece of the jigsaw puzzle.

Notes

1 Jim McGuigan. *Cultural Populism*. (London: Routledge, 1992). Ioan Davies. *Cultural Studies and Beyond Fragments of Empire*. (London: Routledge, 1995).
2 Theodore Adorno. *The Culture Industry*. (London: Routledge, 1991), 85.
3 Raymond Williams. *Marxism and Literature*. (Oxford: Oxford University Press, 1977), 171.
4 Williams. *Marxism*, 97.
5 Raymond Williams. *Keywords: A Vocabulary of Culture and Society*. (London: Fontana, 1976), 172.
6 Williams. *Keywords*, 169.
7 Williams. *Marxism*, 100.
8 Raymond Williams. 'The analysis of culture.' In *Cultural Theory and Popular Culture: A Reader*. John Storey, ed. (Hemel Hempstead: Harvester Wheatsheaf, 1994), 56–63.
9 Matthew Arnold. *Culture and Anarchy*. (Cambridge: Cambridge University Press, 1869).

10 Williams. *Marxism*, 132.
11 Raymond Williams. *Culture*. (London: Collins, 1981), 13.
12 Williams. Analysis, 61.
13 Stuart Hall. 'Encoding/decoding.' In *Culture, Media, Language: Working Papers in Cultural Studies, 1972–79*. Stuart Hall, Dorothy Hobson, Andrew Lowe and Paul Willis eds. (London: Hutchinson, 1973), 128–138.
14 Hall. Encoding, 128–129.
15 Paul du Gay, Stuart Hall, Linda Janes, Hugh Mackay, Hugh and Keith Negus eds. *Doing Cultural Studies: The Story of the Sony Walkman*. (London: Sage, 2013), xxx–xxxi.
16 du Gay, *Doing*, xxx.
17 Stuart Hall. 'On postmodernism and articulation: an interview with Stuart Hall.' In *Stuart Hall: Critical Dialogues in Cultural Studies*. David Morley and Chen Kuan-Hsing eds. (London: Routledge, 1996), 131–150.
18 du Gay. *Doing*, 2.
19 du Gay. *Doing*, 3.
20 du Gay. *Doing*, 5.
21 du Gay. *Doing*, 2.
22 du Gay. *Doing*, 6.
23 Stuart Hoover and Knut Lundby, eds. *Rethinking Media Religion and Culture*. (London: Sage, 1997), 3–5.
24 Hoover. *Rethinking*.
25 Stuart Hoover. *Religion in the Media Age*. (London: Routledge, 2006). Jeffrey Mahan, *Media Religion and Culture: An Introduction*. (London: Routledge, 2014).
26 Heidi Campbell. *When Religion Meets New Media*. (London: Routledge, 2010), 42.
27 Marshall McLuhan. *Understanding Media: The Extensions of the Self*. (London: Routledge, 1964), 7.
28 Neil Postman. *Amusing Ourselves to Death*. (London: Penguin, 1985).
29 Diane Winston ed. *Small Screen, Big Picture: Television and Lived Religion*. (Waco, TX: Baylor University Press, 2009). Bruce Forbes and Jeffrey Mahan eds. *Religion and Popular Culture in America*. (Berkley, CA: California University Press 2017) 3rd edn, 33–118.
30 Pete Ward. *Selling Worship*. (Milton Keynes: Paternoster, 2005).
31 Stig Hjarvard. 'The Mediatization of Religion: Theorising Religion, Media and Social Change.' *Culture and Religion*, 12, no. 2 (2011): 119–135. Stig Hjarvard. *The Mediatization of Culture and Society*. (London: Routledge, 2013). Stig Hjarvard. 'Mediatization and the Changing Authority of Religion.' *Media Culture and Society*, 38, no. 1 (2016): 8–17.
32 Stig Hjarvard. 'The Mediatisation of Religion: A Theory of the Media as Agents of Religious Change.' *Northern Lights*, 6 (2008).
33 Hjarvard. Mediatisation, 6.
34 Hjarvard. Mediatisation, 4–5.
35 Lynn Schofield Clark. 'Considering Religion and Mediatisation through a Case Study of *J+K's Big Day* (The J K Wedding Entrance Dance): A Response to Stig Hjarvard.' *Culture and Religion*, 12, no. 2 (2011): 181.
36 Schofield Clark. Considering, 171.
37 Schofield Clark. Considering, 181.
38 Peter Berger and Thomas Luckmann. *The Social Construction of Reality*. (London: Penguin, 1966).
39 Daniel Stout. *Media and Religion: Foundations of an Emerging Field*. (London: Routledge, 2012), 11.

40 Jeffrey Mahan. *Media Religion and Culture: An Introduction*. (London: Routledge, 2014), 27.
41 Mahan. *Media*, 27.
42 Mahan. *Media*, 27.
43 Mahan. *Media*, 28.
44 Mahan. *Media*, 29.
45 Mahan. *Media*, 30.
46 Mahan. *Media*, 36–46.
47 McGuigan. *Cultural*.
48 Campbell. *When*, 63.
49 Donald MacKenzie and Judy Wajcman. *The Social Shaping of Technology*. (Buckingham: Open University Press, 1999).
50 Campbell. *When*, 50.
51 Campbell. *When*, 58.
52 Campbell. *When*, 58–59.
53 Campbell. *When*, 5.
54 Campbell. *When*, 15.
55 Campbell. *When*, 16.
56 Campbell. *When*, 16.
57 Timothy Hutchings. *Creating Church Online: Ritual, Community and New Media*. (London: Routledge, 2017).
58 Hutchings. *Creating*.
59 Hoover. *Rethinking*, 2.
60 Hoover. *Rethinking*, 6.
61 Hoover. *Rethinking*, 16.
62 Hoover. *Rethinking*, 16–17.
63 Hoover. *Rethinking*, 20.
64 Hoover. *Rethinking*, 36.
65 Hoover. *Rethinking*, 37.
66 Hoover. *Rethinking*, 614.
67 Hoover. *Rethinking*, 615.
68 Hoover. *Rethinking*, 619.

Chapter 2

Celebrity, religion and the sacred self

It has become commonplace, in both popular commentary and academic analysis, to link celebrity and religion. Celebrity Worship is seen as part of the widespread turn away from formal belief; celebrities are proposed as the new alternative religious guides. Celebrities are spoken of as objects of worship and the new gods. The devotion of fans is described as a form of religion, a replacement for traditional ways of worship. The term Celebrity Worship encapsulates the religious overtones that surround the ways in which relationships between celebrities and their fans are described. This widespread assumption, of the connection between celebrity and religion, requires interrogation. There are different levels of association that are implied, in the way that religion is connected with celebrity. At a most basic level, religion in celebrity discourse simply operates as a metaphor. The language of the divine, or of worship, is not meant to seriously imply that celebrities are gods, or that they are really worshipped, but there is rather a slightly ironic, or exaggerated, use of religion, to signify the depth of connection between fans and those they follow. This metaphorical use of religion in some academic work, however, appears to signify a more sustained, or intentional, connection, between the sacred and celebrity representation. There are scholars in Celebrity Studies who argue that celebrity should now be regarded as a substitute for religion, and that it is taking the place of, or functioning in ways that replace, formal religious institutions.

The basic assertion that Celebrity Worship is religion relies, to some extent, on the way that religion is defined. Definitions of religion are, however, many and varied. A note of caution in making a direct analogy between religion and Celebrity Culture comes from the persistent irreverence and mocking tone that runs deeply through Celebrity Culture. This sensibility tempers notions of worship and, on the whole, it does not fit neatly into any formal notions of religion.[1] The lack of a clear, or an unproblematic, fit, however, does not preclude the way in which the widespread use of religious reference and analogy in celebrity discourse does suggest a connection to the sacred. Here, however, what is sacred, or religious, I will argue, is not the celebrity, or even the relationship that fans have with celebrities, but the way in which both of these things are a means to process and to construct a meaningful sense of the self. It is this project of the self that is the new sacred, the new 'ultimate' concern. Celebrity Worship is not a religion, but it points towards the prevailing sensibility of the self, and it is this sacred self that is religious. Celebrities are significant, in a religious sense, only as they form a part of this much larger shift in religious life. Celebrity, then, is deeply religious in the way it operates, not because it acts as a form of religion, but because it forms a central aspect of a change in culture that has had a profound influence on the way that religion is experienced and lived.

Celebrity and the language of religion

The metaphorical use of religion, as a means of talking about the significance of celebrity, is commonplace. The following headlines taken from media at the time of writing illustrate how this connection has become a normal part of celebrity discourse. 'Worshipping Celebrities Brings Success,' says one BBC article.[2] Interestingly, *The Daily Telegraph* uses the metaphor of religion to make the opposite point with their headline, 'The Cult of Celebrity is "Harming Children "'[3] – while a 'Patheos' blog refers to celebrities as gods and goddesses. Speaking about fans as worshippers, and the celebrity phenomenon as a religion or a cult, has been an ongoing feature of the media presentation of celebrities. Film stars have been likened to the gods, and the worship of stars heralded as a new religion from at least the 1950s.[4] Female singers have regularly been spoken of as divas, with both the adulatory and negative overtones that the term brings. In the 1960s, spray-painted graffiti appeared all around London, calling the guitarist Eric Clapton a god, and the behaviour of fans, as they gather to memorialise the death of a pop star or film star, is more often than not described as religious worship. These references to religion are eye-catching, and they signal something of the importance that accompanies Celebrity Culture. To speak of performers as gods, is an exaggerated way of describing their power and influence; it is not so much a theological statement, as simply a mark of admiration. This kind of language, however, has a double inflection. A reference to fan behaviour as worship by the media, might indicate how serious a matter it is for these individuals, but at the same time, it may also signal that such behaviour is unusual, or even misplaced. Ambiguity, ambivalence and double inflection are endemic within celebrity discourse, and this tendency problematises any straightforward, or direct, consideration of the worship of celebrities, as religion.

The religious references that are a feature of a great deal of discussion around celebrity, in many cases, should not be read at face value. To speak of stars as gods and goddesses, or fans as worshippers, in most cases should be understood as a metaphor. This metaphorical use of religion in relation to celebrity and fan behaviour, is evident in the work of academics as well as in the media. The group of psychologists who invented the term 'Celebrity Worship Syndrome,' used what they called the 'Celebrity Worship Scale,' as a means to measure the levels of attachment that are formed between fans and celebrities. Their focus was on obsessive or compulsive behaviour that might be regarded as being pathological in certain individuals.[5] In a subsequent study, Celebrity Worship was defined as, 'an abnormal type of parasocial relationship, driven by absorption and addictive elements,' which can result in significant clinical pathologies.[6] Significantly, from a religious studies perspective, what worship means in this context is never discussed by these researchers, and what it is precisely about fan behaviour that might be considered religious, has no place in the research. In their research into the Celebrity Worship Syndrome, religion really plays no part, other than simply acting as a way of naming the phenomenon. The researchers have nothing to say about the religious significance of what they are setting out to measure. The term effectively functions as a metaphorical flourish that is intended to catch the attention of the wider public. The rhetorical use of ideas, such as worship, cult, god and divinity, as metaphors, by academic researchers and in media reporting, is generally no more than a means to indicate importance, rather than any serious consideration of religion. There are, however, a number of commentators who seek to explore more substantive ways in which religion might be operating in and through Celebrity Culture. Particular understandings of religion and its changing nature therefore occupy a central place in the discussion of Celebrity Worship.

Celebrity gods and the sacred

In *Les Stars*, published in 1957, the French philosopher, Edgar Morin, argued that the motion picture industry had created a new religious cult. The cinema, he said, had become the new temple, or church, and the film had taken the place of previous forms of sacred text. 'Worshipped as heroes, divinized, the stars are more than objects of admiration. They are also the subjects of a cult. A religion in embryo has formed around them.'[7] The movie industry transforms mortals into gods; they are divinised, and then worshipped by the fans, who pay devotion by attending the religious ritual of the cinema. Writing in the United States at the same time as Morin, the Episcopal Priest Malcolm Boyd argued for a very similar religious understanding of films, stars and the cinema. Before he was ordained, Boyd worked as a publicity agent promoting Hollywood movies. In *Christ and Celebrity Gods* he speaks about the processes of marketing and promoting, as an industry that generates a pantheon of stars. 'In the "Age of Publicity", there is now a cult of the stars: in the process of achieving pantheon status, we continually observe the mass media metamorphosis of stars into legends.' Celebrities are divinised and made into gods by the action of the media.[8] They act as symbols or motifs of aspects of life and the audience share vicariously in their lives.[9] Boyd is seeking to develop a theological, or pastoral, engagement with the phenomenon of celebrity, but in doing so, he appears to posit that in some ways the star-making system that he was part of, served to generate a distinctive kind of religious practice.

The semiotic reading of film stars, as gods and goddesses, has become a common aspect of critical commentary on popular culture. A classic treatment of the glamour of Hollywood is Roland Barthes discussion of the face of Garbo in *Mythologies*. In his short essay, on the power of the image in Hollywood, he explores the process of media-generated transformation, that he likens to theosis, i.e. the metamorphosis of a human into the divine nature.[10] A more contemporary exponent of this approach is the American post-feminist critic, Camille Paglia. In Paglia's analysis of music videos that were made by Madonna early in her career, the critic draws attention to the religious energy of the star as a dancer, and her iconic presence in still photography. Madonna, she says, 'has both the dynamic Dionysian power of dance and the static Apollonian power of iconicism.'[11] Paglia's work makes use of the classical gods as a means to develop an analysis that is concerned with archetypes and symbolism. Here, divinity is used as metaphors or archetypes that are seen as powerfully operative in representation. Religion, in this approach, shifts towards a discourse of the self, with the gods standing in for aspects of personality and behaviour. The theologian, Tom Beaudoin, discusses the religious imagery in Madonna's music video as evidence for what he calls, 'irreverent spirituality.' This spirituality can be uncovered, or seen as being active, in and through the music, practices and imagery of popular culture. In discussing the video for Madonna's song 'Like a Prayer', he argues, she is clearly in a Catholic Church, staring at a statue of a black man. The audience might interpret the figure as an image of Christ, but some critics argue that this is a Latin American Saint called Martin de Porres. As the song moves along, the statue comes to life and Madonna and the Saint/Christ figure are seen in a highly sensual and eroticised embrace. For Beaudoin, this is evidence of the subversive approach of popular culture to religious imagery. The sensuality in the video suggests, for him, the centrality of experience as an aspect of spirituality in popular culture.[12] These theological themes are carried by Madonna, who is locating herself within this wider narrative of the divine. Her choice of the name 'Madonna' in itself is something of a clue in this regard. Beaudoin's observations concerning the way in which, through representation, Catholic religious iconography is relocated in individual sensuality and experience, further illustrates how the self is brought to the centre, through the religious inflections found in Celebrity Culture.

There are academic commentators who make more extensive claims about the religious significance of celebrity. John Frow, for example, suggests that the metaphorical and symbolic treatment of religion, in the writing of figures such as Morin and Paglia, does not adequately account for the existence of what he regards as a genuine cult. Drawing on the notions of the sacred and the numinous, taken from Marcia Eliade and Rudolph Otto, in his article 'Is Elvis God?', Frow traces what he understands as a real presence in cultural representation. 'Demi-gods of the type of Elvis and Diana,' he suggests, 'are intercessionary figures, gods in human form, whose presence spans and translates between two worlds.'[13] This notion of presence, he sees as crucially enacted and made manifest in the reproduction of the image and voice of the artist. In the case of Elvis, production of the image takes place through technologies of recording and broadcasting. The real power of Elvis comes from a technology of repetition, seen for the first time in the Sam Phillips, Sun Recording Studios. The real Elvis was, from the very first, a copied Elvis, who earned his authenticity and charismatic force from recording, says Frow.[14] Elvis is recognised, and therefore worshipped, because he is recorded and made present through reproduction. Celebrity Worship is, then, pre-eminently a cult of the dead, whose deities are made alive through the technologies of reproduction. This presence, however, is always carried alongside an ambivalence. The myth of Elvis is always played out alongside impersonations, comic narratives and ridiculous exaggeration. 'The King is a joke, an object of ridicule, as much as, and indeed precisely to the extent that, he is an object of worship and one of the central figures through which American popular culture imagines the relation between the living and the dead.'[15]

These approaches to the celebrity and media representation focus on the religious dynamics at play in representation. Film invites a kind of worship through its representation of the human image as an object of adoration. Edgar Morin, Roland Barthes and Camille Paglia pick up on this generative power within particular forms of image making within media industries, and they draw attention to what is taking place in the relationships that are established between stars. Tom Beaudoin, by contrast, focuses on the specific articulation that takes place in the video imagery of Madonna. Here, the star plays with the divine as sexual partner. These twin themes of the divine in representation have led a number of commentators to assert that celebrity operates as a form of religion in society.

Alongside the discussion of representation and the celebrity as divine image, there are other academic approaches that draw a more direct parallel with the relationship to religion. Chris Rojek places religion at the centre of his understanding of Celebrity Culture. The kinds of relationships that fans develop with celebrities, he says, can achieve an intensity that mimics religious experience. This intimacy, however, carries within it a tension, because the celebrity is also remote from the individual. This means that the relationships that fans have with celebrities, even though they might serve to shape a sense of self, are one sided. Celebrities appear to be known, and yet also not known. They are experienced as special individuals with whom individuals have a deeply held personal connection, and yet they are also somehow beyond touch, or real connection. The tension, between the remoteness and the intimacy that exists between fans and the celebrities that they follow, Rojek likens to religious devotion. Celebrities, he argues, exercise a power in fans' lives that has parallels with the religious figure of the Shaman. The relationship that is generated between fans and the objects of their devotion rests, says Rojek, on secularisation and the way that the sacred and the symbolic shifts and moves, with the decline of formal religious affiliation. 'In secular society, the sacred loses its connotation with organised religious belief and becomes attached to mass-media celebrities who become objects of cult worship.'[16]

Secularisation, for Rojek, does not imply the absence of the sacred, or of religious sensibilities; rather, what is taking place is a gradual takeover of religion by Celebrity Culture. It is a ubiquitous Celebrity Culture that provides, 'the main scripts, presentational props, conversational codes and other source materials, through which cultural relations are constructed.'[17] In a context that is 'post-god', it is Celebrity Culture that serves as an organising framework for belonging in society.[18] In this context, individuals, such as pop musicians and film stars, take on, or attract to themselves, the position of Shamans. Musicians, such as John Coltrane and Miles Davies, he suggests, were able to transport their audiences away from their daily worries into a different world. This ability is associated with magic, or in some cases the devil, and it demonstrates how the musician acts as a Shaman in contemporary culture.[19] The Rock Shaman does not generate a specifically religious devotion in the crowd, their power lies in excitement, and 'mass hysteria.' They are a 'conducting rod of mass desire,' and they 'precipitate semi-orgiastic emotions in the crowd.'[20] While arguing for the Shamanistic tendencies in Celebrity Culture, and in particular in popular music, Rojek is clear that celebrity is often contradictory and multifaceted, and it is a mistake to attempt to generalise about any kind of unified mythic or ritualised, let alone religious, coherence. Nevertheless, says Rojek, there are 'ceremonies of ascent and descent' that, along with related themes of magic and immortality, act as a kind of belief system.

Ascent, or elevation, describes the processes that bring about the transformation of the individual to a state that is above the public. This is achieved through representation primarily, but it is also part of the dynamic that comes with wealth, and the lifestyles that are possible as a result of wealth. The talk show, the celebrity magazine, and celebrity biographies, all serve to build towards the ascent of the star.[21] The celebrity who has been elevated is seen to perform acts of magic. These wonders are evident on the screen, but they are also there in the performance of pop stars on the stage.[22] Magic acts and deeds, are supplemented by the aura that celebrity association gives to material artefacts – the gloves worn by Michael Jackson, or the car that John Lennon once owned. In specific sites, such as the Hard Rock Café, these items that have been touched by the Shaman are put on display in sacred reliquaries. Immortality is guaranteed through media reproduction of images. The star is preserved in their movies and in the photographs that were taken of them. As Graham McCann argues, Marilyn Monroe is immortal because she is always present. 'Monroe is now everywhere yet nowhere: her image is on walls, in movies, in books – all after images obscuring the fact of her permanent absence.'[23] Stars may rise to heights, but they are also frequently seen to descend to the depths. Descent and falling are then the other side of ascent and rising. The mass media that build up celebrities, find it almost impossible not to work to bring them down to size, once they have achieved a certain status.[24] Descent, however, is not simply a media-generated phenomenon, celebrities themselves are perfectly capable of bringing about their own demise through marital infidelity, drug abuse or bad behaviour.

Celebrity Worship, as a new and contemporary expression of the sacred, is a central part of Gary Laderman's understanding of Celebrity Culture.[25] The sacred, as a category, moves beyond, and outside, more formal understandings of religion. In American religious life, there is much, he says, that operates further than the confines of religious traditions such as Christianity, Judaism, Hinduism or Islam. This is the category of the sacred, 'a word signifying religious cultures or communities tied together emotionally and cognitively, but also spiritually and materially by vital rituals, living myths, indescribable experiences, moral values, shared memories and other commonly recognised features of religious life.'[26] The sacred does not rest on one idea of God, or an ordered pattern of religion, rather it describes a religious sensibility that infuses every aspect of life. The sacred is fluid, flexible and messy in character.[27] As religion passes away, the sacred is what is left. It is seen in a variety of different types of cultural activity. In rituals and myths that function in ways that are not entirely like formal religion, and yet offer a sense of belonging and identity. The sacred also gathers community, again not in the structured way that religion works, but through more loose and occasional ties. And within all of these, there are what Laderman calls, rich resources for an ever-present encounter with the sacred, in body and in soul. It is this understanding of the sacred, and how it operates, that he brings into conversation with Celebrity Culture. Celebrities arise in American culture at the point where mainline Protestant religion is losing 'its stranglehold on public culture.'[28] As people grow more distant from God, the media technologies of radio, film, sports and television begin to offer different kinds of divinities to those made familiar by the Church. New divinities in turn generated new forms of devotional practices. Secularisation then did not mean the end of religion but its replacement with new forms of divinisation. Celebrities give rise to passionate forms of worship among their followers. The stars of this new form of the sacred, inspire new religious practices, rituals and mythologies in their audiences. They give rise to new kinds of commitment and moral values that are linked to material rather than spiritual rewards.[29]

Celebrity and non-religion

The academic discussion of Celebrity Culture as religion, has generally situated the approach within an overarching narrative of secularisation. Celebrity is therefore read as replacing aspects of formal religion, or as a cultural formation that functions in a similar way to religion. The problem with this direct parallel between Celebrity Culture and religion is that it runs into the web of issues that are inherent in the fluid and complex nature of what is meant by the term religion. Ironically, it is this problem of the fluid nature of religion that lies behind the resort to notions of the sacred of the numinous in relation to Celebrity Worship. The claim that Celebrity Culture operates as a cult, and that fans are worshippers that share in this religion, is best seen as primarily a metaphor. In popular discourse, there are no specifically religious assertions made, rather Celebrity Worship operates as a means to draw attention to religion-like behaviour. That Celebrity Worship might be 'like' religion has a more substantial claim. This approach to religion and celebrity rests on isolating a particular aspect of an understanding of religion, and demonstrating how Celebrity Culture might, in some way, be working as a replacement. An example might be the extent to which celebrities take the place of more religious role models, seen in the Saints or Shamans for instance. The replacement of religious myths, such as the dying and rising God, by the celebrity narratives that are generated in media culture is again a way to draw parallels between celebrity and religion. It would be possible to add to this the focus on the rituals and gatherings, such as pop concerts, or sporting events, that generate an experience or atmosphere that can be compared to religious behaviour. The changing nature of the sacred also operates as a partial claim to the religious significance of celebrity. The sacred operates in a way that does not require there to be a religious institution or dedicated religious community or set of religious practices.

The religious analogy, however it is framed, has a limited application to Celebrity Culture. One of the main reasons for this lies within the nature of celebrity representation in the media, and in the kinds of relationships that individuals develop with celebrities. There is a deep ambivalence that runs at the heart of every relationship between fans and celebrities, that characterises Celebrity Culture. One of the biggest celebrity television shows in the United States has been 'American Idol'. On the show, members of the public participate in a singing competition. The format is familiar from a range of different shows, where, each week, there is a public vote. The use of the word 'Idol' in the title, carries a range of connotations. In the first instance, it indicates that these people are gods, and yet, in a Christian or Jewish context, the word also means false gods. There is then, a knowingness, or an ironic sense, that these individuals who are performing are not the real deal. The show exists to bring into being false gods, and the audience knows this is the case, even as, by voting, they share in how these idols are made. This kind of insider knowledge and participation is evident in the way that celebrities are both celebrated, and brought down, in media coverage, i.e. what Rojek describes as ascent and descent, in celebrity discourse. Audiences are well aware of this dynamic, to the extent that, even as they might admire or envy their favourite celebrities, they are partly conscious that at some point, through moral failure, avarice, weakness, or foolishness, the celebrity will fall. Such a fall is anticipated with a certain pleasure as part of what it means to share in Celebrity Worship.

Another aspect of this kind of ambivalent relationship is the phenomenon by which fans will both identify with celebrities, and also dis-identify with them. Dis-identification describes how celebrities are regarded negatively, as examples of what not to do, or how not to live a life. Dis-identification is the flip side of identification, and it is as much a part of Celebrity Worship as admiration, or the sense that individuals might be role models. Celebrities are therefore never unproblematically followed or admired. They may equally be ridiculed, ignored, or even despised, and perhaps hated. Ridicule and loathing form part of what celebrity representation and consumption rest upon. Closely related to this is the central role that gossip plays in all aspects of celebrity life. Celebrities are continually being judged and talked about, in both positive and negative ways, and as the word gossip suggests, the chief pleasure in these conversations will be skewed towards the negative. Dis-identification and gossip indicate how Celebrity Culture thrives on misfortune, as well as success, and on characters who exist in order to be examples of what is undesirable, as well as what is desirable. Misfortune and undesirability are only a very short distance from the ridicule and mockery that shapes a great deal of the media coverage of celebrities. In drawing any comparison between religion and celebrity the light-hearted and the frankly unpleasant nature of much of the media culture that surrounds it needs to be considered. The truth of the matter is that religion, and in particular religious people, take what they do very seriously. The predisposition towards levity is one of the reasons why the proposal that Celebrity Culture is a new form of religion lacks credibility. At the same time, there are clearly significant aspects of the relationships that develop between audiences and the way celebrities are represented that carry religious elements. Interpreting these as a form of the sacred or religious in themselves is problematic. My term for this mix of the reverent and irreverent is the term 'para-religion.' Para here indicates something that is similar but not entirely like religion and in some senses its parody.[30] A more helpful approach is to see celebrity as part of a much wider shift in the nature of religion and in particular as a dynamic that is a key driver in the turn to the self as a new sacred or ultimate concern.

Non-religion and the sacred self

The problem with discussions that seek to find a parallel, or indeed a lack of a parallel, between Celebrity Worship and religion, is that they generally rest on an implicit, or an explicit, understanding of religion. As has been noted, this is problematic, in that religion is a difficult phenomenon to define, and Celebrity Culture is a fluid and multi-layered reality. In the study of religion this problem has been central to the fast-developing field of what has been called 'non-religion'.[31] One of the leading figures in the area of non-religion is the sociologist, Lois Lee. Increasing numbers of people in the secularised Western countries are describing themselves as 'non-religious'. Lee argues that approaches to secularisation have been problematic in that they have tended to proceed with the assumption that there is a single, clearly defined definition of religion. This definition is then used to demonstrate the absence of religion in Western societies. The problem with this approach, is that it fails to examine the complexity and nuances that exist in the lives, practices and beliefs of those people who describe themselves as not being religious. Secularisation tends to emphasise how the institutions of religion fare in a changing culture. Lee argues that secular people are not simply living lives that are 'without religion,' because this description is limited, in that it fails to pay any attention to what they might be living with. Secular people, she says, are living with something else. Non-religion, she argues, should be interpreted as a living and energised present, where individuals are actively shaping a non-religious self. Empirical research into non-religion indicates that when questioned, individuals often indicate a range of different identities that might be enacted across different contexts.[32]

The notion of non-religion can be read in connection with two further approaches to the study of religion that have become central to recent academic debates. The first is the notion of 'Lived Religion', most closely associated with the work of Meredith McGuire. In an approach that has many similarities to that taken by Lois Lee, Lived Religion seeks to down play the importance of formal religious institutions, or structured belief systems. Religion, she argues, should not be read in these determined forms, rather it should be examined through the experiences and practices of individual believers. Religion, as it is practiced by individuals, should not be seen as a fixed or even a coherent construct. The individual uses the elements of religious life, symbols, narratives and practices to construct a religious self. This self is fluid and changeable, but it is also social, and developed in relation to others. A formal religious tradition, then, acts a kind of resource that is utilised as a means to generate meaning and significance.[33] Non-religion and Lived Religion are complemented by approaches that deal with the changing nature of the sacred. Gordon Lynch suggests that the sacred offers further ways in which, in a non-religious environment, there are values and norms that persist and continue to carry significance for individuals. The sacred, for Lynch then, indicates what people take as being absolute, or normative, for how we conduct social life.[34] Non-religion, Lived Religion and the shifting nature of the sacred, I want to argue, taken together, indicate a way in which religion and Celebrity Worship should be interpreted. All three approaches situate the religious, or more generally the non-religious subject, at the heart of their analysis. Celebrity Worship is an aspect of this non-religious world, where the sacred has shifted towards the self. What the study of celebrity brings to this conversation is a way of understanding how the choosing self – that is central to both new religious and non-religious forms of practice and identity – comes into being. Celebrity Worship is not an aspect of subjectivisation but a constructive component in how this turn to the self has been generated and sustained, both in wider society and culture, and also in religion and non-religion. This is to say more than simply that celebrity is a missing piece of the puzzle in the academic conversations around theories of media and religion. Celebrity plays a distinctive and fundamental role in how the self is understood more widely in society as a whole.

The turn to the self

The reorientation of religious sensibility, from the authority of religious tradition towards the self, forms a part of a much wider shift in contemporary culture. The self has become the central concern, or project, that structures how people live their lives, and how they relate to institutions, consumer products and social relations. The self has become the epistemological frame through which life is lived and experienced. The sociologist, Anthony Giddens, describes this reorientation towards the self as the 'reflexive self.' Reflexivity refers to a knowing engagement with constructing identity, such that the self becomes an all-consuming project, or endeavour. Identity is not something that is given, says Giddens, it is the result of routine and sustained activities.[35] Maintaining the self as a narrative across time, requires continual attention and focus.[36] This task is made more difficult and all-consuming by the contemporary context, what Giddens calls 'high-modernity.'[37] The experience of the shifting and uncertain context, contributes to the re-orientation of questions of identity, such that they become an overwhelming preoccupation.

In a religious context, these ideas of the self, as the new preoccupation and organising principle, have been widely explored. Wade Clark Roof, for example, situates religious change in America, more generally, in relation to a shift in how the self is understood and performed.[38] He describes this new sense of individuality as, 'the expansive self.'[39] The expansive self, is characterised by a mindset that focuses moral responsibility on how the self is regarded. Life becomes a process of seeking inner meaning and purpose, in and through the elaboration of the self. Roof sees this approach to self as shaping a range of different religious sensibilities from new forms of Pentecostalism to more diffuse approaches to spirituality seen as journeying and seeking.[40] Roof describes this shift in terms of a move away from the question 'How can I be saved?' towards the question, 'How can I feel good about myself?' A very similar focus on the self as a key element in religious change is echoed in the work of Paul Heelas and Linda Woodhead.

Heelas and Woodhead see religious change as being related to a fundamental reorientation towards the self in society.[41] They argue that the turn to the self is a major cultural shift, where objective roles and duties, as a means of organising how people live their lives, have become replaced by the subjective experience.[42] This is not a valorisation of individualism as such, because subjective experience might be individual, or collective. Rather, this move realigns how religion is negotiated and situated in contemporary life. Individuals, Heelas and Woodhead argue, had thought of themselves as playing roles or being subject to external scripts that come from belonging to established 'given orders.' These roles were located in the structure of a past, where family, kinship, community and nation, shaped the sense of self through specific expectations. In this context, the self is understood in and through these external relationships and collectivities. The individual finds value and direction from a structure that precedes and transcends the self. The good life and fulfilment, in this previous cultural paradigm, are seen as sacrificing, or disciplining oneself to downplay personal desires or experience in the light of a higher authority.[43] The turn to the self reverses these relationships. In this context, the experiences and interests of the individual become the touchstone. Living one's life to the best becomes a matter of fulfilling oneself. Rather than submitting to an external higher authority the individual sees themselves as the final authority. The stresses and strains of marriage or parenthood are then reconfigured as a challenge to the self and an environment where there is a challenge where there is an impulse to fulfil yourself as partner or as parent.[44] The turn to the self relocates religious authority and sensibilities in a similar way to that of family relationships. Religion shifts from being an external authority that commands assent and duty to a means to fulfil the self. This leads to a prioritisation of individual agency and choice in relation to religious traditions. The term they give for this is 'the subjectivisation thesis.'[45] The turn towards the self as reflexive project has developed in ways that reshape religion. The ideas of the expansive self and the subjectivisation thesis all point towards the way that traditional forms of religion are being changed. These developments are also part of what is described as non-religion or Lived Religion and they lie behind the shift towards new forms of the sacred. Celebrity Worship should be understood as both a part of these wider developments and also as one of the main ways that these new approaches to the self in religion are created and sustained.

Celebrity and the sacred self

It is in relation to the choices that are made in the construction of the self that Celebrity Culture pays a central role. Celebrities represent possibilities of the self. They signify an ever-changing pageant of different ways of constructing personal identity. Through processes of identification and dis-identification, and the social possibilities of gossip, individuals develop resources that are instructional for their own project. This is what Stuart Hall speaks about when he describes the process of forming identity as a shifting or fluid process of adopting or articulating the self in relation to the media-generated flow of discourse. As has already been noted, 'identities', for Hall, 'are thus points of temporary attachment to the subject positions, which discursive practices construct for us. They are the result of a successful articulation or 'chaining' of the subject in the flow of discourse.'[46] In this context, what is being referred to is the general flow of media. Media has, as its primary content, mediated individuals, celebrities. These individuals are situated in the heart of the vast majority of media representation and they carry associations and influence as a result. The self is constructed in relation to the flow of celebrity images and stories.

David Marshall also sees the emergence of celebrity as located in a much wider shift towards the individual in Western society, art and thought.

Celebrities, he says, 'provide a new representational regime of individuality.'[47] Entertainment, and the narratives and pleasures of a media-generated culture, ensure that celebrities are situated at the 'ideological centre of our culture,' because they express a moment of transcendence, transformation and individuality.[48] Celebrities, he argues, operate as pedagogical aids that facilitate how people generate and construct a meaningful sense of self, in relation to media representation. As such, they form part of the 'structure of feeling' in contemporary culture. Marshall's argument rests in part on Richard Dyer's influential discussion of Hollywood film stars in his book, *Heavenly Bodies*.[49] For Dyer, film stars carry significance in contemporary society because they represent what it means to be human.[50] Stars support the ideological, and the social centrality of the individual. They articulate a narrative of personhood, in the context of change.[51] Celebrity discourses are all constructed in ways that seek to reassure us that we are seeing the celebrity as they really are. In biographies, interviews and photographs, we are invited into the belief that this is what it is like to live an extraordinary celebrity life. We are taken behind the scenes, and given the authentic account of what is taking place.[52] 'Whether caught in the unmediated moment of the close-up, uncovered by the biographer's display of ruthless uncovering, or present in the star's indubitable sincerity and authenticity, we have a privileged reality to hang on to, the reality of the star's private self.'[53] It is in this inner self that the star carries the cultural centre of the authentic individual.[54] Stars then generate in us an affection because they enact ways of being an individual in this particular context. They represent to us what this experience is like, or what it might possibly be like.[55] It is fundamental to the commercial interests of media companies that in representation there are a range of different stars who articulate with the complex dynamics of the self in terms of gender, sexuality, race and social class. The stars then, are 'embodiments of social categories.'[56] Stars are important, because they act out different aspects of life that matter to us, and individual stars matter to us because they represent particular aspects of what matters to us.[57]

This perspective, that sees celebrity as central to the process of developing a sense of self in and through media representation narratives, realigns the idea of Celebrity Worship. Celebrities are not worshipped because they are special in themselves, but because they represent something to fans. Their meaning does not lie in who they are in themselves, but who they are for their audience. What is evident is not so much a cult of celebrity, where individuals are deemed in some way to be divine, but a performance of a different kind of sacredness that operates across contemporary culture. It is the self, and the self as project, that is to be regarded as the 'serious' or normative centre of our culture. Celebrities are nothing like as important or significant as the myriad of ways in which individuals are deeply committed to making their lives meaningful, or well, or whole, or fulfilled. It is this project, or endeavour, that is the new sacred. It is the self that carries religious significance and celebrities are important to it, only to the extent that they might be utilised, or form a means, around which to orientate the self. The theologian, Paul Tillich, describes the human condition as one that is characterised by a series of spiritual concerns. He describes faith as the 'ultimate concern.'[58] An ultimate concern, he says, demands total commitment and it promises total fulfilment. When a particular concern becomes so central that it can be considered an 'ultimate', then it functions in a way that orders other priorities.[59] In contemporary Western society it is the project of the self that has become central. Where the ultimate concern has become the self, celebrity as the mediation of the self plays a central role. It is in relation to the project of the sacred self that Celebrity Worship should be understood.

Notes

1 Pete Ward. *Gods Behaving Badly: Media, Religion and Celebrity Culture*. (Waco, TX: Baylor University Press/SCM Press, 2011).
2 'Worshipping Celebrities Brings Success.' BBC News. Last updated 13 August 2013. http://news.bbc.co.uk/1/hi/health/3147343.stm
3 Lucy Cockcroft. 'Cult of Celebrity is "Harming Children"'. *Telegraph*, 14 March 2008. www.telegraph.co.uk/news/uknews/1581658/Cult-of-celebrity-is-harming-children. html.
4 Malcolm Boyd. *Christ and Celebrity Gods*. (Greenwich: Seabury Press, 1958).
5 Lynn McCutcheon. 'Conceptualization and Measurement of Celebrity Worship.' *British Journal of Psychiatry*, 93, no. 1 (2002): 67–87.
6 John Maltby, James Houran, and Lynn McCutcheon. 'A Clinical Interpretation of Attitudes and Behaviors Associated with Celebrity Worship.' *The Journal of Nervous and Mental Disease*, 191, no. 1 (2003): 25–29.
7 Edgar Morin. *The Stars*. (Minneapolis: University of Minnesota Press, 1972. English translation 2005), 57.
8 Malcolm Boyd, *Christ and Celebrity Gods*. (Greenwich: Seabury Press, 1958), 57.
9 Boyd, *Christ*, 11.
10 Barthes, Roland. *Mythologies*. (London: Paladin Books, 1957. English translation 1972), 56.
11 Camille Paglia. *Sex, Art and American Culture*. (New York: Vintage, 1992), 12.
12 Tom Beaudoin. *Virtual Faith: The Irreverent Spirituality of Generation X*. (San Francisco: Jossey Bass 1998), 80–81.
13 John Frow. 'Is Elvis God? Cult, Culture, Questions of Method.' *International Journal of Cultural Studies*, 1, no. 2 (1998): 202.
14 Frow. Is Elvis, 203–204.
15 Frow. Is Elvis, 204.
16 Chris Rojek. *Celebrity*. (London: Reaktion Books, 2001), 57.
17 Rojek. *Celebrity*, 57.
18 Rojek. *Celebrity*, 58.
19 Rojek. *Celebrity*, 68.
20 Rojek. *Celebrity*, 69.
21 Rojek. *Celebrity*, 75.
22 Rojek. *Celebrity*, 77.
23 Rojek. *Celebrity*, 78.
24 Rojek. *Celebrity*, 79.
25 Gary Laderman. *Sacred Matters: Celebrity Worship, Sexual Ecstasies, The Living Dead, and Other Signs of Religious Life in the United States*. (New York: The New Press, 2009).
26 Laderman. *Sacred*, xiv.

27 Laderman. *Sacred*, xv.
28 Laderman. *Sacred*, 64.
29 Laderman. *Sacred*, 64.
30 Pete Ward. *Gods Behaving Badly: Media, Religion and Celebrity Culture*. (Waco, TX: Baylor University Press/SCM Press, 2011).
31 Lois Lee. 'Secular or Nonreligious? Investigating and Interpreting Generic 'Not Religious' Categories and Populations.' *Religion*, 44 (2014): 466–482.
32 Lee. Secular, 466–482.
33 Meredith McGuire. *Lived Religion: Faith and Practice in Everyday Life*. (Oxford: Oxford University Press, 2008).
34 Gordon Lynch, ed. *Between Sacred and profane: Researching Religion and Popular Culture*. (London: I.B. Tauris, 2007), 5.
35 Anthony Giddens. *Modernity and Self Identity*. (Cambridge: Polity Press, 1991), 52.
36 Giddens. *Modernity*, 54.
37 Giddens. *Modernity*, 12.
38 Wade Clark Roof. *Spiritual Marketplace: Baby Boomers and the Remaking of American Religion*. (Princeton, NJ: Princeton University Press, 1999), 12.
39 Roof. *Spiritual*, 62.
40 Roof. *Spiritual*, 66.
41 Paul Heelas and Linda Woodhead. *Spiritual Revolution: Why Religion is Giving Way to Spirituality*. (Oxford: Blackwell, 2005).
42 Heelas and Woodhead. *Spiritual*, 2.
43 Heelas and Woodhead. *Spiritual*, 3.
44 Heelas and Woodhead. *Spiritual*, 3.
45 Heelas and Woodhead. *Spiritual*, 3.
46 du Gay. *Doing*, 6.
47 David Marshall. 'The Promotion and Presentation of the Self: Celebrity as the Marker of Presentational Media.' *Celebrity Studies*, 1, no. 1 (2010): 35–48.
48 Marshall. Promotion, 19.
49 Richard Dyer. *Heavenly Bodies: Film Stars and Society*. (London: Routledge, 1986).
50 Dyer. *Heavenly*, 7.
51 Dyer. *Heavenly*, 9.
52 Dyer. *Heavenly*, 9.
53 Dyer. *Heavenly*, 10.
54 Dyer. *Heavenly*, 12.
55 Dyer. *Heavenly*, 15.
56 Dyer. *Heavenly*, 16.
57 Dyer. *Heavenly*, 17.
58 Paul Tillich. *Dynamics of Faith*. (New York: Perennial Classics, 1956), 2.
59 Tillich. *Dynamics*, 2.

Chapter 3

The roots and origins of Celebrity Culture

The central argument so far has been that a celebrity is a mediated individual. Stories about people and images of people are central to all forms of media representation and circulation. Media and celebrity are therefore intrinsically and fundamentally related, because celebrity describes what media processes do to individuals. When audiences consume media, they consume people, and these people are celebrities, or they are made into celebrities as they are consumed. It is clear, then, that understanding Celebrity Worship must lie at the heart of any consideration of media because people are so important in media culture. If celebrity is what media processes, in their complexity, do to people, then it also follows that the discussion of the relationship between religion and media cannot be undertaken without a serious and sustained examination of celebrity. People are as fundamental to religion as they are to media representation, so understanding what is taking place in Celebrity Worship is, in effect, common ground in both areas. Passing over celebrity, or leaving it on one side in the discussion of religion and media, is a significant oversight, because neither can be fully understood without a consideration of people. Celebrity is the human shape of contemporary culture and no discussion of religion and media is complete without it.

Celebrity Culture, as we are currently familiar with it, appears to have started in the 1990s. It is at this time that significant aspects of celebrity journalism were developed by a raft of new publications such as *Hello!*, *OK*, *Now*, *Closer* and *Grazia*.[1] Mark Frith the editor of *Heat* magazine, who was at the centre of the rise of Celebrity Culture in the UK, calls the period of the 2000s 'the celebrity decade'.[2] It is at this time that there is a significant shift in the way that the British tabloid press began to cover celebrity stories.[3] A characteristic of this new kind of celebrity coverage is the central role played by individuals, who appear to have no other purpose than to simply be there. As Ellis Cashmore comments, these are people who have not achieved anything specific or noteworthy other than the fact that they are present in the media. This kind of media-driven fame 'celebrifies' by investing ordinary individuals with a heightened significance.[4]

The frivolous nature and altogether pointlessness, of much celebrity media is a constant and enduring trope in both journalism and academic discussion of the field.[5] Daniel Boorstein famously describes the celebrity as a person who is well-known for their well-knownness.[6] Yet alongside the persistent scepticism, and concerns about the effects that Celebrity Culture might be bringing about in contemporary discourse, there has been a growing recognition among academics of the significance and importance of understanding how celebrity operates, and what it might or might not mean. These treatments of celebrity emphasise the way that the media processes act as a 'fame making apparatus'.[7] Celebrity fame, generated by media, acts to ensure that celebrities are central to the sensibilities and experience of everyday life in a variety of different ways. Sue Holmes and Sean Redman argue that celebrities should be regarded as being central to meaning making and idea formation in the modern world. Celebrity is both global in scope and also particularly local in many aspects of consumption. Celebrities guarantee the trans-global marketing of cultural products, such as films or music. As such, celebrities appear to occupy a privileged place at the centre of the media world, and their presence suggests that to achieve celebrity status is to have unique access to the symbolic heart of contemporary culture. Celebrity 'exists at the core of many of the spaces, experiences and economies of modern life'.[8] David Marshall develops a similar approach, arguing that celebrities intersect with every aspect of social life, from politics to economics and all forms of cultural life.[9] One might add religion to this list of areas that in one way or another have been influenced by Celebrity Culture. This is what Chris Rojek calls 'celebrification,' which he defines as, the means by which, 'ordinary identity formation and general forms of social interaction are patterned and inflected by the styles, embodied attitudes and conversational flow developed through celebrity culture.' Celebrities then function both as role models and as social types.[10]

Celebrity and renown

The contemporary manifestation of Celebrity Culture is complex and all-pervasive. The scale and reach of media processes of 'celebrification'[11] is an indication, argues Graeme Turner, that it is likely to have multiple points of origin.[12] While it might be argued that celebrity, as it is currently manifest, arises in the 1990s, it has roots that are much older. Fame and renown, as opposed to celebrity, have been present in human culture from ancient times and there are significant continuities between these older forms and present-day culture.[13] Leo Braudy traces the origination of fame to the fifth and fourth centuries BC. The first famous person, he argues, was Alexander the Great.[14] Alexander was a conqueror, a hero of great deeds, but he also sought a status as one who was distinct, separated and a semi-divine figure. From the earliest period, he ensured that his image was reproduced solely in a form that he approved of, based on designs he commissioned from the greatest artists of his day.[15] From ancient times, then, the presence of the hero, and the reach of the great god-man is made present through representation. Richard Howells develops these themes in his comparison of the images of heroes and saints in the medieval world, and the use of photography in Celebrity Culture.[16] A similar approach is developed by Lee Barron, who traces the connections between representation and the controlling of the image seen in the behaviours of figures such as the actor David Garrick in the eighteenth century, and Louis IV of France, the 'Sun King'. The cultlike nature of celebrity, therefore, has its origins in much older forms of representation that have been powerful as ways to spread influence and power through the reproduction of the image.

These older forms of celebrity illustrate the categories of celebrity developed by Chris Rojek. Rojek argues that celebrity status comes in three different forms: ascribed, achieved and attributed. Ascribed celebrity refers primarily to the way that fame and renown are inherited, as part of a bloodline or family relationship. Examples of this might be the British royal family, or the Kennedys in the US. Interestingly, there are similar celebrity dynasties that have started to function in more recent times – for instance, the Kardashians, the Beckhams, the McCartneys. Through particular actions or achievements, these individuals may develop a particular profile, but the basis for their fame comes, in the first instance, as a given, from their family relationships.[17] Achieved celebrity encompasses film stars, musicians, sporting figures and politicians. These are figures who have risen to public recognition through their own distinctive and often extraordinary achievements. Attributed celebrity arises when an individual comes to public notice through a concentrated representation in the media. Here, the individual is moved into the category of being exceptional, simply through the frequency that they appear, and the spread of their presence across different media platforms.[18] Ascribed, achieved and attributed celebrity co-exist and, in many ways, they show a convergence, as media discourses and ways of reading and consuming celebrities serve to create a homogeneous sensibility. In the contemporary context, everyone in the media – be they a sports star, a politician, or indeed a religious figure – are treated as if they are celebrities. David Giles observes that it is a 'brutal reality' that the media does not make any meaningful distinction between a person propelled into public notice through a reality show, and an extraordinarily talented actor, or a notable world leader.[19]

It is the development of mass forms of media communication that transforms and democratises how fame is spread and manipulated. Technological developments play a crucial role in how Celebrity Culture is generated. Boorstein attributes the starting point of modern Celebrity Culture to what he calls, the 'Graphic Revolution' of the mid nineteenth century.[20] What he is referring to is an explosion in printing and in particular, newspapers, but it is the reproduction of the image, through the invention of photography that, combined with print, generates the most significant shift towards Celebrity Culture as we know it. Celebrities are made by these processes of representation, but they can also be unmade. 'Now when it is possible, by bringing their voices and images daily into our living rooms to make celebrities more quickly than ever before, they die more quickly.'[21]

Roland Barthes' discussion of the face of Greta Garbo touches on the power of cinema to deify through the image of the human face. Audiences, he says, are plunged into the 'deepest ecstasy,' becoming lost in the human image. In Garbo's gaze rendered through film there is something of a platonic ideal in the idea of a human creature.[22] The eulogising of Garbo captures something of the way that film and cinema in particular, served to transform the individual into a new kind of extraordinary being, the star. Joshua Gamson draws a clear relationship between photography and the generation of Celebrity Culture. The image, he argues, increasingly takes the place of the idea in contemporary culture.[23] Technological developments in photography have clearly played a central role in the way that celebrities are represented in the media. One of the most significant photographic innovations was the invention of the zoom lens. Ellis Cashmore points to the publication of images that showed the extramarital affair of Elizabeth Taylor and Richard Burton in the 1960s, while they were filming the movie Cleopatra, as the birth of the paparazzi celebrity photo. Up until the publication of these images, major Hollywood stars, such as Elizabeth Taylor, had been managed by the conventions of marketing and advertising that were able to closely control what was shared concerning the personal lives of their stars. Promotional activities would give a manufactured glimpse behind the scenes, but these forms of publicity were under the management of the star-making system. When Taylor and Burton were pictured in an intimate embrace on a boat in Italy, and these images were reproduced in magazines and newspapers around the world, the rules that controlled the image of Hollywood stars, and for just about everyone else, were changed.[24]

Gossip and personal stories

A major driving force in Celebrity Culture is our human predisposition towards gossip. The photos generated by the paparazzi fed off this hunger for personal and intimate information. The celebrity section of the *Metro* newspaper in the UK is given the title, 'Guilty Pleasures'. This newspaper packaging of pictures and brief insights into the personal lives of a range of celebrities, from A-List film stars to individuals who have featured in reality television shows, acknowledges the slightly tainted feel that gossip occupies in our culture. We are invited to take a sneak look behind the scenes, at what perhaps we should not really know, or indeed be at all interested in, but of course we are anyway. Post the Leveson Inquiry, the intrusion that was a regular aspect of a paparazzi-driven media culture since the 1960s has been somewhat curtailed in the UK and, as a result, most of the images published in *Metro* and elsewhere have been arranged by mutual consent, but they are made to look as if they are taken when the celebrities are caught unaware or off guard. The common element that remains, however, is the continued fascination that is generated around the personal lives of people who are in the media world.

Richard DeCordova traces the origins of the star system in Hollywood to developments in technology and the discourse of acting. The development of more accessible forms of film making and the growth in cinemas saw a shift towards fictional or narrative-based film making. These necessitated the use of actors, not simply to appear in the movies, but also to help promote and sell the product. With more and more films being made, there was a requirement to differentiate between a much greater number of films that were being marketed. It is into this space that the actor moves, and through their use as vehicles to promote and sell films, they are transformed into stars.[25] The emergence of the star turned the individual into a commodity. Central to this process is the way that the star-making system served to develop the personality of the actor, so that they did not simply promote a single movie, but that their appeal became more widespread. By generating an attachment in audiences to individual actors, the Hollywood publicity machine was able to use the star to publicise a series of different products. The star, therefore, says Turner, had both a personal and professional interest in promoting themselves. 'Hence we have the constitution of a new source of information for the media and a new means of constructing identity through the media.'[26]

Developing actors into stars involved a transition from the roles that are specific to movie scripts, to an interest in the individual's 'personal' life. The Hollywood publicity machine carefully managed the way that stars were presented and how their image was developed, through magazine interviews, publicity appearances and most importantly photography. Stars are then created as individuals with lives that are revealed through media accounts. These forms of revelation enable different forms of identification from fans, even as they preserve a distance between the audience and the star. Through the standard industry vehicles of the one-to-one interview, the autobiography and reality television, a kind of intimacy is developed between audiences and celebrities. In these contexts, celebrities perform in ways that demonstrate their authenticity and emotional integrity.[27] The revelation of personal lives, facilitates a media form of intimacy between the celebrity and their audience, and it is this attachment that makes them into such an important commodity for the culture industries. Attachment and intimacy sells.

Gossip concerning the personal details of the lives of stars that goes beyond the onscreen roles that they play, also generates an emotional connection for audiences.[28] Stars, and their private lives, become a part of a shared media world, where the pleasures of talking about the problems and imperfections of another person become permissible. There is an ambivalence around these ways of relating to celebrity lives – they are in some senses a 'guilty pleasure' – but they might also be regarded as serving a significant social function. Marshall argues that celebrities act as some kind of teaching aid in the development of the self. Celebrity gossip, he argues, represents a continued conversation concerning the presentation of the self in a public context. These stories of marital break-up, infidelity, drug taking and squandered wealth, says Marshall, are a kind of morality tale that act as a kind of pedagogy.[29] Celebrity gossip is consumed as an aid to constructing the self in contemporary society. Gossip, then, is the means by which celebrities move from being figures portrayed in the media, to being part of our lives. This process, however, depends upon the distance that a media presence carries with it. Celebrities are not 'real' people. They are one remove from our families or communities, and as a result there is an implicit permission given to speak about them and discuss their behaviour.

Celebrity rests on an illusion of intimacy. The flow of images and stories generate an emotional connection, but this is at a distance. Media acts, then, to build a connection, but it is one that is always slightly at a remove. Audiences experience celebrities as people in their world, and yet the relationships that are a feature of media culture are one sided. Horton and Wohl describe the relationships that are generated through the media with celebrities as 'para-social interactions'.[30] This notion acknowledges that there are often real connections made, as fans interact with the people that they are aware of through media representation, and yet at the same time these relationships are distinct. They exist alongside, or in parallel to, other kinds of relationships. The kinds of involvement that audiences have with celebrities can be varied. Havitz and Dimanche suggest that there are three different levels of relationships that can be discerned in the way that individuals and groups generate connections to celebrity figures. The first they characterise as 'What we do'. This encompasses the regular day-to-day activities of reading celebrity stories in newspapers, or noticing celebrity pictures as they appear in magazines, or watching television programmes that feature celebrities. This kind of low-level interaction is simply a feature of life, or at least a life where there is any kind of consumption of media. The second level of involvement with Celebrity Culture, is described as, 'social identity.' This refers to the consumption of media, with the addition of sharing information and celebrity gossip with friends. This kind of group engagement, with individuals and their narratives, becomes part of a shared conversation. The third level they describe as an 'intense para-social interaction'. Here individuals have developed a deep relationship with a celebrity, such that at times it might be seen as being pathological in nature.[31]

Selling celebrities

Celebrities exist to sell product. They are used by television companies to promote programmes, by the movie industry to sell films, by the music industry to sell records, by the fashion industry to sell clothes, and by charities to generate donations. Selling particular kinds of cultural products, however, is not the limit or extent of their purpose. Celebrities also exist to sell themselves, and if they are successful in developing a profile, they are then more useful as the means to endorse a range of products. The publicity industries work to change individuals into marketable commodities. It is the commodification of people, says Cashmore, that is a fundamental feature of Celebrity Culture. Once they are famous, celebrities are able to enhance their earning power through an association with a range of products, including clothing lines, perfumes, motor cars and electrical products.[32] Celebrities, then, are commodified individuals who exist to sell commodities.[33]

Celebrity Culture arises from the complex interaction of a range of different individuals, organisations and media outlets. Developing a celebrity profile is a process that involves a network of interconnected productive relationships. Celebrity should not be seen as something that is inherent in a remarkable individual, or related to their essence; rather, it arises from a concentration of productive relationships that have at their heart a commercial purpose. As Rojek puts it, 'No celebrity now acquires public recognition without the assistance of public intermediaries who operate to stage-manage celebrity presence in the eyes of the public.'[34] The intermediaries range from media companies, and all the processes of creating and selling media products, to media outlets that are then used to generate interest and sales of these products. Other forms of intermediary are the people that celebrities gather around them, to help them to enhance and promote their own image and career. Celebrity arises from a whole network of individuals, institutions, technologies and commercial interests. Despite the industrial size of the fame-making machine, celebrity publicity, Turner argues, seeks to mask its function. The aim is to generate attention and sell across the range of media content, without appearing to be involved. At the heart of this lies the desire to make sure that, 'advertising appears as news.'[35]

Celebrities are fundamental to commercial processes, because they bring audiences and consumers to particular products. This rests on the kinds of relationships and interest that Celebrity Worship creates among the general public. Interest in the personality and narratives associated with celebrities, becomes articulated or associated with individual products through the action of intermediaries. At the heart of this promotional purpose in Celebrity Culture, is the facility that individuals bring by offering distinctive personalities. Celebrities therefore are developed by the market, such that they represent different, and often opposite, or conflictual, characteristics. The wide range of different celebrity images and personalities mean that producers can sell to a larger audience. For Boorstein, the celebrity is fundamentally an artificial construct of the Culture Industry. He draws a distinction between those who we should rightly regard as being heroes, and therefore achieve fame and notoriety, and those who are well-known because they are always present in the media.[36] Celebrity is the distinctive feature of our modern culture, and this new form threatens to overshadow all previous forms of sainthood, hero worship and notoriety.[37] It is the 'machinery of information' that has generated this new and distinctive celebrity figure. The 'hero', says Boorstein, has a history. They are figures who remain in our cultural memory through legend and historical narrative. The celebrity, by contrast, is locked in the present. As he puts it, 'No one is more forgotten than the last generation's celebrity.'[38] Celebrities are 'pseudo events,' figures constructed simply for publicity, and who exist in newspaper copy and photographs. The figure who is the pseudo-event is eminently disposable. 'Celebrities, because they are made to order, can be made to please, fascinate, and flatter us. They can be produced and displaced in rapid succession.'[39] Rojek takes a very similar view, drawing a distinction between celebrities who may have achieved their fame as say an actor, or as a musician, and what he calls 'celetoids'. The 'celetoid' is someone who has come to public notice through the intense promotion of a range of different media. Examples might include lottery winners, stalkers, arena streakers and the mistresses of public figures. These are people who may be very present one moment in the media, and then forgotten the next.[40]

Cashmore describes the interrelated nature of the productive processes in Celebrity Culture as operating on three main levels. The first is the consumer-driven market economy, which, he says, lies behind a shift in sensibilities towards individual choice and personal preference. The second level is the explosion in different forms of media that arises from technological innovation. The new media environment blurs the distinction between consumers and creators, such that the traditional audience and producer relationships become more complex. The third level, in this network of relations, describes the complicit nature of consumption in the generation of consumer culture. 'Being a consumer no longer meant standing on the outside: it meant being an active player – a creator as well as a consumer of celebrities.'[41] Celebrities then, play a central role in the way that media culture generates attention and desire, and how it seeks to use these to sell products. This process, however, is one which should be seen as a co-creation, between the Culture Industry and audiences, who through consumer choice, and the different forms of participation, share in its creation.

Identification and dis-identification

Celebrities are generated in a media culture with the purpose of selling products. Audiences, however, do not buy things because they are endorsed by famous individuals, rather, they buy in order to be like those celebrities.[42] Consumer products are not simply utilitarian objects in themselves, as commodities and brands, they are objects that are linked to meanings. Celebrities are there to help facilitate this connection. The key element that supports this economic process of linking commodities to meaning arises from the extent to which different celebrities represent particular values.[43] The engine that drives this process comes from the way that audiences develop significant attachments to celebrity figures. Para-social interaction as a theoretical framework, argues Cashmore, does not adequately account for the creative and dynamic ways in which individuals use celebrities as part of their identity construction. Fraser and Brown use the notion of identification to describe how individuals generate their sense of self through the media representation of celebrity. Identification describes how fans, 'reconstruct their own attitudes, values, or behaviours in response to the images of people they admire, real and imagined, both through personal and mediated relationships.'[44] This conception of fan/celebrity relationships reverses notions of individuals being disproportionately influenced by powerful media sources. The fan is not seen as someone who is duped or conned into buying what the media Culture Industry is selling. Identification becomes a way of speaking about the active and empowered means by which celebrity images and narratives become a resource in generating a sense of self.

The process whereby individuals use celebrity as part of generating a sense of self – identification – is balanced by an equally important and probably more pervasive sentiment of 'dis-identification', which, as we have already seen, describes the extent to which audiences make value judgements about the celebrity images and narratives that they consume. Disapproval in this context is just as significant as approval, because the celebrity becomes a means to process values. This might be at the basic level of talking about how a celebrity has handled an aspect of their relationships, or it might be a fashion choice, or something to do with cosmetic surgery. Identification places an emphasis on positive influence and the idea of the celebrity as a role model. Dis-identification recognises that for many people celebrities are better known for poor choices, and lives that resemble a car crash, rather than as figures to admire. These kinds of observations, however, do not diminish the importance that sharing in celebrity media coverage might play in everyday lives. Dis-identification is the process whereby fans make a distinction between themselves and the particular image or narrative that they are consuming around a celebrity or celebrities. The choice to dis-identify is therefore an equally significant aspect of constructing identity in relation to media culture.

The relationship between celebrities and their audiences have changed significantly with the advent of social media. Twitter, for instance, appears to disrupt the communication processes and conventions that have shaped Celebrity Culture, in ways that reposition the celebrity and the ordinary member of the public. The celebrity can use their Twitter feed, or Instagram account, to create a direct connection to their followers. These kinds of interaction give the impression that they bypass the PR machine and formal media. Fans are drawn into an illusion of intimacy, as they seem to share an immediate and behind the scenes connection to the celebrity. Twitter and other forms of social media also carry with them the possibility of a direct interaction between celebrity and individual fans. Pictures can be liked, messages can be retweeted and shared, comments can receive a reply. Social media enable the generation of new and heightened possibilities for identification, as well as being a forum where dis-identification can also be enacted.

Media presentation of celebrity revolves around fostering discourses of approval and disapproval. Celebrity television shows such as *Strictly Come Dancing* or *I'm A Celebrity... Get Me Out of Here*, work by means of a public vote. As *Big Brother* used to say, 'Who goes? You decide.' Power is then handed to the audience, who act as arbiters choosing the fate of celebrity contestants. The media coverage that surrounds the celebrity reality shows, focuses on a continual conversation around what is right or wrong, concerning the contestants. Right and wrong is not, however, entirely confined to what happens on the show. Past relationships and infidelities become part of the coverage, as well as comments and criticism from friends, family and enemies. This kind of material is designed to draw the audience into a debate. Celebrity gossip becomes the means to discuss values. To approve, or not to approve, is part of a social process of discerning a moral position. As the celebrity performances are discussed among friends, or on social media, a discourse around identity and what is acceptable behaviour, and what is not, is evident. Celebrities, as they are gossiped about, act as a barometer of much wider social processes. They enable a discussion about the self and wider social norms concerning personal ethics and behaviour and, of course, dress sense.

Image and bodies: the crucial elements

Celebrity Culture is primarily based on visual images. It is the representation and reproduction of images of the self, on film, in digital media, or in print, that constitute the basic building blocks of celebrity discourse. This focus on visual image means that it is the body that audiences consume. An interest in the human body is not something that has arrived with Celebrity Culture. There are pre-historic figurines that reproduce the female body in an idealised or perhaps a divine form, and in ancient Greece it is clear from art and sculpture that the human form was celebrated as an ideal. The distinct characteristic of Celebrity Culture is that this interest in the body, and indeed idealised and perfected bodies, becomes mediated and reproduced by technologies of representation. An example of this is the impact of the face of the star filmed in close-up and projected onto a giant screen. The image reproduced becomes omnipresent in life in a way that transforms the individual into an enduring part of our lives. It is the image of the star that is the true reality for the fan, rather than actual human presence of a person. The reproduction of an image generates a sensibility where the star is more real than the real. This is what Jean Baudrillard describes as the hyper-real that media creates. This hyper-reality for the large part is not abstract, rather it is embodied in the person of individuals who are mediated. Visual technologies therefore elevate the image of the face and the body as the primary signifier of the self.

The bodies of celebrities are not ordinary bodies, they are bodies that have been worked on, honed and produced. Celebrity, and Celebrity Culture, is intimately connected to the rise of a range of activities that focus on the health, exercise, well-being and the self. One of the reasons for this connection, is that those industries that focus on image and body routinely use celebrities to promote their products. Celebrities are used to promote fashion, cosmetics, hairstyles, sports gear, weight-loss and exercise regimes. Celebrities are intimately connected with the world of cosmetic surgery, with individuals such as Cher or Michael Jackson representing a sensibility where the body is infinitely malleable; while film stars like Arnold Schwarzenegger have built careers on bodies that have been shaped through extreme forms of body building. The celebrity body is increasingly one that has been self-sculpted and produced. For a number of female stars over the age of 25, cosmetic procedures have become routine and well publicised. Individuals such as Nicole Kidman, Meg Ryan, Katie Price and Heidi Montag, have managed to extend their careers through adjusting their bodies through procedures. Lee Barron argues that these strategies have, in part, arisen as a reaction to the ageism that is endemic in the entertainment industry, which celebrates and promotes youthful bodies in preference to those that are older.[45]

One of the features in recent celebrity media coverage has been the rise in stories and pictures that feature the post-pregnancy body of celebrities. These stories celebrate and document the way that celebrities who have given birth are able to 'get their bodies back'. These stories generally focus on the remarkable speed with which individuals restore their bodies to the perfect image of a slim and honed youthful image. As Barron comments, the fact that the media is concerned with the speed of transformation, post-pregnancy, among these women, is an indication that the slim body is the normal body.[46] Celebrity magazines habitually celebrate the achievements of celebrities that have given birth such as Jennifer Lopez, Penelope Cruz, Kate Middleton and Kim Kardashian with headlines such as 'Jaw Dropping Post Baby Bods', 'I Got My Body Back: How She Lost 40lbs in 40 Days', 'My Best Body Ever: How I Did It.'[47] These stories recount the remarkable achievements of celebrity mothers. They not only position the celebrity as one who works on themselves and takes their body seriously, they demonstrate how for these celebrities their body is a project to be forged and honed, and through this coverage the media invite the reader into the same endeavour. The stories offer tips and programmes suggesting that, with effort and application, anyone might be able to do something similar. For Barron, the significance of these stories is that they show how celebrities are a means to promote and normalise a particular sensibility of the body among women more generally, rather than simply, impressionable teenagers. Moreover these stories indicate that the pregnant body is 'abnormal' and every effort should be made as quickly as possible to restore the body to what is regarded as normal.[48]

Celebrity bodies carry significance in more negative ways. Chris Rojek's idea of the rise and descent of celebrities when enacted in media coverage will often focus on the way that this is signified in the body.[49] Descent is signified and confirmed in the bodies of celebrities; sometimes this is characterised simply by weight gain. Celebrities are shown to have, 'let themselves go.' More regularly, however, this failure to work on the self is linked to substance abuse. Pictures appear in the press of celebrities having drunk too much, or being in a state of dishevelment. When Britney Spears was pictured in 2007 shaving her head, it was clear that she was undergoing a significant meltdown. Drug abuse, similarly, signifies the descent of the individual and speaks of failure, weakness and mortality. In these various ways, descent is represented in and through the body. In media narratives, the descent shown in the body of celebrities becomes a morality tale. Audiences are invited to make critical judgements concerning the failure of these privileged and pampered individuals. The failure to live up to the expectations of famous people in this way becomes a resource for a conversation concerning morality and the self, and the body lies at the heart of this discourse.

The work of celebrity

Achieving celebrity status might come overnight but maintaining the attention and regard of the public requires hard work. Celebrities face a dilemma. Audiences identify with individuals because they are 'ordinary'. Emotional attachments that are fundamental to generating the brand of the self, rest in part on similarity and above all, authenticity. Fans want to feel that the celebrities that they follow are being themselves. The notion of authenticity is, however, problematic, as Deborah Root argues, 'the term can be manipulated and used to convince people they are getting something profound when they are just getting merchandise.'[50] Authenticity can be signified by the media representing individuals as having 'natural talent', 'genius' or 'pure artistry.'[51] Attributes such as these can, however, be problematic or contradictory with the expectation that celebrities are somehow 'themselves.' Authenticity, then, is a complex notion that conceals the fundamental purpose of celebrities to promote things and to sell product, while also appearing to be both exceptionally talented and gifted, and yet also 'ordinary' and real. The work of celebrity consists in large part in negotiating these elements and balancing them throughout a career.

The attraction of celebrity-based reality television rests on the way that these programmes promise an insight into well-known individuals. On programmes such as *I'm A Celebrity... Get Me Out of Here*, and *Strictly Come Dancing*, the work of the celebrity is laid bare. There is a clear trade-off taking place between the celebrity who is seeking to enhance, or even relaunch their career, and the rigour and demands of these kinds of programmes. For the audience, the pleasure lies in seeing the celebrity apply themselves to the difficult task of being famous. This task is made manifest within these programmes by dancing or eating disgusting parts of Australian animals, but the underlying narrative rests on what these things reveal about the famous, or indeed the not-quite-so famous individuals who are featured. The format positions celebrities, such that they must compete for attention, and for the public vote. At the heart of this economy of attention there is the question of how 'real' they are being. The guts and determination of an individual is revealed through these testing circumstances, and they are rewarded by the regard of the audience, made evident numerically through votes. Conversely famous individuals can be revealed to be less attractive or capable than they might have been previously understood to be. In these new circumstances, what is revealed is that they are not all that they are made out to be. They are not authentic, in fact there is something that appears to be false or duplicitous about them. Celebrity reality television rests on the assumption that, in order for the celebrity to merit attention, they must put in the hard work.

Working at being a celebrity, and maintaining celebrity status, has become more complex and nuanced with the advent of social media. With platforms such as Instagram and Twitter, celebrities have been able to connect directly with their fans. This has brought benefits in the ability to not only market themselves, but also to promote products to thousands and, in some cases, millions of followers. Fundamental to the connection generated between celebrities and their followers on social media, is the blurring of the distinction between the private and public self. Justin Bieber has made it a regular habit to post romantic and sometimes intimate pictures of himself and his wife, Hailey Rhode Bieber, out shopping in town, embracing while sunbathing and kissing in the street. These kinds of pictures invite his followers into the private moments of his life. Followers can not only feel that they can view and share in these moments, but they can also interact with the posts by likes, emojis and comments. Social media then enables a connection between a celebrity, such as Justin Bieber, and his fans. Fundamental to these connections is the way that, through posting regular images that reveal the private and the personal, the singer builds a brand. Social media generates an expectation that the celebrity is always 'on', and always available. The online brand must be fed with a constant drip feed of revelation and spectacle. One of the dynamics that this flow of images and stories develops in audiences, is what has been termed FOMO, 'fear of missing out'. FOMO describes the anxiety that arises when individuals become concerned that an event is happening elsewhere that they are not aware of. Social media is at the centre of this phenomenon, because the constantly 'on' expectation that celebrities experience, in building their brand, also extends to fans and followers. Audiences experience anxiety because they need to be watching, and in touch with what is happening. The work of celebrity is as much something that has to be conducted by fans, as it is by celebrities themselves.

Elites

Celebrity Culture creates winners and losers. While, through social media use, it could be argued that every individual has access to media, and therefore experiences some level of celebrification, it is also the case that some are more famous than others. Stars, according to the sociologist Francesco Alberoni, writing in 1962, are 'powerless elites'.[52] Those who are famous do not occupy positions of political power, instead they are the object of those who observe them. This relationship is not mutual; the public is a mass audience unknown to the star. Alongside the regard of those who make up the viewing public, stars also benefit from disproportionate wealth.[53] Stars exhibit what Max Weber describes as charisma. By this Weber means 'a quality of being regarded as extraordinary' and endowed with 'powers and properties that are supernatural and superhuman' or sent by God.[54] This does not extend to political power and influence; rather, because of specialisation in societies, it is confined to particular areas of activity. Stars, however, says Alberoni, constitute a power elite. They are a group who have a heightened interaction with each other, and a visibility with the wider public. They relate to each other because of a common business in the entertainment world and they congregate in fashionable places.[55] Through the action of the media, these groups appear to be more closely connected than may actually be the case. Their visibility means that, although they are an elite, they are the subject of collective gossip and judgement by the wider society. In order that they might fulfil this function, stars are required to be visible to the public, and on show. Chris Rojek argues that Celebrity Culture generates a hierarchy of envy and imitation. 'Mainstream celebrities', he says, 'feed the everyday world with honorific standards of attraction that encourage people to emulate them.'[56] He goes on to suggest that this dynamic generates a structure, or a way of cementing or bonding society. Celebrity can be read as a distinct form of social stratification that is distinct from class, race or gender. Celebrity represents a social hierarchy of fame. Individual celebrities embody social position, but they also act as role models and examples. These functions of celebrity shape an environment where individuals measure their sense of selves, and their relative success or failure in relation to celebrities.

Alberoni's notion of the powerless elite, developed during the 1960s, might require some moderation in the light of more recent events. There are, for instance, examples of stars such as Ronald Reagan or Arnold Schwarzenegger, achieving political power. The charisma of the celebrity, in these cases, did not directly result in the ability to exercise power in society but it helped them in the process of gaining office. The idea of celebrities as a new kind of elite that is able to influence and affect the wider society has clearly continued to be the case. With the rise in the various ways in which products and consumer goods of different kinds are promoted by individuals, the commercial power of this elite is a key indicator of their privileged place in society. With the emergence of social media, these factors have become more pronounced, with the direct connection between celebrities and followers being given a numerical confirmation, through likes, comments and shares. Some people quite clearly have a larger public than others, and this gives them financial and social power that is sought after by both industry and politicians. With Donald Trump, politics and celebrity, and the power of social media, have been seen to converge in a new and often alarming way. The notion that celebrities are a 'powerless elite' needs to be rethought, but it is increasingly the case that a new and developing kind of social class has been generated through the action of the media changing individuals into celebrities. The status that this gives, and the wealth and glamour that goes along with it, remain not simply the object of gossip, but of envy and aspiration. Celebrities appear to live in a glamorous world, where backstage, in the green room and at exclusive parties, they meet one another and socialise in a privileged 'club.' These interactions are precisely what Alberoni describes, and they form a central pivot in the attraction that becoming a celebrity plays in the minds of many people. To become a celebrity is to rub shoulders with famous people, and this has become one of the most desired and envied aspects of contemporary Celebrity Culture. Celebrities live a life that many people wish to live, and it is this dynamic that generates their social power. The next chapter takes up this fundamental aspect of Celebrity Worship exploring the different ways in which celebrities become a source for the self.

Notes

1 Lee Barron. *Celebrity Cultures.* (London: Sage, 2014), 100.
2 Mark Frith. *The Celeb Diaries: The Sensational Story of the Celebrity Decade.* (London: Ebury Press, 2008), 3.
3 Barron. *Celebrity*, 100.
4 Ellis Cashmore. *Celebrity/Culture.* (London: Routledge, 2006), 100.
5 Su Holmes and Sean Redmond. 'A Journal in Celebrity Studies.' *Celebrity Studies*, 1, no. 1 (2010): 1–10.
6 Daniel Boorstein. 'From Hero to Celebrity: The Human Pseudo Event.' In *The Celebrity Culture Reader.* David Marshall, ed. (London: Routledge 2006), 79.
7 Graeme Turner. *Understanding Celebrity.* (London: Sage, 2004), 8.
8 Holmes and Redmond. A Journal.
9 David Marshall. 'New Media – New Self.' In *The Celebrity Culture Reader.* David Marshall, ed. (London: Routledge, 2006), 634–644.
10 Rojek. *Celebrity*, 17.
11 Rojek. *Celebrity*, 13.
12 Turner. *Understanding*, 12.
13 Holmes and Redmond. A Journal.
14 Leo Braudy. 'The Longing of Alexander.' In *The Celebrity Culture Reader.* David Marshall, ed. (London: Routledge, 2006), 38.
15 Braudy. The Longing, 46.
16 Richard Howells. 'Heroes, Saints and Celebrities: The Photograph as Holy Relic.' *Celebrity Studies*, 2, no. 2 (2011): 112–130.
17 Rojek. *Celebrity*, 17.
18 Rojek. *Celebrity*, 18.
19 Turner. *Understanding*, 7.
20 Boorstein. From Hero, 79.
21 Boorstein. From Hero, 83.
22 Barthes. *Mythologies*, 56.
23 Joshua Gamson. *Claims to Fame: Celebrity in Contemporary America.* (Berkeley, CA: University of California Press, 1994), 21.

24 Ellis Cashmore. *Celebrity/Culture*. (London: Routledge, 2006), 17–21.
25 Richard DeCordova. 'The Discourse on Acting.' In *The Celebrity Culture Reader*. David Marshall, ed. (London: Routledge, 2006), 91–107.
26 Turner. *Understanding*, 13.
27 Heather Nunn and Anita Biressi. '"A Trust Betrayed": Celebrity and the Work of Emotion.' *Celebrity Studies*, 1, no. 1 (2010): 49–64.
28 Marshall. Promotion.
29 Marshall. Promotion.
30 Donald Horton and Richard R. Wohl. 'Mass Communication and Para-social Interaction: Observations on Intimacy at a Distance.' *Psychiatry: Interpersonal and Biological Processes*, 19, no. 3 (1956): 215–229.
31 Mark Havitz and Frederick Dimanche. 'Leisure Involvement Revisited: Conceptual Conundrums and Measurement Advances.' *Journal of Leisure Research*, 29, no. 3 (1997): 245–278.
32 Turner. *Understanding*, 39.
33 Turner. *Understanding*, 34–35.
34 Rojek. *Celebrity*, 10.
35 Turner. *Understanding*, 26.
36 Boorstein. From Hero, 74.
37 Boorstein. From Hero, 79.
38 Boorstein. From Hero, 82.
39 Boorstein. From Hero, 88.
40 Rojek. *Celebrity*, 21.
41 Cashmore. *Celebrity*, 77.
42 Cashmore. *Celebrity*, 14.
43 Cashmore. *Celebrity*, 175.
44 Cashmore. *Celebrity*, 83.
45 Barron. *Celebrity*, 155–156.
46 Barron. *Celebrity*, 158.
47 Barron. *Celebrity*, 158.
48 Barron. *Celebrity*, 158.
49 Cashmore. *Celebrity*.
50 Cashmore. *Celebrity*, 245.
51 Cashmore. *Celebrity*, 245.
52 Francesco Alberoni. 'The Powerless Elite: Theory and Sociological Research on the Phenomenon of The Stars.' In *The Celebrity Culture Reader*. David Marshall, ed. (London: Routledge, 2006), 108.
53 Alberoni. Powerless, 110.
54 Alberoni. Powerless, 110.
55 Alberoni. Powerless, 114.
56 Rojek. *Celebrity*, 15.

Chapter 4

Celebrity, lifestyle and the self

The phenomenon of celebrity is part of the move in contemporary culture towards the self as a central concern. From home decoration to running, from bucket lists to gardening, from haircuts to styles of parenting, the project of the self infuses every aspect of life. In part, the root of this shift towards the self as a 'reflexive project' lies in the collapse of traditional roles and identities in modernity. The self is no longer prescribed but has to be achieved. At the same time, the compression of space and time that arises from mediation brings opportunity and choice.[1] This new context is one which simultaneously reduces and increases risk for those in the developed world. While key elements of life, such as health or economic prosperity, are insured, for many the sense of self in relation to this world appears to be more problematic. Achieving a self, therefore, becomes a major concern. The self is something that needs to be worked on and maintained. It is quite possible to 'let yourself go', to feel that you are not 'making the most of yourself'. These are the pressures that make identity and the self a central concern. As a result, the self has increasingly become a matter of endeavour and an all-consuming project. The endeavour, or at least the pressure to be making the most of ourselves, has become the central organising framework for Western individuals. The dark side of this compulsion is evident in eating disorders, rising suicide rates, drug taking, and depressive and compulsive disorders. The responsibility to achieve oneself has become a heavy burden. Media representation is a central site for the negotiation of the self. The project of the self is fundamentally related to lifestyle choices and these are generated and circulated through media. The construction of the self takes place in relation to a range of different possibilities that are generated in and through media processes. What is represented in the media are people. Identity and different possibilities of the self are embodied in these people and made present through mediation. Celebrity Worship is primarily a discourse that focuses on the individual and as such it supports a wider shift towards the self through representation and in the consumer identity construction that takes place in relation to this representation.

The personal and the media

In the run-up to the 2015 British general election, the then Prime Minister, David Cameron, is pictured by *The Sun* newspaper making himself a simple sandwich in his kitchen in Downing Street. Mathew Norman, writing in the *Independent* is given the opportunity to critique what he terms, the Richard Curtis 'Nottinghillesque' kitchen of the Camerons. His article draws attention to the Prime Minister's choice of wine, his Jamie Oliver saucepans that are on display, and the top of the range German-made Neff fridge freezer. Kitchens featured quite regularly in Cameron's political career. In a BBC interview in the same campaign, he is shown standing on the touchline cheering on his young son at the local village football team. This cuts to Cameron in another up-market kitchen, this time in his rural home in the Cotswolds, confessing to the BBC reporter Nick Robinson that he plans to run only for one more term, if he is elected as Prime Minister.[2] Kitchen politics were not the exclusive preserve of the Tory Prime Minister during the 2015 election. The Labour leader was also interviewed in his rather humble-looking galley kitchen. The photo opportunity backfired, as it was revealed that this was a second kitchen that had been installed to enable the Milibands to make drinks and snacks more easily. This led to claims in the *Daily Mail* that the Labour leader formed part of a 'North London elite', whose homes were so big that they needed two kitchens.[3] In the same election, Nick Clegg, the leader of the Liberal Democrats was pictured in his kitchen drinking wine with his Spanish wife, while they cooked paella. As the journalist, Jacques Klopp, commented about kitchen politics, 'Each time, the ritual was carefully staged, the relaxed setting rigorously observed. Pullovers and shirt sleeves abound. The children are not far away. A show of real life, neatly arranged for the television cameras.'[4]

Locating male politicians in the kitchen in 2015 was intended to generate a sense of intimacy and informality. It was a clear strategy to promote the politician as an ordinary approachable 'bloke', who made a sandwich, or a cup of coffee, or who shared a glass of wine with his wife while they cooked together. These strategies, for the promotion of a leader during an election, form part of a much larger shift in political discourse towards the personal and the individual. The invitation to view these figures 'backstage' is drawn directly from celebrity discourse. It is an aspect of celebritisation, i.e. the way that celebrity has seeped into every aspect of life. The celebritisation of politics, illustrated by these election interviews, has focused attention on the image and personality of those who seek to be elected. It has been commonplace to decry these kinds of changes, as a distraction from the hard issues related to policy and dumbing down of public conversation. Neil Postman's book, *Amusing Ourselves to Death*, is an example of these kinds of worries. Postman's point is that the grammar of public discourse, as it has been generated through the media, particularly television, has affected wider political and intellectual communication.[5] Celebrity Culture is a central component in the kinds of shifts in thought and perception that Postman is lamenting. Writing about political and news coverage in Australia, Graeme Turner et al identify a widespread shift towards personal narratives becoming the discursive lens through which stories are presented, and issues are understood.[6] They argue that it is not simply a case that there has been a change in the tastes and interests of audiences towards more individualised stories, but that there has been a significant movement in the ways in which political stories and news items are 'produced'. This means that an orientation towards celebrity plays a significant role in how stories find their way into the media, and how they are treated once they form part of media coverage.[7]

Media discourse, and in particular, television, is orientated towards the individual as the central component in narrative construction. John Langer argued that television should be understood as a 'personality system'.[8] The symbolic communication of television rests on conventions and codes that require the consent of the audience. It is in this context of negotiated meaning that 'good television,' becomes a form of communication that personalises narratives through the category of the individual.[9] Langer argues that non-fiction forms of television, such as the quiz show or the talk show, current affairs and news, all form part of a personality system. Often, the television format relies upon an anchor, or an individual, who hosts the show. The personality of these individuals provides the framework around which the shows are based. The same orientation towards personalities is found in drama, where the leading characters are often featured in the names of shows. Advertising also follows this convention, with individuals providing the continuity between one campaign and another.[10] Langer traces a similar shift towards personality in the film industry, where stars shift from being archetypes of virtue, e.g. the good guy or the vamp, to a more psychologised realism that is fed by a desire to see behind the role, to their 'real' private lives.[11]

The idea that television represents a personality system can be extended to all forms of media. Social media, such as Facebook, Snapchat or Instagram, are structured around the representation and performance of the self. More traditional forms of media, such as newspapers and magazines, are similarly part of a personality system. Across all kinds of media platform, the self is the organising framework. This operates at a number of levels. In the first instance, the individual personality is often the lens through which the world is viewed. The self, then, is an epistemological category that helps the viewer to make sense of the world, but it also becomes a means of identification. A good example of this is the BBC charity fundraising event, Comic Relief, that started in the 1988. In 2010, as part of the Comic Relief fundraising initiative, the comedian and actor, Lenny Henry, visited five brothers and sisters, living in one of the largest slums in Kenya. In the film sequence, broadcast as part of the Comic Relief event, he is shown meeting Bernard and his brothers and sisters. The conditions that these children are living in has a visible effect on Lenny that leads him to tears. On camera, he refuses to leave the children until he has been able to ensure that they are moved to a much better location. The improvement in their life situation requires him to make a number of payments himself.[12] Comic Relief, and other fundraising events on television, make use of celebrities in this kind of story. The celebrity becomes an emotional conduit for the viewer. The connection that is generated between the viewer and the celebrity brings an affective dynamic to the viewing experience. As the celebrity is visibly moved, the viewer is also vicariously present and affected. The celebrity represents the viewers, or draws the viewer, into a more intimate encounter with the situation that is being explained. The presence of a personality at the centre of the story makes the story more powerful, or more relatable.

The media convention that places a personality at the centre of stories, marks a significant epistemological shift in contemporary culture. The 'self' becomes the root, not simply to convey knowledge but also to comprehend or to 'feel it'. The individual is situated at the centre of knowing, be the story about a foreign war, or overcoming disability, or giving to charity. Knowing then becomes an embodied personal practice. This change in how things are known, does not simply relate to mediated individuals, or the conventions of media representation. Knowing for the audience shifts in significant ways to become an aspect of the self. The transference, then, is not only at the level of identification with particular personalities, as they are situated in the middle of stories; what takes place is a change in perception more widely. The reflexive project of the self becomes articulated with personal ways of knowing, such that life is viewed through this lens. Celebrities, then, are not simply guides or expert witnesses, they become a resource for instruction and guide to the way that things are known and made meaningful.

The pedagogical function of celebrity

It is people who are central to all forms of media content because they facilitate an emotional connection to the media products. This connection is based upon the relationships that are formed between audiences, and the people they follow in the media. One way of viewing how the interaction between individuals and celebrity operates, is to liken it to flicking through a fashion magazine. When leafing through a magazine, the casual glance that takes place as each page is viewed and then turned involves a complex internal dialogue. At the heart of this conversation is a question, 'Is this me or is this not me?' This goes a little beyond the more obvious, and perhaps surface concerns, 'Do I like this, or not like this?' or 'How much is it?' The question, 'Is this me?' generates involvement and participation, it is a leap of imagination, an assessment of the possibility of the self. The flow of celebrity characters works in a very similar way, only here there are more complex narratives involved that operate over time. Celebrity stories and images are consumed in a very similar way as a kind of 'gossip'.[13] The various activities, infidelities, achievements and family dynamics of people presented in the media generate a fascination and social conversation that is very akin to gossip, where what is taking place, both internally and also socially, is not really about the celebrity themselves. Gossip is a lubrication for the question, 'Is this me or is this not me?' or perhaps it is better expressed as, 'Would I do that or not do that?' or 'Should I do that or not do that?'

The interaction that takes place between celebrities and fans, in this kind of gossip, functions as a kind of educational morality tale.[14] The selves that are at the centre of media representation are not only there to sell product or to draw the audience into an emotional connection to the media content on whatever platform it is generated. There is a level of interaction that takes place that is in the viewer and the listener concerning the construction of the self. This relationship is not exactly akin to the idea that celebrities are role models or heroes. The point of the magazine analogy is that the attachment that the majority of people have with celebrity discourse is partial and glancing, but in the glance, there is this an ontological conversation concerning the self. 'Is this me or is this not me?' In this context, what is 'not me' is possibly more significant that what 'is me'. In other words, as has been argued in the previous chapter, dis-identification is as important as identification. These processes of evaluation and personal reflexivity show how celebrity in media representation draws the audience into a participatory relationship where what is really at stake is not the celebrity but ourselves.

In his preparation for the entering the jungle for the British television show *I'm a Celebrity... Get Me Out of Here*, the DJ Noel Edmunds had been working out. According to the *Daily Mail*, when the 69-year-old Edmunds stripped off for his first shower on the television programme, he revealed a body that would be the envy of much younger men.[15] There were no moobs, no pot belly, but rather a toned and muscled physique. The newspaper then proceeded to explain to the reader the way that this wondrous body was achieved. In the same issue of the *Mail Online*, an article features Kylie Jenner: the headline reads, 'Kylie Jenner gets pulses racing as she flashes her flat midriff during Valentine's Day makeup tutorial.'[16] The story gives an account of a tutorial that Kylie conducted on Instagram, where she has over 125 million followers. The tutorial was an advertisement for her Kylie Cosmetics 'makeup empire'. While Kylie and Noel are admired for their bodies, Celine Dion, in the same week, was coming under scrutiny concerning her extreme weight loss. CNN reported that the Canadian singer was defiant that she felt healthy, and more sexy in her skin. If people do not like what she looks like, they should not take pictures, she said.[17] Meanwhile, the *Daily Express* found a new twist on the royal soap opera speculation concerning the relationship between Meghan Markle and the Duchess of Cambridge. The paper claimed that Markle's wrinkled left kneecap appeared to resemble the face of Princess Charlotte. The kneecap in question is shown alongside a picture of the young royal, Princess Charlotte, so the reader can judge for themselves.[18] These stories are a snapshot of the way that celebrity coverage focuses, not simply on the body and image, but it draws the reader into a participative relationship. It is not simply enough to admire Noel Edmund's body, here the ingredients are made available to follow his exercise regime. Kylie Jenner is admired for her flat stomach, while also giving advice on how to do makeup, and then giving a direct link to where the products can be found. In the coverage of Celine Dion, the question is left hanging – has she overdone the diet? The audience is situated as the judge of what is true or not. The Meghan Markle story invites us to stare at her kneecap and wonder, can we see the face of Princess Charlotte? Each of these stories, while they are concerned with a celebrity, are articulated in such a way that the reader is being drawn into a conversation with the text, which is always about the self. The self of these celebrity individuals who are being put under examination, but also the self of the viewer who is being invited to engage at different levels with these stories.

Kathryn Lofton analyses the news coverage of the singer and actress Britney Spears that became a deluge in 2007. Britney, like all celebrities, Lofton says, is a commodity.[19] Referred to as a single name, Britney, she has been transformed into a product to be sold. As Britney, she is associated in media stories with a range of things. These include: her new CD; an astrological reminder that Scorpios should now 'clean their apartments'; a recommendation that there should be a revival of 1980s music. In all these things, Lofton says, Britney has become a throw-away commodity, something that is used in passing in the most disposable of media stories. Yet 2007 is the year when concern, and a certain moral panic, is associated with Britney, as she goes through a personal meltdown. This is a crisis that is broadcast around the world with images and headlines. The cover of Us Weekly magazine proclaims that Britney is 'SICK!'[20] Inside the magazine, a series of stories concerning her child care, her choice of drinks and her clothes, are put together to illustrate the problems that Britney is going through. 'Does She Even Care?' reads the headline.[21] Worry about Britney was widespread, and even prompted one American pastor to encourage the 8,000 members of his Kentucky mega-church to send letters of support and encouragement to the singer.[22] Lofton describes how the rise and fall of Britney Spears moves through the gears of media representation. From her fresh-faced appearances on the Micky Mouse Clubhouse in the early nineties, to her first hit single, 'Hit Me Baby One More Time'. By 2009, Billboard charts named Britney as the second best-selling act of the decade. Lofton traces Britney's religious history, with its background in the Southern Baptist Bible Belt, and with her advocacy of virginity, to a period when she was influenced by the Hollywood trends towards Kabbalah, and then to the time when she says, 'I no longer study Kabbalah, my baby is my religion.'[23] Britney then, says Lofton, is not simply a product that is sold for American pleasure but she becomes an 'icon of an American ideal, the freely wandering consumer of religious possibility.'[24] Britney clearly occupied a particular space for many Americans. This account of the media representation of the singer Britney Spears, draws attention to the way that celebrity stories, over time, draw an audience into an ongoing and shifting relationship with the star. It is not simply a story about a pop singer, or a child television actor. Britney represented something more enduring, and a relationship that had significance. This kind of connection has enabled celebrities to situate themselves as lifestyle guides presenting different possibilities of the self through a variety of media products.

Lifestyle programmes and the self as project

In the 1990s lifestyle programmes became a major new element in peak time television viewing. In the United States, there was the *Martha Stewart Living* programme, and in the United Kingdom we had Jamie Oliver, Delia Smith and Nigella Lawson. These programmes, each fronted by contrasting celebrity personalities, offered a window into the possibilities of the kitchen and the home. The programmes gave birth to what became known as the 'domestic goddess', exemplified in figures such as Martha Stewart and Nigella Lawson. The rise of the domestic goddess drew upon a middle-class sensibility that sought a certain style and pattern for the home. The message of these programmes, and many others, was clear – the home was where the project of the self was to be nurtured and, above all, fed. The result was that the home, and food in particular, became a site for developing particular kinds of cultural capital or 'taste.' Taste as Pierre Bourdieu would have it generates distinction.[25] In other words, the construction of the self through the material realities of the home and the kitchen translate into social realities.

The rise of the celebrity lifestyle guide corresponds to, and stimulates, the desire to create a particular sensibility, concerning the self and the home. The home becomes a place that expresses individuality and personality, but this embracing of particular forms of 'taste' is located in wider social realities. What is at stake, then, is not simply the construction of the self, but that this self is made in relation to others. The home is not simply a place to live in, it is an expression of the self. This sense of the home as an extension of the self, is what lies behind the success of celebrity magazines such as *Hello!*, which was first published in 1988, and became a phenomenon in the 1990s as part of the lifestyle boom. Each month, on page after glossy page, the magazine shows lavish spreads of celebrities pictured in their perfectly ordered and expensively equipped homes. The diet of perfect homes occupied by perfect families, with perfect smiles, was juxtaposed by pictures of European royal families. Lifestyle and aspiration appeared to have the royal seal of approval.

Until her trial and conviction in 2004, Martha Stewart, through her television shows, magazines and e-marketing, was the lifestyle guru for middle class in America. Her shows presented an image of a perfect home, where everything was given a personal touch. In the 1990s, Stewart was one of the most influential media personalities in the United States, with an appeal that appeared to transcend boundaries. Religious conservatives, according to Junior Bridge, saw Stewart as the champion of domesticity. While for liberals, she represented an independent woman, who did not rely upon men or sexual attraction for her success.[26] Martha Stewart tapped into an anxiety that exists in American working women concerning the home. With women working longer, in more demanding jobs, the fear is the danger that the home becomes a place of chaos where the domestic competence of women is challenged. In this context, Stewart offered a vision of what might be, or even what should be. It is in this ability to focus on the doubt in her audience that Stewart's influence lies.[27] Mason and Meyer's research into the relationship that audiences developed with Stewart's lifestyle world, indicates that there is a significant level of fantasy that operates, as the women they interviewed consume the media products. Stewart's world of wealth, luxury, organisation and elegance is largely unattainable, but nevertheless, it functions as a possibility, or an enticement. Even when the women know that Stewart does not do all these things, and that this is a media production put on by a team, the pleasure in viewing this fantasy world remains.[28] To the extent that some of the things seen in the programmes are attainable, women adapt and work with what they find possible in their own homes. Stewart represents for them a kind of domesticity that has been repurposed from that of previous generations. This is a lifestyle of the home that is a liberated domesticity, one where home-making becomes 'cool again.' Mason and Meyers argue that the fans they interviewed, engage with Stewart as a kind of therapy, or as part of their own self development. They are not simply following Stewart's advice to help them to improve their homes, but they undertake these tasks to make themselves 'feel better.'[29]

Nigella Lawson, in a similar way to Martha Stewart, represents a fantasy lifestyle take on food and the kitchen. Nigella, says Charlotte Brunsdon, is a 'beautiful, glamorous, university educated and upper middle class' woman who first came to public notice by writing recipes in *Vogue* magazine.[30] In her first television programme, *Nigella Bites*, the audience was treated to the wittily ironic and flirtatious sensual enjoyment of food, that has become her trademark.[31] Analysing an episode from the original series, Brunsdon describes how Nigella is pictured with her children eating porridge, preparing a pumpkin and seafood curry, and making bitter orange ice cream. As she is making these dishes Nigella speaks to the viewer and says, 'Cooking something at breakfast time, mad though it seems, I promise you isn't about being any kind of deranged superwoman.'[32] For Brunsdon, what is taking place with this aside is a negotiation concerning a post-feminist identity, with an irony that rests partly on the previous lifestyle programming of similar figures. Nigella's positioning of herself is made possible by the super confidence of figures such as Delia Smith or Martha Stewart. The sensuous pleasuring of yourself through food that Nigella embodies, however, is the opposite of the upper class omnicompetence of Stewart. In 2000, Nigella Lawson published her cookery book *How to be a Domestic Goddess*. For Joanne Holloway, Nigella's positioning of herself situates the cookery writer in a field of post-feminism and fantasy. Nigella's cookery programmes are located in a mediated version of her life. The idealised context for her suggestive cookery demonstrations have a correspondence with her life. As Holloway points out, this shifts over her career, from a programme where Nigella is clearly a mother with two children, in *Nigella Bites* to the newly divorced mother of two in *Nigella Bites II*, and then on to her newly in love and reconstituted family in *Forever Summer*.[33] 'Her cooking style is carefully distanced from the prim and proper efficiency of the (female) home economist and from the decontextualised precision of the (male) professional chef.' She makes a virtue of being clumsy and demonstrates how her own incompetence is a sign that the recipe is foolproof. Above all, the message from Nigella is that cooking should come out of the desire to eat. Her brand promotes comfort cooking that is offered as an escape from the world. Life might be stressful, but 20 minutes stirring a lemon risotto is offered as a mindless moment that is free from stress. For Holloway, the evident pleasure and sensuality that Nigella brings to cooking, and above all eating, is a transformation of feminist discourse around food, where the emphasis has been upon division of labour and women being positioned as a provider of food to others. With Nigella, the meaning and purpose of cooking arises from the desire to satisfy and bring pleasure to yourself. Nigella, Holloway argues, above all, projects the sense of, 'not only a feminine self that eats, but one that is aware of what it wants to eat rather than deferring to the preferences of others.'[34] At the same time, Nigella appears to be aware of the anxieties and pressures that are around the requirement that cooking takes place in a social context. She adopts a sisterly tone, reassuring her viewers that mistakes do happen, and this is okay. If a cake sticks to the tin it is not the end of the world, but through this message she is also acknowledging that cooking brings a pressure to perform. The domestic goddess is often on show.

The cult of fitness

The year, 1981, saw the publication of *Jane Fonda's Workout Book*. It sold almost two million copies in its first two years of publication. The book led to the 'Jane Fonda's Workout' videos, that had sold four million copies by 1987.[35] Jenny Ellison argues that Fonda was at the forefront of a major shift towards exercise as part of a wider lifestyle. 'Fonda,' she says, 'represented the new ideal of femininity in the 1980s: she was athletic, slim and sexy.' Aerobics and aerobic clothing were popular signifiers of this new ideal, and images of women 'working out' were used to sell films, food and clothing in this era. For Louise Mansfield, Jane Fonda was the celebrity fitness guru of the 1980s.[36] Her approach to fitness marked a turning point towards the commodification of women's bodies. The lean and toned look became a signifier of youth and vitality and above all a model for heterosexual femininity.[37] The exercise genre of books and videos created a set of instructions that presented a series of visual and textual instructions on how to create your own sculpted body. For Mansfield, these materials form part of a much wider genre of 'How-to/Self-help' books, videos and programming. In a commercial context, these kinds of products represent a 'strategic, mediated and packaged approach to the selling of fitness.' By the mid 1980s, the sale of health and exercise-related books to women outnumbered sales to men by two to one.[38]

Fitness and exercise books represent a form of education, concerning the body. They are a form of education or pedagogy of the self. The significance of this instruction goes beyond the details of any single exercise regime. The fitness books and exercise regimes are a route into a sensibility where the individual shares in a discourse of instruction that operates both as an intellectual, and an aesthetic, take on the self.[39] The shift during the 1980s was towards individual responsibility for fitness and health. Fonda, interviewed in 2014, claimed that her fitness video lay behind the rise in sales of VCR machines in the United States. It also, says Fonda, brought about a revolution where women were allowed to have muscles. Before the 1980s, health clubs had no provision for women to exercise; the gym was a male only space. Her video brought about a revolution where women saw the value in buying what was then an expensive piece of equipment, because they saw the value in playing a tape over and over again to facilitate exercise.[40] The videos also brought about a massive increase in the sale of lycra and leg warmers to this new market of women who were embracing exercise. This was driven, however, by the interests of those who were concerned to generate a way to sell their products. The aerobics phenomenon for Jane Fonda was about a new direction for femininity. This notion was contested, with some critics observing that the workout was both a means to sell expensive ranges of exercise clothing, while also reinforcing what many saw as conservative views of women and their bodies.[41] While it is not without its critics, the Jane Fonda workout phenomenon illustrates the connection that takes place between media and the facilitation of the self as project. The fundamental element here, is the role that Jane Fonda, as the human face of these developments, plays in bringing about these changes. The exercise regime is not simply fronted by Jane Fonda, it is perceived as credible and worth taking on board because of her championing of the product. The close identification of Fonda with everything that she represented to people, generated an authenticity and an emotional connection that didn't simply result in sales, it changed the way that women felt about their bodies and exercise in general.

The workout craze is part of a much wider obsession that Celebrity Worship has with bodies. This obsession travels a good deal beyond the extent to which someone may be beautiful or attractive. Celebrity bodies are under scrutiny and constant observation. Rebecca Feasey's survey of *Heat* magazine shows the extent to which this celebrity magazine extols the work that celebrities do to achieve, and then to maintain, their bodies. The health and beauty regimes that celebrities undertake as they work on their flawless bodies, says Feasey, are not so much tips for the readers to follow as reassurance of the effort that celebrities put in to achieve their status as extraordinary people.[42] 'The reader is told that celebrities such as Beyoncé Knowles and Elizabeth Hurley are not effortlessly thin women; rather, these performers have to work at constructing and maintaining their perfect physique through a calculated and controlled diet.'[43] Central to the narrative of effort and work, involved in being a celebrity, are the stories that focus on the 'before', and the 'after', of exercise and diet programmes. Readers are given stories that have headlines such as 'tubby to trim' and 'pot belly to washboard'. This kind of coverage reinforces the extreme commitment, and effort, that is required to be a celebrity, and to have a celebrity's body. Feasey's argument is that stars are not presented as creatures who are naturally beautiful, or effortlessly perfect in shape and form. The celebrity body is one that comes when sacrifices are made and the work is put in. Exercise manuals and diet books can be bought, and the reader may choose to try and follow them, but the message of *Heat* magazine is that the extraordinary effort that is required to achieve the same results is what is remarkable in the celebrity. The effect of this portrayal of celebrities, as those who 'put the work in', is twofold. On the one hand, the magazine appears to situate the reader as 'normal' in relation to the extreme efforts that celebrities have to endure to keep their figures. Commenting on Elizabeth Hurley's new swimwear range in February 2005, *Heat* says, 'We don't know about you, but most of us here at *Heat* towers are still trying to fight the flab from Christmas and New Year ... So you imagine our dismay when we spotted these pictures of Liz Hurley ... looking frankly amazing as she posed for a photo shoot for her new swimwear range. But then she does eat just one big meal a day and snacks on raisins. How dull. Maybe we'll keep our curves after all.'[44] The magazine invites the reader into a relationship around the lifestyle of 'normal people', who are in need of recovering from the excesses of Christmas. Hurley, by contrast, is seen as an object of admiration, but also, she is set apart as odd. The celebrity self, it is clear, is slightly strange, and perhaps a little deranged. Yet alongside this message, there is the subtext that reinforces the project of the self as the ultimate concern.

Heat, with its focus on bodies and weight, is not blind to the problems that surround excessive weight loss and dieting. Feasay's research highlights the occasions where questions are raised around how thin a celebrity might have become. Here, the before and after technique, is used to develop a cautionary message for the reader. Celebrities, such as Nicole Kidman, Sophie Dahl and Saffron Burrows, all of whom had been in the past praised for their beauty, health and radiance, were pictured looking very thin and gaunt.[45] *Heat* readers are encouraged to be critical of strict dieting regimes, and to be mindful of the health risks associated with excessive weight loss. In a related area, the issue of cosmetic surgery is also dealt with by *Heat*. Feasay documents the ways in which *Heat* is at pains to show the extent to which cosmetic procedures may not be a miracle solution. Stories warn of 'bulging bottom lips', 'liposuction dents' and 'misshapen breasts'.[46] For *Heat*, she argues, weight loss and cosmetic surgery represent the new celebrity obsessions. The magazine has an overarching narrative that fashion and style are there to be fun, and for experimentation with health and beauty to be part of life choices. Experimentation should, however, take place while resisting the pressure of society to choose what are potentially harmful, or unhealthy, options. *Heat* magazine uses a tone of 'gossip' to consistently both undermine and to promote, the discourses around bodies and weight in Celebrity Culture. The features in the magazine draw the reader into a conversation concerning individual celebrities, but at the same time, drawing the reader into a reflexive consideration of the self. The magazine, then, becomes a resource, where women are able to negotiate their own sense of self, and their personal worlds, in relation to the flow of celebrity representation.[47]

Trajectories

Celebrity Culture is characterised by numerous stories of the rise and fall of famous and talented individuals. Consuming celebrity lives involves the pleasure that is given, not simply by the triumphs and the wonderful achievements of these individuals, but also the fall from grace and the loss of the status as icon. These stories have an intrinsic fascination because of the previous knowledge, and possible attachments that celebrities have generated as they have risen in the public imagination. They are morality tales or cautionary fables concerning people who are part of our lives but who are also unreal. Observing the car crash events that many celebrities manage to manufacture from their extraordinary lives takes place at one remove. Car crashes feature quite regularly in celebrity tales of lives that have taken a wrong turn. The troubled musician George Michael managed to crash his car into a Snappy Snaps shop, not far from his home in the early hours of the morning.[48] According to the *Mail Online*, this was the seventh time that the singer had been investigated by the police concerning driving under the influence of drugs. Shortly after the event, the damaged shop was photographed because someone had sprayed graffiti on it. The graffiti had the witty comment, 'Wham!'[49] In 2018, the British television personality, Ant McPartlin, crashed his mini. His subsequence arrest and conviction for drink driving led not only to a fine for £86,000 and a spell in rehab, but to the unravelling of his television career. His long-term partner, Declan Donnelly, had to team up with Holly Willoughby to present the 2018 series of *I'm a Celebrity… Get Me Out of Here!* The *Daily Mirror* spoke of Ant as both a troubled, and also a beloved star, who was driven to drink over the guilt he was experiencing over his split with his long-term girlfriend Lisa.[50] The celebrity car crash, in media representation, generally operates as a signifier of more than a traffic violation. Car crash metaphorically functions as part of an account of much more serious kinds of personal crises, often involving a combination of drug abuse, alcohol addiction and relationship problems. Car crash, of course, also operates as a metaphor for a life that has gone off the rails and careered out of control.

The car crash celebrity trope features in one of the most dramatic falls from grace that has taken place in recent years. In 2009, the day after Thanksgiving Day in the United States, it was reported that the golfer, Tiger Woods, had crashed his Cadillac into a fire hydrant outside his luxury home in a Florida gated community. The car crash followed closely revelations, in a story in the *National Enquirer*, concerning Tiger and a New York night club hostess. The crash, it was rumoured, came following a fight between Tiger and his wife, Elin. After this story came out, a steady trickle of women shared their stories of sexual encounters with the golfer, including a former Reality TV contestant, a lingerie model and a waitress.[51] As the anthropologist, Orin Stam, says in *The Passion of Tiger Woods*, the bigger a star might be, the bigger the scandal that follows from his or her infidelities, and Tiger was one of the biggest stars in the world at the time. He was one of the most successful golfers that the world had ever seen. He turned professional in 1996 when he was 20. The next year he won his first major, The Masters. He was the youngest recorded winner of this tournament at just 21. As his career progressed, he continued to break records for the number of tournaments he won. At the age of 24, he was the youngest ever golfer to achieve a Grand Slam, wining all the major championships in one year. Tiger, in short, was an extraordinary talent as a golfer, and America is obsessed with golf. It is not insignificant to his celebrity status that Tiger had achieved stellar success in the sport, while also being a person of colour. 'Tigergate', as Stam calls it, demonstrates, 'the breathless reporting of transgression.'[52] The media dissection of a star has a ritualised element to it. There is the deluge of coverage revealing the sordid details, the blogs and tabloids that follow on digging for more infidelities and more details, and this is then followed by the 'teary eyed' public apology and the suggestion that the next visit will be to some kind of rehab facility.[53]

Tiger's 'passion' followed the set pattern of the media trial, condemnation and punishment of a celebrity figure. Tiger's case, says Stam, 'very much followed the expected conventions of celebrity scandal, with its media frenzy, social psychology of public stoning and the opportunity for the repentant sinning star later to be forgiven and reinstalled in the pantheon of the admired'. Central to the stoning of Tiger was the role that race and colour played in the media coverage. In the early years, as he rose in the golfing world, and achieved his first successes, Tiger's mixed-race background made him a flashpoint for racial comment and controversy. As he became the sporting 'icon' who had 'ascended the Mount Olympus of golf legend and American glory', issues of race seemed to recede into the background. Tiger became simply Tiger. The significant factor concerning Tiger, is that he represented a version of multicultural identity and integration that was a contrast to the more controversial racial identities of, for instance, some African American basketball players. This is what attracted Nike to Woods, because he offered them a chance to brand him with a celebration of both multiculturalism and 'colour-blindness', while affirming the centrality of these ideologies to a recast white racial frame. With the revelations concerning his seeming preference for sexual encounters with white women, Stam argues, the issue of Tiger's racial identity suddenly re-emerged, in ugly and unpleasant ways. 'Tigergate' revealed 'an America angry, afraid, transfixed, curious, and resentful about racial politics in both old and new ways.'[54] Tiger's attempt to turn his life around took place in 2009, following a 45 day stay at a rehab centre in Hattiesburg, Mississippi, where he followed the Twelve Step programme for sexual addiction. After the treatment, he appeared on television to make his public apology. The confession took place at the PGA Tour headquarters, near Jacksonville in Florida. His thirteen-minute act of contrition was read out to the assembled media, and broadcast around the world. Tiger's story parallels that of Britney Spears; both narratives function as a lightning rod for debates around morality, identity and the self. They form part of the ongoing flow of representation that is part of the discourse around identity and lifestyle that constitutes Celebrity Worship.

Celebrity fashion retailing

According to *Cosmopolitan*, 'The Nation is Obsessed with Whatever Kate Middleton Wears.'[55] To make things easier the magazine created a click-through gallery of the Duchess's style. The gallery consists of 179 photos showing the style choices, and various outfits, that Kate has worn during her royal duties. Each picture is accompanied by a short comment, setting out where the outfit was worn, but more importantly, a version of the dress, or the bag, or the shoes, is identified, and the price for this item is given. On some pages a weblink is posted, to enable the reader to buy the item online. Beside a picture with the headline 'Visiting a Children's Hospital,' Kate is pictured, alongside her husband Prince William. She is wearing a polka-dot dress and holding a small clutch bag. The dress, *Cosmopolitan* tells us, is from L. K. Bennett and it is available for £325 from www.lkbennett.com. The clutch bag in suede is also available from the same company, and it costs £119. There are a host of websites that facilitate the fashion choices of their readers based around the imitation of celebrities – www.Looklive2.0.com helpfully offers a picture of each celebrity, detailing what they are wearing. These are often very expensive designer brands, so Looklive helpfully has sourced versions of these clothes, that are similar in style and look, at a fraction of the price. An example of this is a picture of the singer Rihanna who is shown walking through New York; she is wearing a matching outfit from the designer Louis Vuitton. The top is a velour multi pocket half zip, and this, the website tells us, can be bought for $2,000. Her multi pocket cargo pants are also velour and at a cost of $1,600. Live click-through links enable the purchase of these items. Next door to these designer purchase opportunities, however, are 'similar' options, such as the white top from LACOS costing $140, and pants from the same supplier priced at $160.

The celebrity imitation fashion websites demonstrate the direct connection that exists between the consumer's construction of the self and celebrity. Here, influence has moved from discourse and participation in gossip, to a concrete financial exchange. During the last decade, there is one celebrity brand that above all others has managed to combine self-promotion with marketing branded products: the Kardashians. Kim Kardashian first came to public notice as the stylist for Paris Hilton, but it was her sex tape that was 'leaked' to the press in 2007 that jettisoned her, and the rest of her extended family, into the celebrity stratosphere. Through a series of Reality TV shows, including the hugely successful *Keeping Up with the Kardashians*, Kim and her family have managed to become style icons. Kim has used social media to build her brand and to market her products. She explains, 'Instagram is my favorite right now, but it changes. Facebook is good for getting the message out, building the brand. Twitter is fun,' she says. 'But Instagram is such a part of your personality. you can put up quotes or photos or anything you want.'[56] Kim's reach on social media is almost unmatched. In 2019 she had 126 million followers on Instagram, and her net worth in 2016 was estimated at $52.5 million.[57] Widely spoken of as a marketing genius, Kim Kardashian has perfected, what the journalist Abigail Tracy calls, the 'freemium' technique of self-promotion. This rests on the principle that the celebrity shares everything about themselves freely on social media and other media platforms. Having hooked her fans on an ever-unfolding personal drama, Kim Kardashian then withholds certain content, and only makes it available via premium sites that her followers must pay for. The psychology behind this strategy is that fans are enticed into paying because they fear what they may be missing out on, or FOMO. As Kim explains, ensuring that she has extra personal content to share on Instagram and Twitter – outside of the free material on her television programmes – requires hard work. She has to generate special trips, or events, that are only accessible to those who pay. The same kind of exclusive package that is paid for, is a feature of her brand of emojis that are called 'Kimoji'. Her fans are able to set themselves apart by having an emoji that features Kim, for instance, bouncing on an exercise ball, as a marker of a privileged and, of course, paid for status. The result, says Tracy, is that Kim Kardashian has managed to create a paywall for her own life, and this is one that millions of followers are willing to pay for in order to get 'exclusive content.'

It is in the area of cosmetic surgery that Celebrity Culture leads to embodied forms of imitation. The use of cosmetic surgery by celebrity fans has been described by Elliott and Lemert as, 'extreme reinvention.'[58] This reaching for surgical solutions to the re-engineering of identity is a significant aspect of the reflexive project of the self. The prevalence of cosmetic procedures, such as liposuction, tummy tucks, Botox injections and facelifts, has accelerated to such an extent that in the United States it is now a multi-billion dollar industry.[59] The rise in the use of medical intervention, to shape and re-shape the self, takes place in relation to a context where, 'altered, enhanced and stretched celebrities' are a feature of media representation. The role of celebrities in the spread of cosmetic surgery, argues Elliott, should not be limited to notions of influence, where the celebrity and Celebrity Culture are seen simply as external influences that exert a power on people's lives. Celebrities such as Demi Moore, Pamela Anderson, Sylvester Stallone, Danni Minogue, Melanie Griffith, Michael Douglas and Courtney Love, have led the way in what has become a wave of self-reinvention as a part of life.[60] Celebrities are followed closely and examined in forensic detail, to reveal where 'work' has, or as not, been done. Celebrity news coverage is filled with webpages that show before and after shots of famous people who have had disastrous cosmetic procedures. CBS News helpfully employed an expert cosmetic surgeon to provide a critical commentary on the results of surgery on 12 famous celebrities. Number eight in the list is actress Jennifer Grey. Now in her fifties, Grey's picture is shown as having undergone a nose job (rhinoplasty), this is set alongside a much younger image taken when she starred in the movie *Dirty Dancing*. The expert, Dr Youn, explains that the actress has had the bump removed from her nose. This he thinks does improve her appearance, however, the problem is that it also alters how she looks, to such an extent that she no longer looks like the character in the movie that made her famous. As Dr Youn says, 'I personally think she looks better since it's just a tad smaller. But the problem is that she doesn't look like she used to.'[61]

Extreme makeover shows on television, Elliott argues, act to normalise and make routine the use of cosmetic surgery. Programmes such as BBC4's *Ten Years Younger*, ABC's *Extreme Makeover*, and MTV's *I Want a Famous Face*, all act to promote cosmetic surgery as a route towards a new self. Fox television's makeover programme *The Swan*, broadcast in 2004, features women who are given an 'extreme makeover'. This includes dentistry, cosmetic surgery, and access to therapists and trainers. Elliott argues that *The Swan* promoted the notion that the self could be redesigned through intervention, and in particular through surgery. At the close of the show in what was called 'the reveal' the contestant would be unveiled on stage in front of an audience consisting mainly of friends and family members. This moment was intended to signify the success and the authenticity of the changes that had been brought about through the programme.[62] *The Swan* illustrates how Celebrity Culture, with its focus on the image and the body, has been a significant engine that has driven the move towards cosmetic surgery. It is not simply the desire to achieve a look that is similar to that of a chosen idol, it is that celebrities embody the message that it is possible to transform the self, and to achieve what you want to be. The re-invention of the self has been fast-tracked by the message that celebrities have worked at the self and found ways to get to where they wanted to be, and this is possible for everyone. Celebrities are part of the endorsing of particular brands of cosmetic products. They offer examples of how to use surgery and more importantly the dangers and pitfalls of extreme re-invention. As Elliott says, 'Celebrity and aesthetic value go hand in hand. In this sense, too, celebrity is the power of authenticating ways of living, certificating styles of self-presentation, and thereby inscribing the individual self in broader structures of power.'[63]

Celebrities and the self

Celebrity Worship lies at the centre of the shift towards the self in contemporary Western culture. This dynamic is evident in a number of ways. The celebritisation of political narratives illustrates how discourse has been altered towards the personal. Politics is not alone in the alteration of sensibilities towards the individual as a lens through which life is viewed and ideas are presented. The same is true for charity work or those in the arts more generally. Magazines, chat shows and social media, all facilitate the personal as a means to draw attention to more 'serious' forms of cultural communication. A similar dynamic takes place in religion where celebrity increasingly shapes how an emotional connection is made to more formal religious traditions. The turn to the self in Celebrity Worship is further illustrated by the overt ways in which celebrities are at the centre of lifestyle choices. Through celebrity driven television programmes, based on the home or cooking, the project of the self is brought centre stage not simply as entertainment but as a means to construct identity. These processes of celebrity influence are even more concrete and material in the spread of websites that market celebrity fashion and promote cosmetic surgery. Here the project of the self is monetised and motivated through celebrity endorsement. Identification and dis-identification are clearly a force that can be chained in a commercial transaction. These kinds of connections are key drivers not simply in the connection between celebrities and the project of the self but in the reason why celebrities are seen as objects of 'worship'. Imitation of celebrity style and body image carries this religion like an overtone. The sacred here is not the individual celebrity but the sacred self.

Notes

1 David Harvey. *The Condition of Postmodernity*. (Oxford: Blackwell, 1989).
2 BBC News. 'David Cameron, "I Won't Serve Third Term" (EXCLUSIVE).' 23 March 2015. https://www.youtube.com/watch?v=rG0T2UqDqO8.
3 Ben Riley-Smith, 'Ed "Two Kitchens" Miliband: Politicians and the Photos that Inadvertently Come to Define Them.' *Telegraph*, 17 May 2019.
4 Jacques Klopp. 'Britain's Party Leaders Throw Kitchen Sink at the Election.' *Business Insider*, 1 May 2015.
5 Postman. *Amusing*.
6 Graeme Turner, Frances Bonner and David Marshall. *Fame Games: The Production of Celebrity in Australia*. (Cambridge: Cambridge University Press, 2000), 1.
7 Turner. *Fame*, 2.
8 John Langer. 'Television's "Personality System."' *Media Society and Culture*, no. 4 (1981): 351–365.
9 Langer. Television's, 352.
10 Langer. Television's, 635.
11 Langer. Television's, 345.
12 YouTube. 'Lenny Henry is Reunited with the Five Orphans He Met in 2010'. www.youtube.com/watch?v=851VkU5CbNc.
13 Marshall, The Promotion.

14 Marshall. The Promotion.
15 Helen Carroll. 'How Noel Edmonds, 69, got Tarzan's body for the I'm a Celebrity jungle – Using Electromagnetic Mats, Japanese Workouts and a Glass of Champagne a Day.' *Daily Mail*, 27 November 2018.
16 Annita Katee. 'Kylie Jenner Gets Pulses Racing as She Flashes Her Flat Midriff During Valentine's Day Makeup Tutorial.' *Daily Mail*, 31 January 2019.
17 Lisa Respers. 'Celine Dion on Criticism She's Too Thin: "Leave Me Alone."' *CNN Entertainment*, 31 January 2019.
18 Carly Read. 'Royally Bizarre: Princess Charlotte's Face "Appears" in Meghan Markle's Knees.' *Express*, 17 January 2019.
19 Kathryn Lofton. *Consuming Religion*. (Chicago: University of Chicago Press, 2017).
20 Lofton. *Consuming*, 106.
21 Lofton. *Consuming*, 107.
22 Lofton. *Consuming*, 112.
23 Lofton. *Consuming*, 111.
24 Lofton. *Consuming*, 111.
25 Pierre Bourdieu. *Distinction: A Social Critique of the Judgement of Taste*. (London: Routledge, 1984).
26 Ann Mason and Marian Meyers. 'Living with Martha Stewart Media.' *Cinema Journal*, 44, no. 2 (Winter, 2005): 110–116.
27 Mason and Meyers. Living.
28 Mason and Meyers. Living.
29 Mason and Meyers. Living.
30 Charlotte Brunsdon. 'Feminism, Post feminism, Martha and Nigella.' *Cinema Journal*, 44, no. 2 (Winter, 2005): 113.
31 Brunsdon. Feminism, 113.
32 Brunsdon. Feminism, 114.
33 Brunsdon. Feminism, 182.
34 Brunsdon. Feminism, 182–183.
35 Jenny Ellison. 'Not Jane Fonda: aerobics for fat women only.' In *The Fat Studies Reader*, Esther Rothblum and Sondra Solova, eds. (New York: New York University Press, 2009), 312–19.
36 Louise Mansfield. '"Sexercise": Working Out Heterosexuality in Jane Fonda's Fitness Books.' *Leisure Studies,* 30, no. 2 (2011): 237–255.
37 Mansfield. Sexercise.
38 Mansfield. Sexercise.
39 Mansfield. Sexercise.
40 YouTube. 'Jane Fonda on Her Legendary Workout Videos.' www.youtube.com/watch?v=8YEMrzoRsRY.
41 Mansfield. Sexercise, 13.
42 Rebecca Feasey. 'Get a Famous Body: Star Styles and Celebrity Gossip in Heat Magazine.' In *Framing Celebrity: New Directions in Celebrity Culture*. Su Holmes and Sean Redmond, eds. (London: Routledge, 2006), 186.
43 Feasey. Get, 186.
44 Feasey. Get, 187.
45 Feasey. Get, 187.
46 Feasey. Get, 188.
47 Feasey. Get, 190.
48 Rosie Swash. 'George Michael. Arrested After Crashing Car into Shop.' *The Guardian*, 6 July 2010.
49 Artlyst. 'George Michael Wham Graffiti Poster.' 14 September 2010. www.artlyst.com/news/george-michael-sentenced-latest-wham-graffiti-photo/

50 Emmeline Saunders and Frances Kindon. 'Troubled Ant McPartlin's Car Crash Revealed to be his Third in Three Weeks.' *The Mirror*, 20 March 2018.
51 Orin Stam. *The Passion of Tiger Woods.* (Durham: Duke University Press, 2011), xi.
52 Stam. *Passion*, xvii.
53 Stam. *Passion*, xvii.
54 Stam. *Passion*, xvii.
55 *Cosmopolitan.* 'The Nation is Obsessed with Kate Middleton's Amazing Style.' 6 March 2019. www.cosmopolitan.com/uk/fashion/celebrity/g3517/kate-middletons-outfits-style-fashion/
56 Danny Sullivan. 'Kim Kardashian Talks Social Media: Loves Instagram, Twitter is Fun, Facebook for Branding.' *Marketing Land*, 6 February 2013. https://marketingla nd.com/live-blog-kim-kardashian-talks-social-media-brand-building-more-32738.
57 Abigail Tracy. 'The Genius of Kim Kardashian.' *Vanity Fair Hive*, 10 June 2016. www.vanityfair.com/news/2016/06/kim-kardashian-kimoji-entrepreneurship.
58 Anthony Elliott and Charles Lemert. *The New Individualism: The Emotional Costs of Globalization.* (London: Routledge, 2006).
59 Anthony Elliott. 'I Want to Look like That: Cosmetic Surgery and Celebrity Culture.' *Cultural Sociology*, 5, no. 4 (2011): 463–477.
60 Elliott. I Want.
61 CBS News. 'Celebrity Plastic Surgery Disasters.' www.cbsnews.com/pictures/celeb rity-plastic-surgery-disasters/8/
62 Elliott. I Want.
63 Elliott. I Want.

Chapter 5

The presentational self

Social media and digital technology have democratised celebrity. The culture of celebrity has been built on processes of representation. The reproduction of the image, or the song, or the moving picture, was controlled by cultural industries, and the numerous professionals that specialised in producing mediated individuals. Representation was limited in its dimensions in the legacy media. The performance of the self as a mediated individual relied upon access to television, radio, print or film. These were the means to representation, and hence to becoming famous and a celebrity. For those not represented in the media, options were limited to the process of consumption. These might be both creative and absorbing, such that fans could develop their own cultures of consumption by making use of stories and images producing their own individualised events or styles. These fan cultures in turn were processes of representation and production. What fan cultures had in common with mediated individuals was that they relied upon 'the media industry.' Digital media turned these relations of production and consumption around, and brought about a decisive shift in Celebrity Culture, from the 'representational self' to the 'presentational self.'[1]

Social media and the democratisation of celebrity

The shift towards an environment where the mediation of the self becomes a widespread phenomenon is linked to technological changes. In particular, the shift from what is known as web 1.0 to web 2.0, brings about a change in the use and social dimension of the Internet.[2] This shift was from the web as a source for consuming information and entertainment, to a place where individuals and communities interacted and participated.[3] Fundamental to these changes was the emergence of social networking sites in the first decade of the 2000s. This led to an explosion in interactivity; suddenly the web was a forum for actively sharing the self. With these developments, the mediation of the self became not simply a possibility, but an everyday reality for millions of people. Posts could go viral and reach around the world. The status of celebrity was no longer confined to those individuals who found a way to be featured in the legacy media. Mediation of the self was in the hands of the individual, and this meant that celebrity status was democratised. The 'celebrification' of the self, through social media, is not solely, or even primarily, to be understood in terms of the spread and scale of social media activity, it is also a way of presenting the self that is shaped by media. Individual identity becomes a complex reality that is performed both online and offline. This shift towards a participatory media culture means that previous distinctions between producers and consumers or celebrity and audiences have collapsed.[4] These changes have accelerated the dynamics that enhance and support the turn to the self in wider society.

Celebrity Culture has become characterised by a shift towards the ordinary. Ordinary people, through Reality TV and social media are being transformed into celebrities, says Joshua Gamson, and famous people are increasingly being represented as ordinary.[5] This process has been facilitated by the rise of Reality TV and the participatory practices linked to web 2.0. Celebrity consists in the generation of a commodity, Gamson argues, and that celebrity is embodied attention. 'The value of the celebrity inheres in his or her capacity to attract and mobilize attention, which is then typically attached to other products (a television show, a magazine cover, a record album) or sold for cash directly to people making those other products.'[6] This economy of attention is facilitated and controlled by media industry processes. The key requirement of this industry is not that celebrities are particularly talented or able but simply that they are willing to be made visible. The distinguishing feature of celebrities is that they generate narratives of their own lives that are offered to the public in the form of entertainment. This overall shape to the way that celebrity operates, says Gamson, produces an environment that is hospitable to the development of 'the ordinary.'[7]

The Internet produces different kinds of celebrities to those that feature in the Hollywood dominated media industries. These might include those who simply have a particular quirk in their character or an unusual event that makes their videos 'go viral.' A good example of this is the video on YouTube 'Charlie Bit My Finger'. This is a family video of a young boy sticking his finger into his younger brother's mouth. As a result of the video, Gamson says, both of the boys became unlikely stars.[8] The rise of social media has enabled the development of the American interest in the spectacle of ordinary people who become celebrities. Celebrity, it is claimed, has become available to anyone no matter how unexceptional they might be. This is the 'lionization of the ordinary.'[9] The result has been that, at least to some extent, the entertainment and publicity technologies of Hollywood have been bypassed, but this is only an aspect of what is taking place. There has been a partial decentring of Celebrity Culture. On the one hand the power of the audience to create celebrities has become amplified and enabled by social media. These processes take place largely away from the powerful interests associated with traditional media. At the same time the commercial interests of these established groups remain primary, and this is illustrated by the way that online celebrities seek to convert their fame into more traditional forms of media, such as television.[10] Parallel to this, traditional forms of media have readily identified that online celebrity can be a source to discover new talent, indeed online success can be regarded as a way to take away the problems associated with breaking new stars. The shift towards the ordinary has, however, generated a culture where the ordinary individual is not only performing themselves online, but they are also seeking to be watched. This work of being open to observation shapes how the self is understood in new ways, not least because of what the awareness that being watched brings to the individual, as they are conscious of this fact. Life observed, followed and liked, becomes a legitimating feature of daily reality. What is real is what has been posted and liked. This is an environment where everyone has become a star. The ordinary experience of life is not just one in which we are watching but one in which we are being watched. Performing the self online is built on this expectation.

Reality TV

Reality TV represented the first significant move towards a media environment where 'ordinary' people could become celebrities. With shows like *Survivor*, launched in the US in 1992, the global franchise of the Dutch show *Big Brother*, which started in 1999, and *American Idol*, which first broadcast in 2002 and *The Great British Bake Off* in 2010, the phenomenon of members of the viewing public becoming the stars of primetime shows became a major part of Celebrity Culture. As the name suggests, Reality TV has its origins in the television genre of factual programming. These kinds of programmes historically had never attracted significantly large audiences and primetime slots. With the emergence of *Big Brother*, and shows like it, everything changed.[11] Fundamental to the popularity of these programmes was the opportunity that they gave for individuals from the general public to be present on TV in unscripted situations. The format featured people who were not performers or stars. Ordinary voices were celebrated in primetime television, and through this media exposure these people were given the potential to become household names. Reality TV was, therefore, a means to transform individuals, from quite humble or unlikely backgrounds, into celebrities. Chris Rojek refers to these kinds of celebrities as 'celetoids.' Celetoid is defined as 'compressed, concentrated, attributed celebrity.'[12] The individual is famous solely through media-generated processes. The celetoid rises to public consciousness very quickly, but then is forgotten within a very short space of time.[13] The attractiveness to the media industry of the ordinary person who is transformed into a celebrity by television, comes from the ready availability and accessibility of these people. Stars have agents and managers, and they employ publicity companies, and these all seek to control the narrative, and limit the availability of their clients. In the person made famous by Reality TV, the media guaranteed a steady flow of famous people who relied on exposure to maintain their fame.

With the promise of celebrity status, individuals could then become the subject, not simply of the television show, but of any number of spin-off stories concerning their personal lives and loves. Graeme Turner argues that Reality TV reflects the ongoing concern of the media industry to seek to control the process whereby people achieve fame. Rather than being just an end user of celebrity, television companies and executives seek to manufacture their own home-grown stars.[14] Celebrities can therefore be produced in ways that bypass the requirement to be a skilled actor or performer. There is no need for any kind of lengthy or demanding apprenticeship in a craft or training in an artistic discipline. As Turner puts it, 'Those who participate do not want to be singers, or actors, or dancers necessarily: they just want to be on television.'[15] Reality TV has transformed the relationship between broadcasters and audience, bringing about what Henry Jenkins refers to as 'convergence.'[16] The emergence of the new formats, that have become known as Reality TV, did not just change who and how celebrities were made, it also brought about a new relationship with audiences. Reality TV enabled a shift from the viewer, as a passive audience, to a new kind of interactivity. In 2003, the US reality music show, *American Idol*, was receiving more than 20 million phone messages or texts per episode.[17] These levels of interaction show how the celebrity shaping formats were a significant draw for audiences who wanted to share in making their own idols.

Reality TV is a vehicle to generate viewers and advertising income, and it has the added spin-off of allowing television companies the possibility to manufacture celebrity, in ways that suit their economic interests. These dynamics, however, are built upon the interest that is generated among audiences by the spectacle of ordinary people being placed centre stage. The appeal of these programmes rests on the 'self' revealed, exposed and challenged through the particular format of the show. In shows such as *Big Brother*, individuals were placed under surveillance in unprecedented ways. Their actions and interactions were not simply recorded and broadcast, they were poured over and commented upon, not just within the show but also through the avalanche of media coverage that accompanied each episode. *Big Brother* in its first series used 'experts' in body language and psychology to inform the audience of the significance of certain gestures, or forms of communication. Narrating and revealing personal identity, Biressi and Nunn suggest, is one of the crucial ingredients in Reality TV. The programmes construct a world that claims to present the 'real feelings' of 'real people'. This access to 'reality' lies at the heart of the way that these formats present a credible view of the individual.[18] In the Reality TV world individuals are thrown together in an unscripted environment where 'matrices of jealousy, rivalry, distrust and erotic attraction' can be played out in front of the audience.[19] The self-performed, therefore also becomes the self-revealed and laid bare. This dynamic of self-revelation is structured into the format of reality shows, through the device of the private interview or dialogue room. In *Big Brother* contestants are invited into the 'Diary Room', where they are asked to sit in the 'Diary Chair' and talk in a frank way to an anonymous voice representing 'Big Brother'. These moments are designed to reveal what is happening behind the action, and as such, they are another device that enables the viewer to garner additional insights into the personalities and motivations of those who are on the show.

Reality TV feeds, and has in many ways generated, a widespread desire to become a celebrity. The shows have spawned a number of media careers, and they function in the popular imagination in a similar way to the lottery, where the individual can overnight win big. Instant fame, however, is not the primary function of Reality TV for the viewer. What this format offers, is a steady flow of lives to consume. Celebrity fame is bred from self-revelation, and what is revealed is fodder, not only for the tabloid press, but for fans to follow. The narratives that are generated by Reality TV become a fruitful source for gossip, speculation and above all, self-examination. The ordinariness of the contestants in these shows facilitates processes of identification and dis-identification in ways that more traditional celebrities fail to achieve. Quite simply, audiences can believe that a particular individual could be them, because that is actually the case. This close association, and the detail and nature of the revelation that Reality TV generates, means that fans are able to process their sense of themselves, in relation to the selves that are placed on show and put up for comparison by the media. Reality TV is therefore the most raw, basic and affectively dynamic form that brings about the mediatisation of the individual and it is a key ingredient in Celebrity Worship.

Understanding the selfie

The rise of the selfie represents a significant development in the representation of the individual in a mediated culture. Katrin Tiidenberg suggests that, as a phenomenon, the selfie is not entirely new; there are, for instance, significant continuities with practices associated with the previous technology of the instant Polaroid camera.[20] Rather than being a completely new phenomenon, the selfie operates a coming together, or a convergence between technology and representational practices.[21] The selfie brings together three elements in a new configuration. The photographic object, the representation of the self or an object that has been taken by oneself, and the third is a digitally networked object.[22] Although these three elements have a significant history that predates what has become known as the selfie, e.g. in photographic self-portraiture, it is the combination of elements that marks the selfie as distinctive. Tiidenberg argues therefore, that for something to qualify as a selfie, all three of these elements must be simultaneously present: photographic object, visual self-representation and network. Selfies then are defined as 'self-representational, networked photographs.'[23] Selfies do not have to be an image of a person's face, they simply have to be a self-representation. Neither do selfies have to be shared. They can be taken for personal pleasure and stored on a phone or other device, but the possibility that these images might be networked should be a possibility.

Digital technology and social media mean that the selfie is generated on a device that has the capacity of connecting to millions of similar devices around the world. This creates the possibility, as Tiidenberg expresses it, of 'the number of potential eyeballs that can see it.'[24] Digital technology, then, enables an exponential increase in the number of pictures that are created, and the ease with which they can be taken. This new facility is combined with the possibility of an audience of hundreds, or possibly millions, when these pictures are shared. Sharing photos does not simply increase the audience for an image, it also brings a new kind of social dynamic. Photos that are shared operate in networks to develop conversation, connection and community. Images are able to move between individuals and groups, bringing new kinds of relationships. The result is that photos operate as a kind of 'social currency.' 'By posting a well-chosen image at the right time in the right place, we can say, "I am who I claim to be", "I belong" or "I understand the rules of this community."'[25] Profile pictures, on social networking sites and dating apps, can be regarded as early versions of the selfie. In these contexts, images are not simply concerned with looks. These images are self-representation in photographs that are used to communicate a number of nuanced messages about the self. Photos are often updated and changed for a range of reasons. Images that show the individual having fun or being funny are generally preferred. Women seem to be drawn towards images that portray them with friends and family or celebrating a special occasion. Men on the other hand tend to show themselves engaged in activities. Men are also much more likely to upload a video of themselves. The visual clues that are contained in photos are used by followers and viewers to assess the authenticity of the person's profile. Claims made by an individual can be judged against the kinds of images that they regularly post of themselves.[26]

Taken together the sum of everything posted online can be seen as a 'networked self-representation.'[27] The presentation of the self in these ways is fundamental to social media. For Dannah Boyd and Nicole Ellison, social media is defined as web-based services that enable individuals to create a profile that can then be viewed, either publicly or semi-publicly. This bounded system, then supports the articulation of a group of users who share a connection. The individual who has created the profile is able to view and negotiate a way through the various connections that are made. The self, and how the self is performed, is therefore central to how social media operates. Profiles and posts are constructed in order to attract attention – likes and shares are everything. The selfie, then, should be read not as an isolated object, or practice, but as a part of this wider flow of self-representation within a networked online environment. As Tiidenberg expresses it, selfies are experienced by people 'within an endless flow of posts, other people's posts, relationships, people, platforms, visual tropes and popular norms.' The practice of taking a selfie involves a whole series of activities that may include: 'posing, editing, posting, saving, sending, deleting, hashtagging, commenting, captioning, liking and reposting selfies.'[28] These practices support a particular performance of the self, but they also imply a notion of the presence of the self. Selfies are a particular form of making oneself present in the world. Social networking sites enable the individual to create a steady flow of images and words that reinforce the sense that the individual has a presence and exists in relationships that are in a context. A selfie can simply be a way of letting our family and friends know that we have arrived at a particular location; it can, however, also be used to convey a message, for instance photographing ourselves next to a gay pride flag. Selfies also can be a way to perform the self that we wish to be seen as. Selfies, then, might be a means to garner attraction on, for instance, a dating site, or they can be used as a form of marketing to make money.[29] Selfies are not simply a performance of the self, they also provide an opportunity, and perhaps an invitation, to comparison. Understanding the self, in relation to others, is fundamental to identity formation and construction. The selfie can read as operating as a part of these processes. Social media platforms have increased the possibilities for comparison of the self in almost unlimited ways. The flow of images that come across the screen represent an environment that is participative and interactive. Social media is 'social', it takes place through a series of relationships. The self online is therefore not an isolated individual but a networked person. Posts are sent to people or they generate likes and comments. It is this networked representation of the self that creates a link between selfies and Celebrity Worship. Through social media and representation, the distinction between the celebrity and the audience collapses and the distinction is simply how many followers and likes are created by each person. This scale does not detract from the ways in which each are part of the same representational system. These interactions enable a level of self-reflexivity. Through interaction it is possible to develop a sense of what is socially attractive or what 'look' is better than another look. Here, celebrity posts and images are part of the wider flow that forms part of the discourse. The selfie is therefore a part of the continual revision and development that is the project of the self.

A significant aspect of the selfie relates to self-discovery and self-understanding. Photographs are linked to specific events and emotions; for instance, the photos taken at weddings or birthdays carry memories and feelings. Selfies operate within this affective economy of the photograph. They are self-revealing. This revealing of the self, however, takes place in public. The selfie has a power because it is a self that is being seen by others. 'Being seen,' is an important aspect of developing identity. To be seen is to be present and hence to be recognised. Being seen situates us in a network of relationship. This is one of the reasons why selfies have continued to increase as an online practice: they make us feel good. Selfies are a way of being affirmed and recognised by others. This kind of recognition operates as part of Celebrity Worship. Social media brings about a seeming democratisation of celebrity. The validation that social media offers, brings benefits in terms of being encouraged in the performance of identity. As Tiidenberg expresses it, the selfie is 'about being seen as what I choose to share with you, through things, people and places important to me.'[30] The ability to manufacture and reproduce the self, as an image that is shared through networks of relationship, is a significant empowerment of the self. It is the means by which each one of us, in our own way, are celebritised. An important aspect of this empowerment is the way that selfies are used as a means to situate the self in relation to particular places, events or objects. Taking a selfie in front of a piece of art or at rock concert inserts the individual into a flow of significance. The self then becomes a pivot to read these events or objects. The self is in relation to the world and more significantly perhaps becomes a means to read the world.

Facebook and the self

When Facebook was launched in 2004, as a means for intercampus socialising in Harvard University, it represented a shift in the presentation of the self online. The initial requirement that those who signed up needed to give an institutionally registered email address, and to use their real names, represented a significant shift in online identity. Prior to this point the performance of self on the Internet was shaped around anonymity and the use of aliases.[31] Facebook changed this 'virtual' self into a presentational self. On Facebook, people were seeking to share a version of themselves with their existing friends, and with those who they have yet to become friends with. This dynamic of generating friends eventually meant that the site had an inbuilt motivation towards shaping the performance of the self, in ways that were attractive and attractional. Zhao et al researched a group of early Facebook adopters. They found that these Facebook users developed a number of strategies to present versions of themselves to selected audiences on Facebook, actively choosing who they would share stories with, and how these stories were constructed. Photos and specific narratives were presented, where identities were chosen to facilitate a performance of the self, as for instance highly social. This was achieved by including a number of photos with groups of friends, or through highlighting particular forms of consumer choices, or cultural activities, in stories that were posted.[32] These forms of communication, Zhao et al argue, demonstrate a tendency to 'show' the self through intermediaries. For these Facebook users, their performance of the self was enacted through the people they were with, and by means of the things that they chose to buy, use and appreciate.[33] A common element found in the research was there was a strong motivation to be seen as 'being popular among friends.' The users in the sample were also concerned to present themselves as being well-rounded, with a range of different social activities and also to be thoughtful, for instance, by demonstrating a depth of reflections upon life.[34] The researchers concluded that these identities were a performance of a hoped-for, or an aspirational self. This was a self that was distinct from the possibilities of the more anonymous selves represented in virtual worlds, but also disconnected, or perhaps not yet achieved, in the offline world.[35] The hoped-for selves, however, indicate the extent to which Facebook supports the generation of complexities of the self. These online identities are not unreal or virtual, rather, they are aspects of a complex self. The hoped-for self, and the offline self are interconnected.

A key dynamic in social networking sites, such as Facebook, is the driving force of visibility.[36] Visibility relates a range of discursive activities that shape the performance of self through social media. The launch of Facebook and other networking sites coincided with the development of digital photography. This meant that taking, reproducing and sharing images, became cheap and accessible to all. Photographic images have been central to the performance of the self online, but it is significant that the written text has also been fundamental. On social media, the use of language has been central, such that one commentator speaks of 'writing oneself into being.'[37] The presentation of the self online has certain limits, for instance, tone of voice, or facial expression is excluded. This enables a forum, where identity can be constructed in a way that enables a range of choices about the performance of the self. At the same time, the relatively limited range of clues that are available in performing the digital self, means that generating a sense of authenticity requires a level of attention and hard work.[38]

Negotiating the demands and perils of performing an online self in social media has become a significant challenge. Donna Freitas identified the need for American college students to be continually attentive to their online profiles. In her research, she identified what she calls the 'happiness effect', where students feel that they are under constant pressure to present themselves online through a narrative of happiness and success. Fundamental to this sense, that what should be posted is only what is positive, upbeat and, if possible, funny in ways that show them in a good light, is the overarching understanding that the purpose is to achieve maximum attention. Attention in social media is numeric and continually accessed through likes, shares and comments. Posting stories, then, is motivated by the desire to be successful and popular, and to be seen as being that kind of person. Social media posts and profiles on Facebook and Instagram are not watched solely for the posts, they are monitored by friends and followers who can measure the relative popularity of others. This means that an individual can make judgements about the pictures that they post, and the images that they present. Many of those who were interviewed by Freitas were acutely aware that they were constructing an idealised and unrealistic image of themselves but they also knew that posts that revealed their struggles, or indeed any strong or controversial opinions, were not just unlikely to benefit from likes and shares, but they might also draw adverse comments and disapproval. This awareness of the constructed nature of the self, extended to how individuals viewed the posts that came into their feeds. There was a knowing realisation that the over perfect and happy narratives that they saw in their friends' social media were unreal, and yet at the same time, they found that it was almost impossible to not continually compare their lives with what appeared to be the more successful lives of others. Envy and self-doubt were part of the experience and the pressures associated with consuming social media.[39]

Freitas found that students would adjust their sense of who they were, and how they presented themselves, in reaction to the feedback that they were getting to the pictures that they were posting. These reactions took place in live time as a flow of interactions between comments and likes and posts. This awareness of the self in relation to a watching audience led to students carefully curating their online persona for maximum effect. An added pressure was the realisation, often reinforced by college authorities, that an online profile will be researched by potential employers or indeed by the college itself. There was, then, a heavy responsibility to ensure that negative or problematic images were not posted, and this extended to a vigilance around the images and messages posted by other friends or groups. The expectation that an online profile requires attention and effort, led to many speaking of about social network activity as 'work.' The self that is created online was increasingly regarded as a brand. Online activity is an arena where many see themselves as generating, editing and cultivating, their own personal image. Branding means that the self has become something of a business that needs to be marketed and protected. The language of business was very common, Freitas found. 'The idea that we can, "advertise ourselves" through social media is common, and one student went so far as to say that the image one cultivates on social media, "can even be used to create a business of being "yourself" online."'[40] The control and professional approach that students adopted, in relation to publicly visible social media sites, was in marked contrast to the way that they interacted on platforms that appeared to guarantee anonymity or privacy. Here, college students would engage in practices that were designed to be outrageous and unacceptable in any other sphere. Photos would emphasise rule breaking, criticism of others would be brutal and often obscene. Freitas comments that the work hard, play hard, mentality that shaped the daily lives of these students appeared to be extended to their online selves. On Facebook and Instagram everything was perfect but on anonymous sites such as Yik Yak they revealed their dark sides.[41]

Self-branding and micro-celebrity

The notion of the self as a brand has grown in significance, such that it has been commonplace as a prerequisite for success in business, academic life, or in developing a small business.[42] Transforming the self into a brand involves the utilisation of media processes, in order to market the earning power of individual. The opportunities and possibilities for self-branding have increased exponentially with the emergence of social media. Khamis et al argue that social media 'tacitly promises fame', and, as a result, the possibility of wealth to 'ordinary individuals.'[43] The ability to project a self-image through social media, leads to a widespread belief that anyone can be famous. This possibility, however, argues Khamis et al, is largely an illusion. The multiple platforms and applications that characterise new media generate an arena where projecting the self takes place in an increasingly competitive environment. This leads to what has been termed an 'attention economy.'[44] This describes an environment where 'an unprecedented number of communicators compete across more screens for increasingly distracted, dispersed and privatised audiences.'[45] Self-branding therefore becomes an attention-seeking device, to try to gain an advantage through developing the individual as image. From 2000, self-branding became a widespread activity, not simply for those from whom it was normally expected, such as musicians, sportspeople or TV personalities, but much more widely. Social media was very quickly grasped by 'ordinary individuals' as a route to becoming celebrities. Individual brands could be developed in the first wave of digital technology through websites and blogs, but with the launch of Twitter, YouTube, Facebook and Instagram, these possibilities, Khamis et al argue, accelerated and served to emphasise the extent to which individuals could use these sites as a means to 'package, perform and sell a lucrative personal brand' across a number of online sites.[46] The convergence of media technology allows for multiple points of access and a range of interrelated and supporting forms of self-branding and the rise of what has become known as the micro-celebrity.

Self-branding and micro-celebrity are based around developing clear and consistent narratives that are designed to be attractive across a range of audiences. Fundamental to this is the way in which social media collapses specific contexts and flattens the audience into a single group of consumers. In this arena, projecting the self, through representation that can be consumed by a diverse range of people, becomes a fundamental strategy.[47] Effective self-branding requires the ability to 'embed' the narrative of that particular individual into their media flows through 'likes, shares and comments.' These participatory practices are fundamental to the development of micro-celebrity. The generation of an individual narrative enables the performance of the self, as a product, to be consumed. This consumption is not passive, but facilitated, and enhanced through the actions of followers and friends. Self-branding requires that the individual who seeks to be a celebrity, is willing to nurture and feed their audience, in order that it might grow, thus yielding social, and possibly economic, benefits.[48] Khamis et al call this process of generating a brand – through sharing, liking and interacting – a process of 'self-mediation.'[49] Social media does not simply enable the projection of the self on a global scale, it also has inbuilt mechanisms that support the measurement, and hence reward, for this activity. The metrics that are a feature of developing followers, friends, likes and shares, allow for the measurement and comparison of success. These factors are visible and evident, and they encourage the culture of micro-celebrity by offering a precise account of what it means to be famous.

Micro-celebrity was first coined as a term by Theresa Senft, who researched what were called 'cam-girls.' These were young women who were early adopters of digital technology, using it to broadcast themselves on the Internet.[50] Senft argued that micro-celebrities were distinct from previous forms of celebrity. The celebrity image generated via traditional forms of media involved the manufacture of distance and mystique. By contrast, the cam-girls that Senft researched, sought – through a variety of tactics – to collapse the distinction between private life and media-generated representation. Micro-celebrity is constructed around the development of emotional connections between the audience and the media-generated individual, such that there is an expectation that what is being broadcast is an unedited display of the 'real' self. This connection between the micro-celebrity and their audience is further enhanced among the cam-girls by the realisation that fame rested on the co-creation that takes place online between individuals. This is again distinct from other forms of celebrity where fame may arise from particular talents or abilities[51]. Alice Marwick developed Senft's idea of micro-celebrity in her research into tech industry workers in San Francisco during the early 2000s. Marwick found that the use of social media by these workers, as a networking tool, required them to continuously curate a performance of the self online that appeared to be authentic and interactive. These representations of the self, involved the individual projecting themselves as a celebrity, whatever the size of their audience.[52] Social media enable the individual to promote themselves in ways that do not directly rely upon the gatekeepers that are associated with legacy forms of media such as radio, magazines or television. The reach of these forms of media can be enormous. An example of the reach of micro-celebrity is Cayla Friesz, a high school student from Indiana, who showed pictures of herself, her friends, food, and trips out, on Instagram. Her posts have been seen by more than 35,000 followers.[53] Friesz represents an individual who has become, what Alice Marwick calls, the 'Instafamous.'[54] These kinds of activities support a growing culture where the private self is broadcast and exposed in ways that appear to turn the self, inside-out. David Marshall refers to this as 'the ubiquity of the exposed public self.'[55] Fundamental to this shift is the sensibility that regards being and identity as something that is linked to the experience of being observed. Micro-celebrity, and social media in general, frames a culture where self must be broadcast to be real and this is a fundamental dynamic and driver in Celebrity Worship.

The micro-celebrity is able to make use of the same processes of representation and publication as those of established stars to generate their own presence online. This means that the individual is able to replicate or situate themselves in parallel ways to established celebrities.[56] As a result, celebrity has become less about something that a person 'is', rather it describes something that they do. '"Celebrity" in the social media age is a range of techniques and strategies that can be performed by anyone with a mobile device, tablet, or laptop.'[57] Marwick argues that micro-celebrity should be interpreted as simply the latest development in how we interpret how people are using the Internet as a more participatory, self-promoting and interacting arena.[58] Social media becomes a place where micro-celebrities 'hang out' and seek attention – as Molly Soda, a blogger on the site Tumblr, puts it, 'I hate it when someone asks me what I "do," like your job is supposed to define you or something. I'm doing me, you're doing you, some people are better at getting attention for it than others. There's no shame in that.'[59] For a micro-celebrity like Molly Soda the activity undertaken in self-promotion is not a kind of work, it is just 'being me'. This activity, however, is linked to the desire for attention in the competitive space of the Internet. Why she receives so much attention – she has 30,000 followers – rather than other people who also desire attention is not entirely clear and Molly Soda herself is resistant to analysing what is taking place. Marwick suggests that what appears to be the case is that just the act of creating a consumable persona, interacting with readers, and sharing personal stories and images of yourself, does not guarantee an audience.[60] At the same time, the development of broadband Internet has created an environment where micro-celebrities see themselves as being 'always on.' This leads to a stream of sharing details of themselves. Being always on, also relates to the potential audience where attention is constantly being sought by a series of notifications and alerts. This brings a further level of magnitude to the competitive world of online celebrity. Crystal Abdin describes how the scale and the dynamics of micro-celebrity have evolved in recent years. In its origins, micro-celebrity was restricted in its scale compared to more traditional forms of celebrity. This distinction has changed, and Internet-based celebrities have now become as significant as other kinds of celebrities and in some cases their following and reach exceeds other kinds of celebrity. Micro-celebrity, in its origins, was confined to social media, and other Internet forms of communication. This has also changed, with individuals operating not simply across Internet platforms, but also becoming a feature of the coverage in mainstream media. The audiences of micro-celebrities were generally limited to small niche groups, who picked up on their activities online. With the generation of social media algorithms, and the crossover to other forms of media coverage, the global impact of micro-celebrity has become a much more significant feature of the current scene. This growth in reach and popularity has enabled micro-celebrity to transition from a hobby, or an amateur leisure activity, to become a career with the possibility of earning a very healthy wage. The practice of micro-celebrity, says Abdin, has also undergone something of a change. In the early stages of Internet celebrity, the practice was for individuals to primarily focus on personal stories, and thereby generate intimacy and interaction. These aspects of micro-celebrity continue, but they are increasingly anchored by content that is aimed to demonstrate some core activity or skill that can be shown through social media posts. This kind of content has a more substantive character based on shared activities and interests. These changes have shifted the primary location of Internet-based celebrity from the intimacy of the bedroom and the personalised spaces that illustrate the private life of the celebrity, to more public arenas. The influence of these practices is not limited to the bedroom, increasingly they have become a presence in the boardroom.[61]

Closely associated with micro-celebrity has been the rise of a new kind of individual who is able to use their profile across social media platforms to generate income. These individuals have been labelled 'influencers.' Abdin traces the origins of the present day influencer to earlier iterations of a commercialised personal presence on the Internet through websites and blogs in Singapore. In the 2000s, a new kind of 'blogshop' industry began to develop where blogs were used in ways that facilitated online sales and shopping. As part of this activity, some of the bloggers started linked sites, where they would narrate their lives, offering personal stories that illustrated the promotion of products.[62] A number of these blogshop activities grew rapidly, and as a result they led to connections with manufacturers and the launch of related retail outlets. Inspired by this success, Abdin recounts how young women began to take up this activity of blogging about their lifestyle activities, while simultaneously promoting products on their websites.[63] With the advent of social media apps in South East Asia, a number of these women transferred their activities onto these new forms of communication, and the influencer as we recognise it came into being. These developments soon led to the creation of agencies that specialised linking clients, who wished to advertise their products, with the influencers. These connections produced lucrative income streams for the women, who would develop stories around their lives and these products.[64] Income can be further generated by influencers by producing 'advertorials' – these are short films that promote a product and are paid for directly by their clients. The second major way to monetise a presence on social media is to sell advertising that will be shown on their blogs and social media. Generally, these advertisements can be banner posts that give a direct link to the commercial sites where products can be bought. A third way to generate income is for the influencer to sell products themselves on their own dedicated websites.[65] The rise of the influencer has become a feature of mainstream celebrity discourse where individuals such as Kim Kardashian and Gwyneth Paltrow have monetised their brands by promoting endorsed products online. Here traditional celebrities are picking up on developments elsewhere.

The democratisation of celebrity

Celebrity Worship has been transformed, such that is has become an aspect of everyday life. Through Reality TV and the selfie, the focus has shifted from extraordinary individuals to the celebrity – a status that is interwoven into life. Ordinary celebrities have at the same time, through social media, begun to transform themselves into influencers and micro-celebrities, such that these developments are mimicked by more mainstream celebrities. These convergences are the active and energising features of contemporary Celebrity Worship and they fuel the turn towards the self as the ultimate concern and the new dimension of the sacred. In the following chapters, these aspects of Celebrity Worship are traced in relation to specifically religious themes as Celebrity Worship becomes a driving force for the turn towards the self in religious practice and discourse.

Notes

1   Marshall. New Media, 638.
2   Tim O'Reilly. 'What is Web 2.0: Design Patterns and Business Models for the Next Generation of Software.' *Communications and Strategies* 1 (2007): 17–38.
3   Philip Sergeant and Caroline Tagg, eds. *The Language of Social Media: Identity and Community on the Internet*. (Basingstoke: Palgrave, 2014), 2.
4   Sergeant and Tagg. *Language*, 4.
5   Joshua Gamson. 'The Unwatched Life Is Not Worth Living: The Elevation of the Ordinary in Celebrity Culture.' *Theories and Methodologies,* 126, no. 4 (2011): 1061–1069.
6   Gamson. The Unwatched, 1066.
7   Gamson. The Unwatched, 1063.
8   Gamson. The Unwatched, 1066.
9   Gamson. The Unwatched, 1067.
10 Gamson. The Unwatched, 1068.
11 Anita Biressi and Heather Nunn. *Reality TV: Realism and Revelation*. (London: Wallflower Press, 2005), 2.
12 Rojek. *Celebrity*, 20.
13 Rojek. *Celebrity*, 21.
14 Turner. *Understanding*, 53.
15 Turner. *Understanding*, 53.
16 Turner. *Understanding*, 59.
17 Henry Jenkins. *Convergence Culture: Where Old and New Media Collide*. (New York: New York University Press, 2006), 59.
18 Biressi and Nunn. *Reality*, 96.
19 Biressi and Nunn. *Reality*, 98.
20 Katerin Tiidenberg. *Selfies: Why we Love (and Hate) Them*. (Bingley: Emerald Publishing, 2018), 18.
21 Rojek, *Celebrity*.
22 Tiidenberg. *Selfies*, 19.
23 Tiidenberg. *Selfies*, 21.
24 Tiidenberg. *Selfies*, 34.
25 Tiidenberg. *Selfies*, 34.
26 Tiidenberg. *Selfies*, 35.
27 Tiidenberg. *Selfies*, 36.
28 Tiidenberg. *Selfies*, 47.
29 Tiidenberg. *Selfies*, 64.
30 Tiidenberg. *Selfies*, 92.
31 Shanyang Zhao, Sherri Grasmuck and Jason Martin. 'Identity Construction on Facebook: Digital Empowerment in Anchored Relationships.' *Computers in Human Behavior,* 24 (2008): 1816–1836.
32 Zhao, Grasmuck and Martin. Identity, 1825.
33 Zhao, Grasmuck and Martin. Identity, 1826.
34 Zhao, Grasmuck and Martin. Identity, 1826.
35 Zhao, Grasmuck and Martin. Identity, 1828.
36 Sergeant and Tagg. *Language*, 6.
37 Sergeant and Tagg. *Language*, 6.
38 Sergeant and Tagg. *Language*, 9.
39 Donna Freitas. *The Happiness Effect: How Social Media is Driving a Generation to Appear Perfect at Any Cost*. (Oxford: Oxford University Press, 2017).
40 Freitas. *Happiness*, 77.
41 Freitas. *Happiness*, 135–140.

42 Susie Khamisa, Lawrence Ang and Raymond Welling. 'Self-branding, "Micro-celebrity" and the Rise of Social Media Influencers.' *Celebrity Studies*, 8, no. 2 (2017): 191–208.
43 Khamis. Self-branding, 194.
44 Khamis. Self-branding, 194–195.
45 Khamis. Self-branding, 195.
46 Khamis. Self-branding, 195.
47 Khamis. Self-branding, 195.
48 Khamis. Self-branding, 196.
49 Khamis. Self-branding, 196.
50 Crystal Abdin. *Internet Celebrity: Understanding Fame Online.* (Bingley: Emerald Publishing, 2018), 11.
51 Abdin. *Internet*, 12.
52 Abdin. *Internet*, 12.
53 Khamis. Self-branding, 199.
54 Khamis. Self-branding, 199.
55 Khamis. Self-branding, 199.
56 Alice Marwick. 'Instafame: Luxury Selfies in the Attention Economy.' *Public Culture*, 27, no. 75 (2015): 137–160.
57 Marwick. Instafame, 2.
58 Marwick. Instafame, 8.
59 Marwick. Instafame, 10.
60 Marwick. Instafame, 11.
61 Abdin. *Internet*, 14–15.
62 Abdin. *Internet*, 73.
63 Abdin. *Internet*, 75.
64 Abdin. *Internet*, 76.
65 Abdin. *Internet*, 78.

Chapter 6

Celebrity and religious change

Celebrity Worship lies at the heart of the media processes that are bringing about religious change. This is basically because Celebrity Worship focuses attention upon the self as the centre of a narrative. This is as true of film, as it is of radio, or social media. In all kinds of media communication people are fundamental, not only to what is communicated but also to the way in which communication takes place. Celebrity is therefore the human face of media communication. The emotional connection and attachment that is generated by media, arises from people, and these people are the substance and content of Celebrity Worship. Celebrities are mediated selves, the self, represented and performed, across media platforms. The self, therefore, is fundamental to understanding media. What follows from this argument is that as the complex relationship between media and religion has evolved, mediated individuals have been a generative force for change. This change has a key dynamic that revolves around the shift of focus from religious tradition and authority, towards individual choice as the organising principle. So, just as the celebrity is the human face of every media-generated story, the 'self' is situated as the centre of religious life. Celebrity Worship thus becomes an amplification system to this reorientation of how the self is situated in relation to religious traditions. The accelerant that has boosted this change has been the idea of choice. With the self at the centre of a religious narrative, then the emphasis moves from acquiescence to agency. Selection, however, also leads to the fragmentation of religious traditions. The religious self is free to choose, to edit, and to combine, across religious traditions and non-religious sources. The self as a selecting and constructing agent brings about a change in how religion is present in the lived.

The change that Celebrity Culture brings is not to be confused with any direct notion of influence. Celebrities do not generate religious change simply by what they say, or indeed by the things that they endorse. Celebrity Worship forms a part of the wider shift towards the self in society. This shift to the self, arises as a cultural formation in relation to media representation. Drawing on the perspective of Cultural Studies, the turn to the self is articulated with processes of production, representation and consumption. This pattern of cultural meaning making suggests that a shift to the self will develop out of a network of different actors, institutions, technologies and social relationships. The point here, is that people form the substantive content of each of these aspects of cultural production. Celebrity Worship runs through all the elements of cultural meaning making, but how it operates is variously articulated. This chapter explores the role that celebrities play in bringing about fundamental changes in religion. Three case studies illustrate these changes. The first looks at the role that individuals such as Madonna have played in popularising the Jewish teaching of Kabbalah and the spread of the Los Angeles based Kabbalah Centre that was founded by Rabbi Philip Berg. The second case study focuses on Oprah Winfrey and her use of her celebrity status and power in the media industry to promote a distinctive vision of the spiritual life. The third case study focuses on the One Love concert that was organised by Ariana Grande as a response to the Manchester terror attack in 2017. These case studies serve to illustrate how processes of production, representation and consumption align in generating new religious practices and perspectives. Celebrities lie, then, at the heart of a particular structure of feeling, to use Raymond Williams' term for culture.[1] This sensibility arises through a particular relationship with media production and representation. The 'influence' of celebrities is diffused throughout this process, not simply causing the structure of feeling but functioning as a part of it. Individual celebrities are seen to be, in these case studies, agents who facilitate these changes. They are articulated in the complex interaction of acting in relation to each of the moments of cultural meaning making.

Kabbalah: the celebrity religion of the self

In 2013, Rabbi Philip Berg died. Berg was a Jewish rabbi who had come to fame through founding the Kabbalah Centre, firstly in New York, and then in Los Angeles, in the 1980s. The centre has branches all over the world including in London, Toronto, and it is now run by his wife, Karen Berg, and their son, Michael Berg. Kabbalistic teaching and practice originated in thirteenth century Spain, from where it spread around the world.[2] By the eighteenth century, Kabbalah, and those traditional Jewish groups who adhered to it, were regarded as marginal by the majority of the Jewish communities. In the late nineteenth and early twentieth centuries, as Kabbalah was largely rejected within modern Judaism, it began to attract non-Jewish followers in the West, who were influenced by romanticism and attracted to esoteric forms of knowledge.[3] In the 1970s, Jewish groups began to rediscover Kabbalah, and a number of different schools were established, including the school of Yehuda Ashlag, and it was within this group that Philip Berg received his training.[4]

Contemporary Kabbalistic teaching and practice, according to Huss, is eclectic and diverse but in many instances, it has crossed over with aspects of New Age religion. Characteristics of New Age religion – such as the anticipation of spiritual transformation, psychological accounts of religious beliefs, the sanctification of the self and a belief in the inherent compatibility of spirituality and science – are shared by many of the new forms of Kabbalistic groups.[5] At the same time, contemporary expressions of Kabbalah, including those pioneered by Philip Berg, have embraced what Huss terms, a postmodern spirituality that downplays doctrinal formulation. Kabbalah has been repackaged as a 'practice' that no longer requires a coherent narrative of belief to sustain the various activities such as meditation or healing.[6] These activities are rather located in a spirituality of the self, and of personal transformation.[7] The turn to the self, then, is paralleled by a move away from more propositional, or doctrinal ways of speaking about faith. The turn to the self, decentres one kind of rationality that is based upon texts, and replaces it with another that is related to experience. Kabbalah, then, is effectively redefined through prioritising the self.

The Kabbalah Centre received a considerable boost when, in 1996, Madonna started to attend classes. At the time, celebrities such as Roseanne Barr and Sandra Bernhard, both of whom have a Jewish background, were already attending meetings at the centre, but it was Madonna's interest in Kabbalah that resulted in a significant rise in media interest in Philip and Karen Berg and their teachings.[8] A number of other celebrities were moved to take up Kabbalah, encouraged by the interest that Madonna showed. These included: Ashton Kutcher, Demi Moore, Donna Karan and, more recently, Ariana Grande. Interest in Kabbalah is often associated with the wearing of a red string bracelet and indeed, celebrities are seen as supporters when they have been photographed wearing one of these items. A pack of red bracelets can be purchased from the London Kabbalah Centre for around £18. The purpose of the red string is to ward off the evil eye.[9] Celebrities, such as Paris Hilton, Lindsay Lohan and Nicole Richie have been photographed by paparazzi, sporting the red string bracelet. Those attracted to Kabbalah have also included royalty, with Princess Eugenie having been photographed wearing the red bracelet.[10] The Centre also markets Kabbalah water at $4 a bottle. The water, it is claimed, has healing properties. Madonna was reported to have tried to fill her swimming pool with bottles of this water. Financial demands on individuals who connect to the Centre can be significant. The model Jerry Hall said that she eventually left Kabbalah, because the expectations were so heavy. She told *Index Magazine*, 'We had a fantastic time with the Kabbalah Centre for about a year, they give very practical advice on day-to-day stuff, like how to be a better parent. But we couldn't go through the Door of Miracles unless we gave the Kabbalah people ten per cent of our money, so we couldn't study it anymore.'[11] Despite these financial issues, Kabbalah has continued to thrive. In 2015, The Kabbalah Centre in London was said to have around 1,000 members and it was planning a £5 million extension.[12]

Berg was a former insurance salesman, and his wife Karen was his secretary. He discovered Kabbalah on a trip to Israel and started to instruct people from his insurance office.[13] At the Kabbalah Centre, Philip and Karen Berg developed a form of Kabbalah that emphasised the transformation of the self and the benefits of specific practices. At the same time, the specifically doctrinal, or theological aspects of Kabbalah, were deemed to be less significant. An example of this shift towards practices over theology is found in the use of the Zohar. In traditional forms of Kabbalah, the Zohar has been the key foundational text. Zohar in Hebrew means, splendour or radiance, and the group of books that form the Zohar include commentaries on the first five books of the Old Testament known as the Torah. The Zohar also includes discussion of mysticism, the nature of God and the relationship between universal energy and humanity. Theologically, it is part of the genre of Jewish literature known as Midrash, that acts as commentary on scripture. The Zohar is written mainly in Aramaic, with a mixture of medieval forms of Portuguese and Spanish. At the Bergs' Kabbalah Centre, there was no requirement to study the text in the original language, or indeed in translation. Instead members were taught to run their finger over text, so that they might absorb the teaching without reading.[14] This practice is understood by the Kabbalah Centre to be a kind of meditation, that enables the participant to participate in the harmony and different processes that are within the divine.[15] The religious roots of Kabbalah, within Judaism, or indeed the notion of formal religion at all, has become less significant for those affiliated with the Kabbalah Centre. Interviewed in *The Guardian* newspaper in 2015, Marcus Weston, who teaches in the London Kabbalah Centre explained,

> When we say Kabbalah is a spiritual wisdom, it sits diametrically opposed to religion. In religion, you can blame someone, or God, because ultimately God ... is a punishing or rewarding energy or person. In spirituality, it doesn't exist. In spirituality, it is 100 per cent a spiritual fabric of causes and effects, meaning that each word, thought and action that you plant has an energy to it.[16]

Philip Berg's version of Kabbalah was intended to bring a vision of spirituality to a wider public and most crucially to non-Jews: gentiles. He sought to both simplify, and to popularise elements that he had drawn from Kabbalistic teaching. This vision in itself, as Jody Myers argues, was a radical move away from the traditional Jewish thinking, where Kabbalah was regarded as a 'hidden knowledge' that was limited to a small number of male devotees.[17] In the 1980s, Berg began to be influenced by marketing executives, who inspired the way that he began to develop his organisation.[18] His approach emphasised those aspects of Kabbalah that had relevance to all humanity, and that linked to New Age themes. In the Kabbalah Centre the term God is avoided in favour of references to a non-personal absolute idea 'the Light.'[19] The Kabbalah Centre provides courses that enable those who participate to identify their impulses, and channel these in a direction that will benefit their soul. A further distinctive aspect of the practice taught by the Kabbalah Centre is the way that meditation is to be practised. Meditation is taught in a manner that encourages the participant to engage for minutes or even seconds. Individuals can do this in a communal setting, or on their own, and there are no set requirements or rules given as to how it should be conducted.[20] Karen Berg describes Kabbalah as something akin to a therapeutic process. Those who practice Kabbalah, she suggests, will be enhancing themselves, and generating a distinct kind of consciousness. 'Kabbalah,' she says,

> is a study that expands consciousness and understanding … Kabbalah also helps us to, without any trace of shame, recognize the part of us that is perhaps not as enlightened, a part of ourselves that we are not always proud of, and gives us the tools to transform that quality within us. The more we can become the person that our soul wants us to be, the more complete we feel. I think this applies to you and me and to the most powerful people in the world.[21]

While the practices of Kabbalah are distanced from formal religion, they are firmly located in a spirituality of the self. On her official website, Karen Berg speaks about each individual containing, a 'spark of God that can be bound together to create transcendence beyond all difference.'[22] In her ethnographic study of the Kabbalah Centre in Los Angeles, Jody Meyer observed that the practice and commitment levels of the members varied, with those at the centre of the organisation being more intense in their practice and in their beliefs. Madonna, speaking in 2015, is clear that she does not regard herself as affiliated to any specific religious group. She does, however, practise Kabbalah, she keeps Shabbat, and she held a bar mitzvah for her son. She does not call herself Jewish, rather, she regards these rituals as 'the Tree of Life consciousness.' These ideas connect her to being what she terms, an 'Israelite,' rather than 'Jewish.'[23] A similar kind of religious eclecticism can be seen in the religious sensibility of Lindsay Lohan, another celebrity follower of Kabbalah. Lohan told Elle magazine, in 2006, that Kabbalah was linked to karma. She explained, 'I would never steal anyone's boyfriend. It's bad karma and I'm a big believer in karma – hence the fact that I've studied Kabbalah.'[24] In recent years, there have been reports that suggest that a number of the more high-profile celebrities have started to drift away from the Kabbalah Centre. Sandra Bernhard, one of the Centre's first celebrity members, who introduced Madonna to Kabbalah, told Women's Wear Daily,

> I went in 1995 before there was any hoopla and I got the best out of it. Then the wheels started to fall off. I'm not nearly as involved with that place as I was. Unfortunately, money corrupts everything, even spirituality. And it's hard not to get caught up in the excitement of glamour and fame.[25]

Kabbalah, it would seem, is something of a self-improvement 'kick' that is taken up by celebrities for a while, but then it is also dropped when their interests move on. It is a spiritual lifestyle, rather than a lifetime religious commitment.

The role that celebrity has played in the success of Kabbalah is complex. The high profile given to the movement through individuals such as Madonna clearly helped the Bergs and the Kabbalah Centre to expand their activities. The celebrities, however, did not formulate the way in which Kabbalistic teaching and practice are realigned towards the self. What is evident, however, is that there is a symbiosis between the kind of religion that the Bergs started to formulate and the sensibilities of many celebrities. This connection replicates a more widespread shift towards the New Age in the US and around the world. Celebrity involvement forms a part of this, rather than being its cause. At the same time, the celebrity presence at the activities of the Kabbalah Centre contributes to the plausibility of this innovative religious formation. The mediation of the religious practice of Kabbalah, is extended through the products that the Kabbalah Centre marketed. These products allow a shift between religion and style in the wearing of the red string bracelet. This commodification becomes a means for the discourse of Celebrity Worship, that revolves around image, style and fashion, to merge with the new religious form. The image of Kabbalah is then carried in celebrity representation. Wearing the bracelet, of course, does not imply any specific religious practice or commitment. The symbol operates as an addendum to the self as personal style, and this echoes the way in which many began to interact with Kabbalah, as a lifestyle option that for a period was enriching. Celebrities then passed through the religious style choice, much as they might a diet or an exercise regime. What this illustrates is the way that religion, as lifestyle choice, shifts the nature of belonging in radical ways from those that are more regularly understood in traditional religious forms.

Oprah and the religion of the self

Kabbalah has managed to spread itself and gain influence because of high-profile celebrity endorsement. This popularity has been celebrity generated. The celebrity effect upon the particular religious practice served to springboard the Kabbalah Centre and the Bergs into popular consciousness. At the same time, while the celebrities involved in Kabbalah have given a high-profile lift to the religion, in large part it has not been the case that they have been active evangelists or teachers. The next case study, by contrast, explores how Oprah Winfrey has used her media profile to actively promote a particular religious vision. Oprah may not be an evangelist as such, but she is clearly a religious influencer, who has used her media empire to try to bring about a change in American religious consciousness.

In her book, *Oprah The Gospel of an Icon*, Kathryn Lofton explores the religious message and significance of Oprah Winfrey.[26] Oprah, she argues, is a person who is also a product. By making herself the product Oprah blurs the line between what is religious and what is not religious. Making herself the product, however, is itself mediated through the generation of the wide range of material products that she sells. These products are sold across a range of media platforms and through them Oprah, according to Lofton, shows how religion is shifting in contemporary American culture.[27] Through her media empire, Oprah promotes the things that she likes, and the things that she needs, alongside the things that she believes. These messages are not just product placements, they are also 'proposals for a mass spiritual revolution, supplying forms of religious practice that fuse consumer behaviour, celebrity ambition and religious idiom.'[28] The products, then, are situated in Oprah's choice and tastes. Through the products she offers a version of herself, but this is intended as a means for the audience to reinvent themselves. What is generated through this commercial activity, as a result, says Lofton, is a 'story about ourselves.'[29]

Lofton describes how Oprah went through a kind of conversion experience around the purpose and function of television. As a result, over a four-year period, *The Oprah Winfrey Show* was transformed, from a chat show that dealt with the usual fare of tragic lives and break ups, to a new kind of programming, that focused on the power of media to transform lives. Rejecting what she described as 'trash television', Oprah embarked on a corporate makeover towards, what she called, 'Change Your Life Television.'[30] The goal was to bring about a change in people's lives that brought fulfilment and happiness. This was intended to generate an inner revolution in her audience. As Oprah described it, 'I am talking about each individual coming to the awareness that, "I am creation's son, creation's daughter. I am Spirit come from the greatest Spirit. I am Spirit."'[31] The change in *The Oprah Winfrey Show*, towards this transformative agenda, quickly spread across the range of products that formed her media portfolio. The explicitly stated aim of enterprises, such as *The Oprah Book Club*, *The Oprah Magazine*, and her radio show *Oprah's Soul Series*, was to influence her audience to generate new lives and new selves.[32] Oprah's vision, then, represents a religious self that can negotiate and operate in a secular environment. The roots of this lie in her own childhood and family upbringing within the Protestant Church. These religious roots, however, function, says Lofton, as a Christian preamble to her project.[33] Oprah rejects formal religious institutions and belief, as control and oppression. But this position is something of a sleight of hand, for she is happy to embrace theological positions that accord with her particular vision.[34]

Oprah's religious message moves some way beyond her roots in the Church. What she offers is a place of meaning, or a means to find a way to move through the 'pulverized space' of contemporary society. She creates a place of gathering, and spiritual refreshment, in the 'thronged silence,' and she does this through a series of branded products, for example: 'Make the Connection,' 'Live Your Best Life' and 'Use Your Life.'[35] Her message encourages a focused attention and quest for personal growth, as a 'transcendent possibility.'[36] Central to this project is the reframing of consumerism, as an explicitly spiritual enterprise. Learning to shop for quality products is the route towards embracing the best that we can be. What develops is a kind of spiritual capitalism, where a discerning purchase is designed to change the experience of living.[37] The spiritual value of shopping is demonstrated in the Oprah store in Chicago, where shoppers can select what they choose, from nine hundred products that reflect the consuming interests of Oprah herself.[38] While religious tradition is suspect, Oprah fully embraces the notion of spirituality. This, says Lofton, is a 'non-dogmatic dogma that encourages an ambiguous theism alongside an exuberant consumerism.'[39] Central to this new religious formulation, is Oprah's use of the term 'Spirit.' Spirit crosses the boundaries of everyday life and lifts the individual into a new transcendent reality. The focus on Spirit represents the possibility of a new self. Oprah there-fore speaks of Spirit, as a way of connecting to the life that you want. 'Spirit is not religion; it's just about what is really great about yourself and remembering to live that way.'[40] Spirit then, is an ethic and a sensibility for consumption, where Oprah has preselected the products that are designed to enable personal transformation. Life is not seen as a place to be good, but rather as a project where each individual is seeking continually to be better. The goal is to be always moving forwards to a grander vision of the self.[41] Oprah does not present herself as a religious guru. What she offers are not rules for life, or indeed a prescription. Her vision for the transformation of the self is framed as her own choices and preferences. In doing so she leaves open the choices that individuals might make for themselves. Indeed, it is this encouragement to make individual choices and to feel free to select and to consume, for personal fulfilment and well-being, that drives her media empire. This leaves Oprah in a flexible and ambiguous position as guide, without being an authority, and as a teacher who does not have the answer, only 'her answer.'[42]

The religious vision and media strategy of Oprah Winfrey, is a move beyond the celebrity endorsement seen in the first case study concerning Kabbalah. Oprah is a powerful and connected media figure who is using her position to both con-struct and promote a religion of personal transformation. Oprah is important, then, because she represents a new kind of religious authority that comes from media visibility. The source of her power and her influence come from her celebrity status. This position gives her, not simply a platform, it also gives her an alternative source of authority to that which generally operates within formal religion. Given this position, Oprah is able to choose how she designs religion. She selects from what she wants and rejects those things she does not. The key criteria throughout, is the overriding concern for the self. This religious vision, however, much like Kabbalah, is extended and accessed through commodities that are sold. These products become the means to generate the transformation of the self. This pattern of religious practice mirrors the prevailing dynamics in Celebrity Worship more generally where audiences generate a relationship to a celebrity through the pur-chase and use of material objects or products.

One Love

In the two previous case studies, celebrities play a distinctive role in promoting and influencing the spread of forms of religion that are innovative. The religious media strategy that Oprah Winfrey has pursued, shares key perspectives with the form of Kabbalah that Madonna and other celebrities have embraced. Both are fundamentally oriented to a form of religion that is focused on the self. Religion is a therapeutic, or a life-enhancing practice that is taken up by individuals. Religion, then, is an aspect of the reflexive project of the self. At the same time, this religion of the self is constructed from elements of more traditional or formal kinds of religion that are lifted from their location in established communities and institutional settings and used as free-floating spiritual reference points. This detachment from formal religion is driven from a sensibility of self. A major factor in this process is the belief that individuals have the right to select and chose from any, and all, religious forms of knowledge and practices. Choosing, both constructs new religious formations, but it also reconfigures religious authority, away from formal or institutionally ordained leaders, towards the individual. In this new context, media representation plays a pivotal role, firstly, because it operates as the discursive source from which aspects of religion might viewed and chosen. Secondly, media representation demonstrates the possibilities of different kinds of religious lifestyle choices. It is in this context that Celebrity Worship plays a fundamental role. Celebrities are the human face of choosing. Celebrities carry the affective possibility of representation, and what it might mean to embrace a religion of the self. They are the selves at the centre of self-religion. In the final case study in this chapter, the focus is on how celebrities are able to use their media presence to reconfigure religious discourse in the context of one of the most pressing issues in contemporary society: terrorism.

'One Love Manchester' was a response to the bombing of the Manchester Arena by a suicide bomber. The bomb exploded as the crowd were leaving the Ariana Grande concert and 22 people were killed, and 250 people were injured. 'One Love Manchester' was a benefit concert that was organised by Ariana Grande and her manager two weeks after the terrorist attack. The concert was held at the Old Trafford Cricket Ground, and was attended by 50,000 people. The event raised over £2 million and this was used to support those affected by the bombing. The artists who appeared at the event alongside Ariana Grande included: Justin Bieber, The Black Eyed Peas, Chris Martin, Miley Cyrus, Marcus Mumford, Niall Horan, Little Mix, Katy Perry, Take That, Imogen Heap, Pharrell Williams, Robbie Williams and Liam Gallagher. With this line-up, the event featured the kind of mainstream pop that the fans of Ariana Grande would be familiar with. A distinctive aspect of the concert was that running through the event were a number of religious elements. These religious elements were explicit in many of the things that were said by artists as they performed on the stage, and in the response of the crowd. There were also religious elements both explicitly and implicitly in the songs that were sung. Taken together the event had some of the characteristics of a religious gathering. There was, however, no formal religious presence there – for instance, the event did not have any religious figure speaking to the crowd. Nevertheless, during the event, religious messages and themes were continually repeated.

Many of the performers at 'One Love Manchester' had religious back-grounds. Ariana Grande was Catholic, but she is now reported to follow Kab-balah. Ariana left the Roman Catholic Church in protest because of the church's attitude to gay people. Her brother is gay, and she objected to recent papal announcements on sexuality, and, as a result, she decided to renounce her faith. Scooter Braun, her manager, who was the producer of the event is Jewish. Marcus Mumford's parents founded the Vineyard Church in London. Marcus was brought up in an evangelic-charismatic Anglican home before his parent joined the Vineyard. Justin Bieber was raised in an evangelical house-hold. His mother wanted him to be a youth minister, and then eventually he reignited his faith through the Australian mega-church, Hillsong. In recent times, he has become quite an advocate of evangelical Christianity. Katy Perry was brought up by ministerial parents, but famously sang the song 'I kissed a girl and I liked it.' She has said:

> I don't believe in a heaven or a hell or an old man sitting on a throne. I believe in a higher power bigger than me because that keeps me accoun-table. [...] I'm not Buddhist, I'm not Hindu, I'm not Christian but I still feel like I have a deep connection with God. I pray all the time – for self-control, for humility. There's a lot of gratitude in it. Just saying 'thank you' sometimes is better than asking for things.[43]

Gary Barlow, singer with the band Take That, is reported to have said, 'I do think about religion loads: it seems like quite an old-fashioned thing now but I've started to consider what goes on out there. You do as you get older.'[44] The lead singer of Coldplay, Chris Martin, originates from a family that are also evangelical Anglicans. He expresses his own religious affiliation, however, with more ambiguity. He told one reporter, 'I'm an all theist. I'm always trying to work out what "He" or "She" is. I don't know if it's Allah or Jesus or Mohammed or Zeus. But I'd go for Zeus.'[45] Will.i.am from The Black Eyed Peas was brought up as a Baptist. Much like Chris Martin, he adopts a fluid approach to religious identity,

> If it's the Torah, if it's the Koran, if it's the Bible, if it's ... whatever ... you shouldn't be disrespecting people's vehicle to enlightenment ... Muslims are great, Jews are great, Buddhists are great, Hindi are great, Christians are great. There's great people everywhere.[46]

Many of the performers at the concert had a connection to the Christian reli-gion. This connection, however, in a number of cases, is fluid rather than formal. The celebrities, when they are interviewed are open to religion, but they are often unwilling to locate themselves firmly within a particular religious tradition. There are similarities here with the fluid approach to a specific religious affiliation that Madonna adopts when asked if she regards herself as Jewish, or the reluctance that Oprah Winfrey shows to the institution of religion. The fluidity reflects a shift in culture towards choice, and the way this generates a sensibility that wants to keep options open. At the same time, religion is not rejected or necessarily seen as undesirable. Rather, religion is regarded as part of a lifestyle choice and a way to enrich life, but this is firmly based on individual choice. Being against a particular religion is regarded as problematic, then, because it is disrespectful of the individual choices of others. It is the self that chooses what is sacred rather than the specifics of the religion in question. At the same time, throughout the concert, several of the performers reached into their religious understanding for something that they could use to say something that was a response to the experience of the terror attack. As a result, religious elements drawn largely from a shared Christian heritage, were brought into the space created by this event. They served as a resource for hope and resilience in the face of the collective trauma that had been shared by the people of Manchester. These religious elements can be divided into three groups. The first are those aspects of the concert that are explicitly religious in their message or origins. The second are aspects of the performance that take on a religious or spiritual meaning in the context of the event, and the third relates to the response of the crowd.

The most obvious religious aspect of the concert is possibly the title, 'One Love'. The theme of love as a response to terror was repeated numerous times throughout the concert both in the things that artists said, but also in the lyrics of the songs. The title 'One Love' echoed the use of this term by Bob Marley in his song 'One Love / People Get Ready.' In the song, Marley calls people to get together to 'feel alright.' Together they can share one heart.

The origins of the notion of 'One Love' came originally from a Christian theology that identifies God as love and those who love as participating in God. These ideas are reshaped within Rastafarianism, which advocates a connection between celebration, community and well-being. Bob Marley was a follower of Rastafarianism and it is in this religious sense that he uses the term 'One Love'. Choosing the title 'One Love' for the Manchester Concert does not signify a direct location of the event with Rastafarianism, rather what might be happening is the taking up of this term that has become animated in popular culture. The term is emptied of its original theological ecology, and then relocated in a new context where the meaning becomes fluid and open to reconstruction. This does not mean that there are any specific theological or religious connections being made. Unlike Marley, those at this event are not promoting any particular religion, but the emotional content that is carried in the title sets the atmosphere for the event. There is a religious connection, then, that operates at an affective level, which can be seen as a recurring motif throughout the concert.

While there were no prayers on stage that involved the audience, Ariana Grande and her mother did lead prayer backstage, before the start of the event. This is a practice that many American popstars, like Lady Gaga and Madonna, have been known to do before they go on stage, and it may not have been a specific response to this event, although it will have had a particular emotional connection for the artists. This was not a normal concert, and at her last performance Ariana Grande knew some of her fans had been murdered. There were, in addition, worries about the safety of people at this event with some staying away out of these concerns. At the very start of the concert, Marcus Mumford invited the crowd to hold a minute's silence to remember those killed, as a result of the terrorist attack. This act in itself is not specifically religious, but it framed the event ritually as distinct from simply being entertainment, and it set the tone for some of what was to follow. Prayer, however, was explicitly referred to by the actions of some members of the crowd. Images were shown of fans holding small posters that had the 'One Love' logo and the invitation, 'Pray for Manchester.'

Several of the artists appearing at the concert included specifically religious elements in their performance. Following the minute's silence, Marcus Mumford performed his song 'Timshel,' which has its roots in the Bible, but also draws inspiration from John Steinbeck's novel, *East of Eden*. The song speaks of death coming to steal your soul and freezing your mind. Death is at the doorstep, but there is hope, because it will not be able to steal who you are. There is hope, the song makes clear, because despite the presence of death each of us is 'not alone in this.' When the crowd applauded at the end of this song, Mumford shouted out, 'Love casts out fear.' This appears to be a quotation from the New Testament, 'There is no fear in love, but perfect love casts out fear; for fear has to do with punishment, and whoever fears has not reached perfection in love.'[47] Justin Bieber shares a Christian upbringing and commitment with Marcus Mumford, and like Mumford, he also drew on this to offer something to the crowd as a source of hope. During his time on stage, where he performed solo with a guitar, Bieber said: 'I'm not going to let go of hope. I'm not going to let go of love. I'm not going to let go of God. Put your hand up if you're not going to let go.' Later in his performance he said: 'God is good in the midst of the darkness. God is good in the midst of the evil. God is in the midst, no matter what's happening in the world, God is in the midst and he loves you and he's here for you.' The idea that the love of God is present in the context of violence and suffering, is picked up in the lyrics of The Black Eyed Peas song, 'Where is the love.' The song speaks about people being killed and children crying. There is a prayer in the song calling out to God to help and the chorus repeats the title of the song, 'Where is the love?' In its performance, the song acts as a kind of lament, and something of an anthem for the event. This sense is reinforced by the fact that Ariana Grande joins the band on stage to sing 'Where is the love?' with them.

Alongside these explicitly religious aspects of the concert, there were a number of songs and performances that can be read as playing a religious role in the event. These might be regarded as secular hymns. The message they carry is also of love and longing, but in the context of this event they carry strong overtones of resistance and resilience in the face of direct, and life-threatening, attack. The underlying message, running throughout the concert was, 'You might kill us, but we are still going to live this life. There might be horror and terror, but we are still going to celebrate our music, our way of being.' In addition to this, both in the songs, and in what was said by performers, love was promoted as a better way, and the best response to hatred. An example of a secular hymn is Pharrell Williams' song 'Happy' – in this context the meaning of the song suddenly shifts in performance. There is an articulation that takes place between the song and this particular event. In the background to this performance is the fact that, three years before, a group of Muslim girls in Iran had made a video of themselves dancing to this song. They were arrested and sentenced to up to a year in jail and 91 lashes. At the time, Pharrell used his Facebook account to object to the treatment of these girl saying, 'It is beyond sad that these kids were arrested for trying to spread happiness.'[48] Pharrell's performance, with the theme of resistance and the power of love, was emphasised when he said: 'I don't see, hear or smell any fear here this evening. All I feel is love and positivity.'[49] Katy Perry, like Pharrell, also spoke a message of love. During her appearance on stage she asked the attendees of the concert to reach out and to touch the person next to them. 'It's not easy to always choose love, is it? Especially in moments like these, right?' she said. Perry's words reflect the widespread fear that this concert might also prompt a further terrorist attack. Perry also repeats the quotation that Justin Bieber used earlier. 'It can be the most difficult thing to do. But love conquers fear,' but she made a further inflection by adding, 'and love conquers hate. And this love that you choose will give you strength, and it's our greatest power.' Then, building on the event as a show of defiance and resistance she said: 'We will not be silenced,' and she sang the song 'Roar.' It is a great feminist song, or at least an iconic song of female power. This is again an example of an artist at the concert asserting something in the face of what the terrorist, and the ideology that lay behind his actions, would seek to deny. In this context, Take That's song, 'We Can Rule the World,' might also be read as a message concerning the right to live a life, and the sense that with love rather than hate, 'Our values will triumph.' This aspect of the concert was picked up in the subsequent press coverage. As a reporter from *The Telegraph* newspaper expressed it, 'In a sense, though, this concert was not really about the music being performed on stage, it was about the place music plays in the lives of free people. It was a gathering in aid of our right to gather, a party about the fundamental humanity of partying.'[50] At the end of the event, Ariana Grande sang 'Somewhere over the Rainbow.' The song evokes childhood, having the feel of a lullaby. The lyrics express a wistful hope that somewhere there is a place where things are different, where the dreams that we have really do come true. This is a place where bluebirds are able to fly and if they can travel there, then perhaps, we can as well. A Christian heaven is not mentioned but the affective pull of this dream lies deep within the longing of the song.

The 'One Love' concert shows how, in response to an extreme event, celebrity musicians are able to generate a particular religious or spiritual sensibility. The theme of love is picked up and repeated a several points throughout the concert by the performers. As they do this they draw directly upon theological resources that have their roots in the Christian tradition. They do this, however, as a fluid form of theologising that is shaped around the intention of helping the audience to generate a spiritual energy that is resilient but also political in nature. Love as it is spoken of here acts both as balm and ethic. Where the love has its origins and roots is not articulated. Love has then both a reference to the divine but also to the collective will of those on stage and in the crowd to act and think differently than those who have tried to kill them. Here then the sacredness of the self is more than individual self-fulfilment or transformation. Ostensibly what the performers and the crowd do at the event is reach out to a self that is strengthened in response to real world events. The sacred self, then, operates in a way that mirrors the resilience of more formal religious commitments, or at least at this concert, the possibility that this might be the case, begins to become evident. The celebrity performers at the event are fundamental to this new kind of religious formation. At a visceral level, they hold within themselves an authenticity that supports the emotional and affective connection that facilitates the particular religious response. The celebrities make the message plausible and believable, but it is also the case that they are able to function in this way because they are on the stage. Celebrity status then projects them into the place where they have a voice. In this context, their specific response situates them alongside traditional religious leaders and politicians. As pop performers they have an authority that they choose to make use of not simply to entertain or to raise money for charity but to generate a religious message. Religion here needs to be used with caution. What is not being offered is any kind of coherent belief system or any attempt to recruit people to a particular religious group. What is offered are resources or specific theological elements drawn mainly from a Christian heritage. This case study, then, serves to show how religion and religious sensibilities form a part of a valued and valuable theological capital. They are there to be drawn upon and made use of. The context that this takes place within suggests that some aspects of religion have a significant continuing value, but they do so as they are articulated in relation to the sacredness of the self. These themes are explored further in the next chapter through music videos and performances.

Notes

1 Williams. *Marxism*.
2 Boaz Huss. 'The New Age of Kabbalah: Contemporary Kabbalah, the New Age and Postmodern Spirituality.' *Journal of Modern Jewish Studies*, 6, no. 2 (2007): 107.
3 Huss. New, 108.
4 Huss. New, 110.
5 Huss. New, 110.

6 Huss. New, 119.
7 Huss. New, 114.
8 Harriet Ryan. 'Philip Berg Dies: Controversial Kabbalah Rabbi with Celebrity Followers.' *The Washington Post*, 21 September 2013.
9 Harriet Sherwood. 'Preaching to the Converted: How Kabbalah Keeps on Growing.' *The Guardian*, 26 October 2015.
10 Sherwood. Preaching.
11 Emily Marthe. 'Why Celebrities Stopped Following Kabbalah.' *Vice*, 21 May 2017. www.vice.com/en_us/article/mbqvmy/why-celebrities-stopped-following-kabbalah.
12 Sherwood. Preaching.
13 Marthe. Why.
14 Sherwood. Preaching.
15 Jody Myers. *The Kabbalah Centre and Contemporary Spirituality*. (Northridge, CA: California State University, 2008).
16 Sherwood. Preaching.
17 Myers. *Kabbalah*, 10.
18 Myers. *Kabbalah*, 10.
19 Myers. *Kabbalah*, 10.
20 Myers. *Kabbalah*, 11.
21 The Kabbalah Centre. 'Karen Berg'. https://kabbalah.com/en/people/karen-berg.
22 Kabbalah. Karen.
23 Ynet. 'Madonna: I am Not Jewish, I am an Israelite.' 23 May 2015. www.ynetnews.com/articles/0,7340,L-4640263,00.html.
24 Marthe. Why.
25 Jacob Bernstein. 'Stand Back: Sandra Bernhard Speaks Her Mind.' *Women's Wear Daily*, 4 June 2009. wwd.com/eye/people/stand-back-sandra-bernhard-speaks-her-mind-2156863/.
26 Kathryn Lofton. *Oprah The Gospel of an Icon*. (Berkeley, CA: University of California Press, 2011).
27 Lofton. *Oprah*, 2.
28 Lofton. *Oprah*, 2.
29 Lofton. *Oprah*, 2.
30 Lofton. *Oprah*, 4.
31 Lofton. *Oprah*, 4.
32 Lofton. *Oprah*, 5.
33 Lofton. *Oprah*, 13.
34 Lofton. *Oprah*, 49.
35 Lofton. *Oprah*, 7.
36 Lofton. *Oprah*, 32.
37 Lofton. *Oprah*, 36–37.
38 Lofton. *Oprah*, 38.
39 Lofton. *Oprah*, 49.
40 Lofton. *Oprah*, 49.
41 Lofton. *Oprah*, 92.
42 Lofton. *Oprah*, 209.
43 Lorie Johnson. 'Music Superstar Katy Perry Denounces Her Devoutedly Christian Upbringing.' *CBN News*, 20 April 2017. www1.cbn.com/cbnnews/entertainment/2017/april/music-superstar-katy-perry-denounces-her-devoutly-christian-upbringing.
44 Clemmie Moodie. 'Gary Barlow on Shedding Five Stone – But He Didn't Need a Fad Diet to Do It.' *Mirror*, 30 November 2013. www.mirror.co.uk/3am/celebrity-news/gary-barlow-shedding-five-stone-2866963.

45 *NME.* 'Coldplay's Chris Martin Declares Religious Belies – Daily Gossip.' 3 June 2008. www.nme.com/news/music/daily-gossip-587-1333314#zj6rr0aMzwwIMzuP.99.

46 Moodie. Gary.

47 1 John 4:18 *New Revised Standard Version* (NRSV).

48 *BBC News.* 'Iran: Happy Video Dancers Sentenced to 91 Lashes and Jail.' 19 September 2014. www.bbc.co.uk/news/world-middle-east-29272732.

49 Helen Pidd and Josh Halliday. '"Let's Not Be Afraid": Ariana Grande Returns to Manchester.' *The Guardian,* 5 June 2017.

50 Rebecca Hawkes and Tristram Fane Sanders. 'Ariana Grande One Love Manchester Concert: Fans Shower Ariana with Praise after Moving, Joyous Night.' *The Telegraph,* 5 June 2017. www.telegraph.co.uk/music/what-to-listen-to/ariana-grande-one-love-manchester-concert-live/.

Chapter 7

Celebrities as theologians of the self

In February 2012, the *New York Post* ran a picture on its front page with the title 'Beymaculate Conception.'[1] The image that went with this headline showed the singer, Beyoncé, as the Virgin Mary. She is pictured kneeling in front of large display of flowers, in a pose that is frequently seen in images of the Virgin. She is wearing a veil and she is holding her bare, and obviously pregnant, belly. As well as the veil, she is wearing mismatched underwear, a black bra and pair of blue silk knickers. For Katie Edwards, the image is a challenge to a dominant white portrayal of the divine. The Virgin in Christian art represents authority and virtue and she is 'white'. Beyoncé, says Edwards, is re-appropriating the attributes of the Holy Mother into a black identity.[2] Edwards' point is that the artist is provoking a reconsideration of what it means to be black, a woman and a mother, and the reference to the Holy Mother is a means to generate this shift in thought. The religious symbolism of the Virgin, therefore, offers a rich vein of reference for the artist to seize upon, and to re-imagine, as part of the wider conversation concerning the self in contemporary society.

The use of religious imagery and symbolism by celebrities suggests a significant area of consideration in the debates around the relationship between religion and media. Celebrity brings a human face to this conversation and the humanity of the celebrity indicates the centrality of the self to how religion and media interact. At the heart of this conversation, then, lies a question concerning the meaning of the kind of representation seen in the pictures of Beyoncé as the Virgin Mary. Adopting and adapting the symbols of religion in pop music videos and images, has been a characteristic feature of the work of a number of artists. This chapter centres on the way that religious symbols are used by three musicians: Lady Gaga, Ariana Grande and Beyoncé. Each of these singers, in their lyrics, music and videos, have made use of Christian, and other forms of religious narrative and imagery, as part of their performance. The analysis of the work of these artists, acts as a further case study that explores how changes in religion are related to media representation and how Celebrity Worship is an agent in this change.

The videos that form the basis for this analysis are Lady Gaga's, 'Judas' and 'Born This Way;' Ariana Grande's 'You Believe God is a Woman' and Beyoncé's 'Formation.' These videos illustrate how, in the media processes of production and representation, aspects of religious narrative and symbol are linked to discourses concerning celebrity and the self. Popular music and music video, in particular, lend themselves to the fragmentation of imagery, as they make use of multiple references that combine a range of different perspectives and ideas. Understanding how meaning is being made in these videos, requires a notion of the elements or 'bits' of religious traditions that are taken up and made use of by the artists, directors and stylists that combine to create music videos. These 'religious bits' are a kind of theology, in that they carry meaning concerning the divine, albeit variously understood. The use of these fragmented theological elements in the videos is itself an act of theologising. Stephen Roberts argues that Lady Gaga should be regarded a public theologian, in that she takes religious stories and symbols and reworks them into a new configuration.[3] The same, I would suggest, is true of Ariana Grande and Beyoncé. What these artists are doing can be described as a theology, even though it may not be intended as such. They are making use of theological symbols and narratives, that have been fragmented and lifted out of the traditions and institutions where they have had specific uses and meanings. Now as religious 'bits,' they are reused, but in order that this can take place, they are taken out of their previous location, in coherent and organised traditions with their recognised forms of community, authority and practice, and made fluid in representation. The 'religious bits,' however, retain a reference to the sacred and the divine. They are therefore 'theology,' but theology that is made use of in relation to a different kind of conversation that revolves around questions of identity and the self. The image of Beyoncé as the Virgin, for instance, is intended to say much more about Beyoncé than it does about the Holy Mother. At the same time, the sacred in this image, and in the videos that are analysed in this chapter, is not replaced entirely, or secularised. Instead what is apparent is that, even as the theological elements of religious tradition are linked to a conversation about the self, the cultural, and to some extent, the spiritual power of the Holy Mother remains as part of the representation. The divine then persists, as a ghost or a shadow in the background. As this realignment of the religious to the self takes place in representation, the celebrity figure plays a central role in generating the emotional space and authenticity where these new connections can be forged and carry significance. What this illustrates, is the way that celebrity is a fundamental and powerful dynamic in how religion is being reshaped in the representation of popular culture.

Music video and articulation

Music video and musical performance generate a multi-layered and complex arrangement of symbols. In the videos of Ariana Grande, Beyoncé and Lady

Gaga, religious imagery and symbolism merges with those that denote race, gender, sexuality and power. With this kind of practice, multiple forms of reference are self-consciously and intentionally woven into the practice of making music videos. The generation of such multi-referential images might suggest that what is taking place is akin to denoting the fragmentation and therefore incoherence of meaning. Stuart Hall makes reference to this possibility in music video in discussing the emergence of MTV. Fragmentation and a 'plurality of codes,' he points out, citing Walter Benjamin, is a characteristic of the modern era.[4] He argues, however, that reproduction and multiplicity does not mean that there is a collapse in representation as a site where coherent meaning is generated, rather it is in the complexity of representation evident in music video that a new sophistication in the ability to both encode and decode is evident.

> We have all become, historically, fantastically codable encoding agents. We are in the middle of this multiplicity of readings and discourses and that has produced new forms of self-consciousness and reflexivity. So, while the modes of cultural production and consumption have changed, qualitatively, fantastically, as the result of that expansion, it does not mean that representation itself has collapsed.

This perspective suggests that the religious imagery used in music videos should be treated as the construction of new religious perspectives.

Religion going Gaga

Lady Gaga, born Stefani Joanne Angelina Germanotta, burst onto the music scene in 2007, when her first two singles, 'Just Dance' and 'Poker Face', sold millions around the world. She has said that the name Gaga was taken from the Queen song, 'Radio Gaga.' Gaga is, however, suggestive of baby talk and carries the additional reference of ways of speaking and communicating that are nonsense. It is also a word that can be used for the behaviour of fans at a concert, when they might be referred to as, 'going gaga.' This cocktail of meanings associated with the word, gaga, corresponds with the artist's assertion that she is not real. Ashanka Kumaris argues that both Lady Gaga and Beyoncé, through their names, generate and exchange between the performer and the audience. They effectively offer a challenge to the individual to name themselves and therefore create multiple voices as the fan engages with them.[5] Lady Gaga's statement, 'I am not real, I am theatre' was made at the MTV awards in 2011, when she spent the whole event dressed as her male alter-ego, Jo Calderone. Her performance of multiple selves has become a key element in how she has negotiated celebrity, and it has in turn served to catapult Lady Gaga into the public eye, most notably when she wore the infamous meat dress to go the MTV Music Awards. Her outlandish clothes have also included a dress that was entirely made up of Kermit the Frog puppets.

In her construction of herself, Lady Gaga draws on surrealism, performance art and an aesthetic drawn from horror and shock art. Richard Gray argues that Lady Gaga is a modern shape-shifter, who is constantly changing, and as a result seems to defy any clear classification or interpretation.[6] Gaga consciously sets out to transmit a range of different messages about race, gender, class and sexuality. Central to her manipulation of herself, as a source of meaning, is a camp performance and a queer sensibility. As Jen Hutton expresses it:

> Gaga's performances are not only camp but a type of genderfuck, a position that can be tied to the concept of the monster. By no means is it meant to be a pejorative comparison: it's just that her performance destabilizes what we perceive as "normal" and, more importantly, works against it, thus opening up a frank discussion about (sexual) transgression. Gaga is queer because she's anything but straight – which is to say that she is dissolving the sexual binary and maintaining a "slightly uncomfortable" space that is in direct opposition to heteronormative behaviour.[7]

Gaga's art plays with different versions and possibilities of the self with the intention to undermine assumptions and set patterns through the use of shocking imagery and an exaggerated camp irony. In the two videos that are described – see Box 7.1 and Box 7.2 – this dialogue concerning the self is given an explicitly religious orientation, such that theological themes and symbols are taken up as part of this conversation about the self.

Box 7.1 'Judas' video description

The opening sequence shows a biker gang in leathers riding along a highway. Lady Gaga is pictured on the back of one of the bikes wearing a large cross. As the gang ride past the camera it is revealed that each of the bikers has a name written in silver studs on their leathers: Philip, Thomas, Judas, John. These are the disciples from the gospels transformed Gaga style. As the song starts, Lady Gaga is shown, this time riding on a bike with her arms around a man who is wearing a gold and sparkling crown of thorns. The lyrics start with a chant 'Judaaas, Judah ah ah, Gaga.' Then they speak of a relationship with Judas. When Judas comes to her, she is willing to wash his feet every day with her hair. Judas may betray her 'three times,' but she is still in love with him. She is a 'Holy fool' and it is so cruel, but she is still in love with him. In these sections of the video there is a dance/orgy scene, with the disciples and the key characters of Jesus, Judas and Gaga acting out a three-way relationship. Gaga speaks the next lyrical section where she says in a biblical sense that she is beyond repentance. She is a 'fame hooker, prostitute wench,' who vomits her mind. Towards the end of the video, Gaga is shown in a large bath/jacuzzi with both Jesus and Judas, where she washes both of their feet. This is sequenced with images of Gaga on a rock being deluged by what appears to be a huge tsunami-like wave that sweeps her away. This cuts again to Gaga with Judas and Jesus in the bath.

Here, in a new musical section of the song, Gaga sings, 'I wanna love you but something is pulling me away from you. Jesus is my virtue but Judas is the demon I cling to.' At the end of the video she is pictured in a white dress being stoned by a group of men and women. The song ends with the opening Judas chant repeated and a close-up of Lady Gaga with the heavily reverbed phrase 'Gaga' left hanging without any musical backing.

The 'Judas' song was a single that was released in 2011 from Lady Gaga's second studio album, 'Born this way.' The music video that accompanied the song was directed by Lady Gaga and her choreographer, Laurieann Gibson. In the video, the gospel narratives are mined for symbols that speak not so much of the Christian faith, as of an inner and more personal turmoil. Lady Gaga describes the religious elements of the video as a metaphor, or an analogy. These elements function as a point of reference for a consideration of forgiveness and betrayal. The religious symbols speak of the darkness in an individual, that Gaga says, in the end shines, and shows a greater light that the individual can experience. As she described it on MTV, 'So the song is about washing the feet of both good and evil, and understanding and forgiving the demons from your past in order to move into the greatness of your future … I just like really aggressive metaphors – harder, thicker, darker – and my fans do as well. So it is a very challenging and aggressive metaphor, but it is a metaphor.'[8] For Gaga, 'Judas' is about honouring the darkness that is within you, because it is only by looking at what is haunting you that you can learn to forgive yourself. The song, then, is primarily concerned with a conflict within the individual, and the way in which darkness and light interact. As the lyrics of the song put it, she is a 'Holy Fool' who, even when life is cruel, and relationships are cruel, cannot help returning to what she calls 'evil things.'[9] The theme of the self-divided, or made up of both darkness and light, is developed further in the 'Born This Way' video where theological ideas are also woven into the representation – see Box 7.2.

Box 7.2 'Born This Way' video description

The video opens with a unicorn in a triangle with an urban nightscape in the background. This cuts to Lady Gaga, also in the triangle, sitting on a throne holding her legs open with what appear to be gynaecological stirrups. Over this image Gaga speaks, what she calls the 'Manifesto of Mother Monster.' We are told that on G.O. A.T. – A Government Owned Alien Territory in space – 'A birth of magnificent proportions took place.' This was an infinite birth, that heralded the beginning of a new race. This is a race within humanity that tolerates no prejudice, no judgement and advocates instead 'boundless freedom.' But at the same time, as the 'Eternal Mother' gives birth, another birth takes place; that of evil. As these words are spoken, Gaga is shown with two heads facing in opposite directions, Janus-like, giving birth. The mother, we are told, is split in two, between two forces. It seems easy to gravitate towards good. Mother Monster, we are told, then wondered how could something that is so perfect be protected without evil? Gaga is then seen in a leather bikini that is decorated with silver studs and chains, dancing with a group and she speaks these word, 'It doesn't matter if you love him or capital H.I.M. Just put your paws up cos you were born this way baby.' After a full three minutes of introduction, the techno dance track for the sons kicks off. The lyrics speak about the words that Gaga's mother spoke to her telling her that she is a superstar and there's nothing wrong with loving who you are "Cause he made you perfect babe.' I am beautiful in my way sings Gaga because, 'God makes no mistakes.' The chorus is an anthemic disco melody with the lyrics declaring that to be 'born this way' is to be on the right track. In the middle of the video there is a voguing dance sequence, and Gaga chants, 'Don't be a drag just be a queen.' A different lover is not a sin. The scene shifts to Gaga wearing a tuxedo jacket, white shirt, bow tie and black trousers, in heavy skeleton makeup, reminiscent of the decoration seen in Mexican celebration of the Day of the Dead. 'In the religion of the insecure I must be myself, respect the truth.' In a second voguing section Gaga says, if you are broke or evergreen, black, white, beige, Lebanese or Orient. Whether life's disabilities have left you as an outcast or bullied or teased 'Rejoice, love yourself today because baby, you were born this way.' The video ends with a return to the triangle and the unicorn, but this time there is a female mounted on its back. This image fades into Gaga in her Day of the Dead makeup.

Lady Gaga's artistic representation has, from the first, been a conversation about a self-divided. Her second single, 'Poker Face' describes her bi-sexuality, and how she is out with her boyfriend, when she realises that she desires a woman that she sees. The conflicted or agonised self, is also central to her portrayal of herself as a 'Monster.' Gaga regularly speaks of her fans as little monsters, and herself as Mother Monster. Monster is a term that deals with her own sense of otherness, with all her sexual and gendered ambiguities. Yet this monstering of the self, functions as a source of strength and affirmation. In her 'Manifesto of Little Monsters,' Gaga talks about the way that her fans operate their cameras as a heroic act. The Manifesto says that the fans are like kings and queens writing their own history, and within this dynamic process she locates herself as the court jester. In an interview with *Rolling Stone* magazine, Gaga speaks about her relationship with her Little Monsters. 'I love what they stand for. I love who they are. They inspire me to be more confident every day. When I wake up in the morning, I feel just like any other insecure 24-year-old girl. But I say, "Bitch, you're Lady Gaga, you better fucking get up and walk the walk today," because they need that from me. And they inspire me to keep going.'[10] At the heart of this concern for her fans, is a message concerning self-acceptance, and being free to be yourself. Gaga wants her fans to celebrate who they are, including the things that they do not like about themselves.[11]

'Born This Way,' is the anthem that celebrates and proclaims Lady Gaga's message of the acceptance of difference and otherness. Religious references and symbolism are a central aspect of the message of the song and the music video. The opening sequence represents a creation myth, Gaga style. Here she is portrayed as the female divinity located above the planet, giving birth to a new race. This gives rise to a new order of things, where there is acceptance and inclusiveness for all. The message is clear, you may love him, or H.I.M., it doesn't matter, because each of us is 'born this way.' Here the divine and sexuality are articulated. Birth is attributed to the divine, 'he made you this way baby.' The divine then, is appropriated to Gaga's vision of self-acceptance, and in particular, to the freedom that is there in this new race, for all of those considered other because of their sexuality or gender. Richard Gray argues that what is significant in Lady Gaga's vision for society, is that empowerment is extended to all people.[12]

Throughout her career, Lady Gaga has maintained a strong Catholic identity that comes from her family. Norman Reedus, who played Judas in the video, described her in an interview as 'super catholic' and how she would always get people together before she did any performance to pray.[13] In 2016, the singer posted a picture of herself on Twitter, with her elbow resting on the shoulder of a Catholic priest, as they ride on the New York subway. The priest is Father John P. Duffel and it is evident from the post that Lady Gaga has just attended mass and she remarks on how much she appreciated his homily 'I was so moved today when you said: "The Eucharist is not a prize for the perfect but the food that God gives us."'[14] Her identification as a Catholic, while advocating progressive viewpoints, has ensured that Lady Gaga has often been criticised by religious commentators. These critical conservative voices have not gone unremarked upon. In an Instagram post, Lady Gaga responded to Becky Roach, who criticised her for being a Catholic celebrity with a Hollywood lifestyle. Gaga wrote,

> Dear, Becky Roach. Mary Magdalene washed the feet of Christ and was protected and loved by him. A prostitute. Someone society shames as if she and her body are a man's trashcan. He loved her and did not judge. He let her cry over him and dry his feet with the hair of a harlot. We are not just 'celebrities', we are humans and sinners, children, and our lives are not void of values because we struggle. We are as equally forgiven as our neighbour. God is never a trend no matter who the believer.[15]

Writing in *The Washington Post*, Guthrie argues that at a time where conservative religious voices dominate public discourse, Lady Gaga is significant, because she champions a vision of empowerment, grace and self-acceptance. Gaga theology, he argues, is summed up in the lines from her song 'Hair,' 'I just wanna be myself / And I want you to love me for who I am … this is my prayer.' Gaga should therefore be regarded as a progressive Christian theologian in the public sphere.[16]

Madonna, Ariana Grande and the 'God is a Woman' video

Lady Gaga is not simply appropriating religious imagery to shock or make an impact, though she is certainly doing that. In the videos and songs, it is clear that a new kind of theological construction is taking place. Theological narratives and symbols are used as part of Lady Gaga's project concerning questions of identity. The link between identity and religion is also evident in Ariana Grande's video 'God is a Woman' – released in 2018, as the second single of her fourth studio album, 'Sweetener.' The song was co-written by Ariana Grande, Rickard Göransson, Max Martin and Savan Kotecha. The video was directed by Dave Meyers – see Box 7.3.

Box 7.3 'God is a Woman' video description

The video opens with Ariana standing on top of the Earth surrounded by planet dust. She is wearing thigh-length silver boots with high heels. This cuts to her pictured from above, she appears to be naked, smeared in paint. She is lying in an artist's representation of what might be interpreted as female genitalia. In the next scene, she is raised on a four-poster bed with several male figures, also naked, writhing around in foam. The lyrics speak of sensuality and female power. 'You, you love it how I move you, You love it how I touch you, My one, when all is said and done, You'll believe God is a woman.' The scene shifts to Ariana pictured as a giant on a stool, that is placed on a book; in the background there is a model that appears to represent the high rises of a city. Standing on the book there are miniature male characters, most seem to be middle-aged and overweight. They take it in turns to pick words off the page and throw them at Ariana. These include the words: 'Bitch,' 'Fake,' 'Little Girl' and 'Anything.' These insults appear as cartoon speech bubbles, and they bounce off an indifferent giant Ariana. At several points in the video, Ariana is pictured with the heads of wolves, or dogs, coming from behind her head. Later she is kneeling on all fours, with male figures who seem to be suckling from teats, that appear from her body. Just over halfway through the video, Ariana is shown wearing a military style biker helmet with the addition of her trademark bunny ears attached. She is holding a large two-handed sledgehammer. The music stops, and Madonna recites words from the movie Pulp Fiction, 'And I will strike down upon thee. With great vengeance and furious anger those who attempt to poison and destroy my sisters. And you will know my name is the Lord. When I lay my vengeance upon you.' These are a paraphrase of Ezekiel 25:17. Ariana then hurls the sledgehammer, and it smashes a glass dome that is high above her. Throughout the video there are short images of Ariana sitting astride the world, her legs apart, standing in the biker helmet between her own parted legs, kneeling in oriental costume inside a triangle holding her two hands so that they resemble the female sexual organ surrounded by astral images. These images include: Ariana in a schoolgirl's uniform walking a tightrope holding on to balloons, and standing wearing a crown in front of a monumental door. As the chorus is repeated, 'God is a

Woman,' Ariana in a white robe is shown dancing in the middle of large crowd of women, who are also wearing white robes. Many of these women have their arms in the air, as if attending a charismatic, or a Pentecostal worship service. In the closing sections of the video there is a pastiche of Michelangelo's The Creation of Adam on the Sistine Chapel's ceiling. Ariana is pictured as God is reaching out with her finger to a black female figure who is naked apart from a fig leaf.

'God is a Woman' is a powerful and enchanting enticement of female empowerment. The overt sexuality of the piece links sensuality to divinity. As the journalist Alexis Rhiannon says, the video, with its opening sequence of Ariana gyrating at the centre of the Milky Way situates female sexual energy at the centre of the universe. The song includes allusions to prayer and the practice of confession, with references to kneeling down and a blessing that comes from confession. These, however, are linked with the suggestion of sexual acts. The various images that imply divinity, or semi-divinity, such as the image in the triangle and Ariana sitting astride the world, are located in the personal narrative. An example of this personal dimension to the video is an image where she is walking the tightrope. This, says *Vigilant Citizen*, is a reference to the way in which Ariana has, since she was a young girl, had to find her way along the tightrope of fame and the entertainment business.[17] The video in the depiction of the three-headed wolf and the suckling image make references, not so much to divinity, but to mythology with the three-headed Cerberus and the Romulus and Remus myth, where the twins who founded the city of Rome are said to have been suckled by a wolf. The layering of different images in the video should not be read as an attempt to develop a coherent or argued theology. What is generated by the video is an atmosphere that locates the song, and the idea of female sexuality, as in some way divine. The chorus that runs through the song, then operates as the key theological theme that these other ideas are nested around. 'God is a Woman' is a dialogue about the self, that appropriates the idea of 'God,' to the experience of sex and female power.

Beyoncé and 'Formation'

The film maker, Melina Matsoukas, described, in an interview with *The New Yorker*, how she went about making her video, 'Formation.' At an initial interview, the video maker explained how Beyoncé told her that the video should explore the impact that the history of black slavery has had upon the black family and 'black men and women – how we are almost socialised not to be together.'[18] With this initial idea, Matsoukas then went away and began to explore how she might develop the visual imagery in the videos. Her creative process might be described as that of a bricoleur where she spends time browsing online and in art books, searching for the elements that she will bring together in the piece. 'I treat each video like a thesis project she said.'[19] When she found the plantation house set that she used in 'Formation,' she instructed her art assistant to transform the building into something that resembled the movie 'Gone With the Wind.' She describes the next process as 'blackifying the house,' hanging pictures that represented black people in clothes, postures and live situations that would have more usually been associated only with the power and privilege of white people in the South. 'I wanted to turn those images on their head.'[20] The video 'Formation' was released in 2016, ahead of the album 'Lemonade' – see Video description 7.4. Beyoncé performed the song the next day in a guest appearance at the Super Bowl half-time show and then the song became the title for the Formation World Tour that followed the release of the album.

Box 7.4 'Formation' video description

The video's opening sequence shows Beyoncé on the top of a police car that is marooned in flood water. The voice of the artist Messy Mya, who was murdered in New Orleans, is heard asking 'What Happened After New Orleans?' The music track starts with minimalist repeating synth notes that are more of an alarm than music. The lyrics are a defiant assertion of black identity and the power of sexual allure and wealth in the face of those who seek to do her down. Beyoncé is the one who slays and rocks her Givenchy dress. She is proud of her afro hair and her negro nose, because her Daddy comes from Alabama and her mother from Louisiana. Formation is a call for the ladies to get co-ordinated and to join together. The line, 'Get in Formation,' however, when it is sung can also be read as get 'information.' Empowerment then comes from joining together and from knowing what is going on. What is going on as the rest of the 'Lemonade' video album makes explicit is that Beyoncé has been betrayed in love by her husband Jay-Z who she married in 2008. Throughout the 'Lemonade' album, Beyoncé processes this experience of infidelity and break-up, through the lenses of black identity, history and religion. In 'Formation' the message is clear. If the ladies are to avoid elimination, socially and emotionally, they need to show co-ordination. Beyoncé leads the way as she makes clear in the lyrics, she takes what is hers, she is a star who 'goes hard.' She is a black Bill Gates in the making and if you play your cards right so can each of the women also be a black Bill Gates. She is a polite capitalist who celebrates the power of money. Stay gracious but the best 'revenge is your paper.'

The music video switches rapidly between different scenes and merges sections where Beyoncé is singing and dancing, and clips, images and scenes that are edited into these sequences – the performance sections with Beyoncé on the police car that sits in flood water. This conjures up the disaster of Hurricane Katrina that devastated parts of New Orleans in 2000. The disaster and in particular, what happened in its aftermath, had a marked impact on poor black communities. In quick succession, there are images of a streetscape and a young boy on a bike, a poor New Orleans street, a concrete underpass, a preacher in a black church, the naked torso of a muscular black male, flooded houses, and the police. Set in this quick succession of images, there is the first glimpse of Beyoncé on the porch of a large Southern-style house flanked by black men in suits – some wear a hat that looks like a fez and Beyoncé is wearing a large wide-brimmed hat that casts a shadow, such that it is not possible to see all her face. After a return to the scene on the top of the police car, the singer is next seen, dressed in an elaborate white period dress, holding a white umbrella in the interior of a very impressive Southern American house. The next scene shows her dancing, dressed in thigh-length stockings and a body suit. This is reminiscent of her stage persona, Sasha Fierce, and it coincides with some of the more sexually explicit lyrics in the song. There are two other set dance sequences that appear throughout the video. The first is located in a street with Beyoncé dancing with a group. The second is set in a swimming pool picking up on the water imagery that is a recurring trop throughout the 'Lemonade' video album. There are other clips where Beyoncé appears; a recurring image is where she is filmed leaning out of the window of a vintage car that turns in a circle on a dirt road. These set performance scenes repeat throughout the video; in between there are a number of different short clips, which include: an image of Beyoncé's daughter in a white dress with her hair flowing, a black cowboy riding on a horse, a group of older black women marching in protest, pictures of Mardi Gras, and young men street dancing. There is also an image of a line of police officers facing a very young black teenager dancing and a graffiti-sprayed image is displayed on the screen, which says, 'stop killing us.'

The video of 'Formation' is a complex multi-layered construction. It exemplifies the notion of articulation where a series of different and contrasting symbols, images, narratives and sonic experiences are interwoven. The film is a collaborative construction between Beyoncé and her cowriters Asheton Hogan, Khalif Brown and Michael Williams and the film maker Melina Matsoukas. In addition to these people who are credited for their work, there is a whole host of stylists, hair and make-up artists, musicians, dancers, publicists and film makers, who collectively share in generating the four minutes and forty-seven seconds that comprise the 'Formation' video. All this work is intentionally creating the rich symbolic mix that makes up the video. In the 'Lemonade' videos as a whole, there are three interrelated dominant narratives. The first has already been mentioned, it is the problems that Beyoncé has experienced in her relationship with the singer, Jay-Z. The second key narrative relates to black history and identity. For Inna Arzumenova, 'Formation' is a cultural moment that stops time. It is a piece that focuses on black resilience in the face of oppression. 'Beyoncé's ultimate project,' she argues, 'is about positioning black communities, black activism and black art as enduring weapons against racial violence, reincarnating black pasts to rearticulate and strengthen black futures.[21]' In 'Formation', Beyoncé performs a range of different black subjectivities. This is characteristic of Beyoncé's performance style and imagery, that Aisha Durham says, enables the artist to span both black and middle-class white audiences. She is a central figure in Feminist Studies, Durham suggests, because she shows how celebrity and hip-hop culture is constructed around a negotiation of the self and sexuality, in a context of contested gender and racial identities.[22] As is evident from 'Formation', Beyoncé adopts a range of different personae in this one video. Durham, commenting on her earlier work, argues that Beyoncé performs competing black femininities in such a way that at one point she is the good girl and at another the bad girl.[23] This complexity situates Beyoncé in a space where black subjectivity is being worked out in relation to both personal and structural, forms of hardship and oppression.

The religious symbolism in 'Formation' is woven into the complex interplay between personal narrative, and discourses of black femininity and social hardship. The first line makes reference to those who are haters and speak about the 'illuminati mess.' This is a reference to conspiracy theorists who speculate that Beyoncé and Jay-Z subscribe to the Masonic theological system of thought popularised in the *Da Vinci Code* by Dan Brown. This seeming dismissal of this thinking at the start of the song, is made more complex by the image of Beyoncé on the porch of the house in her broad-brimmed hat where she is flanked by black males, some of whom are wearing fezzes. This appears to be a reference to the nation of Islam, some of whom adopted the fez, and were explicitly linked to Masonic lodges and practices. In the 2018 video 'Apeshit' recorded with Jay-Z, Beyoncé and her husband are filmed in front of the 'Mona Lisa' – this is the picture that is at the heart of the Dan Brown novel. Beyoncé is therefore playing with these references both in 'Formation' and elsewhere.

Throughout the video there are very short sequences that explicitly reference the Christian religion. A picture of Dr Martin Luther King is shown, taken from a newspaper with the headline, 'The truth.' Repeated in the video, there is picture of a small neighbourhood black church, with an elderly male preacher at the front, and mainly female worshippers actively receiving the message. 'Formation' also links images of the American South, with deeper and more mystical notions, of the relationship between the world of the dead and world of the living symbolised by the water imagery. This notion is picked up in the Mardi Gras images that also draw on the relationship between the living and the dead. The blogger, Natrice, likens the water images in 'Formation' to the notion of the Kalunga line in the religious thought of the Congo.[24] At the end of the 'Formation,' Beyoncé is shown disappearing beneath the flood waters. Water imagery is repeated throughout the 'Lemonade' Videos. In the video for 'Hold Up,' Beyoncé is again submerged under the water in an extended sequence. As the song starts, however, she bursts out of a large wooden door in a gushing tidal wave. Here the singer is shown dressed as the Yoruba water goddess and the symbol of fertility, Oshun. Beyoncé is,

Floating on a gush of water and an equally flowing yellow dress, smashing hydrants with glowing laughter and a buoyant reggae beat, Beyoncé is Oshun, the Nigerian, Cuban and Brazilian orisha of sweet water, sexuality and creativity, whose generosity makes life worth living and whose wrath begins with rolling laughter that foreshadows disaster.

Dressing as a divine figure is something that Beyoncé has frequently resorted too. The 'Beymaculate Conception' image is an example of this, but there have been other occasions where she has portrayed herself as the Virgin Mary. On the birth of her twins she again dressed as the Virgin, this time in a flowing blue robe and a veil, holding her children, who were a month old. In 2012, she recreated Michelangelo's 'Pieta'. The images in 'Lemonade', prompted the journalist, Omiseke Natasha Tinsley, to say that, 'Lemonade' is black woman magic.[25]

Reversing dominant stereotypes runs throughout the 'Lemonade' piece. At the end of the song, 'Freedom,' Hattie White is shown speaking to the crowd at her birthday in 2015. She says, 'I had my ups and downs, but I always find the inner strength to pull myself up. I was served lemons, but I made lemonade.' The oppression and disadvantage that is part of the black experience is continually linked to a personal narrative of success in 'Lemonade.' As Beyoncé says in the lyrics at the end of the 'Formation' video, 'The best revenge is your paper.' Material success as a response to betrayal is intertwined with religious consolation. At the start of the 'Hold Up' video, Beyoncé recites the poetry of the British Somali-born poet Warsan Shire.

Fasted for 60 days … confessed my sins and was baptized in a river. Got on my knees and said "Amen" and said "I mean" … I drank the blood and drank the wine. I sat alone and begged and bent at the waist for God … and plugged my menses with pages from the Holy Book. But still inside me coiled deep was the need to know, are you cheating on me?

Here the Christian notions of baptism, fasting, the Eucharist and the Bible are embedded in the experience of relationships that have been betrayed. The same pattern of association between religious symbol and personal life shapes 'Lemonade'. Each video in the series is given a title. The titles: Intuition, Denial, Anger, Apathy, Emptiness, Accountability, Reformation, Forgiveness, Resurrection, Hope, Redemption, also combine religious and personal narratives. Taken as a whole, the 'Lemonade' album develops a profound account of the breakdown and restoration of a relationship. Woven throughout the piece is also a consideration of what it means to be black, and to be a woman in US society. In this construction, religious themes and images function as symbols and signifiers of the divine, and of structural issues and problems in American society. At the heart of the piece, however, is Beyoncé and her manipulation of herself and her own representation in relation to the themes she is exploring.

These in turn are focused primarily on questions of identity and empowerment. Theological notions are utilised in this larger project of the self, but they gain traction and carry authenticity in and through Beyoncé, as a celebrity figure. It is what Beyoncé represents, and not simply what she sings that carries the creative energy of the project.

Celebrity and the changing nature of religion

The theologian, Vincent Miller, criticises the way in which religious images and symbols are commodified in contemporary culture. Commodification, he argues, lifts elements of a tradition out of their firm location in religious communities and fragments them.[26] The analysis of the videos in this chapter in many ways confirm the process of fragmentation and dislocation that Miller is so concerned about. In the music videos, religious ideas, narrative, symbols and artefacts, are taken up and made use of. Through articulation these 'religious bits' take on new meanings and are re-appropriated into new kinds of theological understanding. The worries expressed by Vincent Miller and others are not entirely misplaced, in that with Lady Gaga and Ariana Grande, it is clear that traditional understandings of sex, gender and sexuality associated with religion are being challenged. God is seen to be the one who has made people this way, and God is located as a woman whose sensuality is the mystical experience that leads her partner into a new appreciation of the divine and that God is a woman. Similarly, Beyoncé appears to be indicating that the things of the Church, and the ways in which the Church might speak to, and of women and their social situation, are limited in their efficacy. As Candice Bender argues in 'Lemonade,' Beyoncé takes the message that the black Church offers to women, that through spirituality and faithfulness they can endure the suffering that they face, in relationships and in society, and she turns them on their head. Beyoncé's message is an assertion of female sexual power, and of the redemptive possibilities of the US dollar for black American women. For Benbow, Beyoncé represents a generation of black women who are refusing to follow the directions of their Church. The 'Lemonade' video represents, she says, a moment where it is clear that these young black women will no longer refuse to make lemonade out of the lemons that they have been given in life.[27] The album 'Lemonade,' then, can be read as a journey from the positioning of black women as subject to the abuses that relationships with black men place upon them to a new affirmation of themselves. Black women she suggests have been taught by the Church to be selfless, but in this video album we see Beyoncé on a journey towards self-acceptance. 'While Beyoncé may have embodied this position at the beginning of "Lemonade," she walks completely away from it when she learns to love herself. As she journeys toward wholeness, she puts herself first – something many churched women are taught not to do.'[28] Redemption and reconciliation with her estranged lover come on her own terms and where she is empowered. For Benbow, the message is that black women have had a hard life forced on them, but it is in these circumstances that they have found ways to thrive.

Religious notions of the divine and associated practices, narratives and symbols are used in the videos as a form of theology. This is enabled by the ways in which media representation, particularly music video, has a cultural logic that entails a multi-layered form of signification. The technology, therefore, lends itself to a complex and playful, or even irreverent, interplay of different theological ideas. In each of the videos, however, what lies at the heart of this kind of theologising, is the centrality of the self, as a point of reference and concern. It is how the self is constructed, and made to feel powerful and meaningful that energises the vision of these music videos. The dynamics of a particular religious vision is, however, subtly different artist by artist. For Lady Gaga, the vision is for a new race that is inclusive of difference, Beyoncé on the other hand seems to celebrate a particular black identity and Ariana Grande links the divine to female empowerment. Lady Gaga situates her narrative of the divine in a struggle concerning the self as a monster; Beyoncé and Ariana Grande in contrast present a more singular empowered self that fights against structural evils of those who abuse and kill. All three, however, are highly political in the issues that motivate and inform this kind of theologising.

The theology that takes place in these videos is not an ecclesial or Church-based theology. While it is clear that in many ways these artists, through the re-articulation of theological images and themes within a conversation about the self, effectively subvert or alter what might be seen as received ways of speaking about Christian divinity or religion, this is not the primary purpose of what they are seeking to do. The intention is not to generate a new religious sensibility. What takes place in these videos is the reformulation of theology to a new purpose. The intention then is to use the continuing cultural religious and spiritual power of the divine as a means to enhance the more immediate and pressing concern, which is the self, and how the self might be accepted and empowered in various ways. It is in this context that celebrity as a construct plays a central role in how religious themes are relocated to a conversation concerning the self.

Figures such as Beyoncé, Ariana Grande and Lady Gaga are central to this process. In the first instance, it is the cultural and economic power that comes from being a celebrity musician that enables them to do this kind of theologising. They are able to speak in new ways, precisely because they are wealthy, successful and talented artists. From this celebrity position, they can utilise the processes and possibilities of media communication. Celebrity then is a self-fulfilment in that being well-known enables further well-knownness to take place, and in this context, what is being spread around in the flow of media discourse by these artists is a public form of theologising. Celebrity then is also significant in that it means that this theologising is heard. Hearing here involves not simply clicks, viewings and sales, it also refers to the ways in which songs become part of people's lives. These songs implant their lyrics, and their images, in the heads of those who listen to them and watch them repeatedly. Celebrity, however, also operates on a third level, in ways that bring authority to these theological forms of representation. Authority here does not come from scholarship, or from a formal position within a religious organisation. The authority that celebrity offers comes from the emotional attachment that these individuals are able to generate among their audiences. These theological ideas have significance, not so much because they are coherent, persuasive or canonical, but because they are created by people that matter to their fans. Celebrity, then, is a form of authenticity in the contemporary theological dialogue that acts as the power that lies behind the way that religion is changing shape in our society through media representation.

Notes

1 *New York Post*. 'Beymaculate Conception.' 2 February 2017. https://nypost.com/cover/covers-for-february-2-2017/.
2 Katie Edwards. 'How Beyoncé's Virgin Mary Imagery Challenges Racist, Religious and Sexual Stereotypes.' *The Washington Post*, 14 July 2017. www.washingtonpost.com/news/acts-of-faith/wp/2017/07/14/how-beyonces-virgin-mary-imagery-challenges-racist-religious-and-sexual-stereotypes/?utm_term=.40219f3afbfa.
3 Stephen Roberts. 'Beyond the Classic: Lady Gaga and Theology in the Wild Public Space.' *International Journal of Public Theology*, 11 (2017): 163–187.
4 Stuart Hall. 'On Postmodernism and articulation: an interview with Stuart Hall.' In *Stuart Hall: Critical Dialogues in Cultural Studies*. Edited by David Morley and Chen Kuan-Hsing. (London: Routledge, 1996), 137.
5 Ashanka Kumari. '"Yoü and I": Identity and the Performance of Self in Lady Gaga and Beyoncé.' *Journal of Popular Culture*, 49 no. 2 (2016): 403–416.
6 Richard Gray, ed. *The Performance Identities of Lady Gaga: Critical Essays*. (Jefferson, NC: McFarland, 2012), 15.
7 Jen Hutton. 'God and the "Gaze": A Visual Reading of Lady Gaga.' *Chicago Art Magazine*, 2 July 2010. http://chicagoartmagazine.com/2010/07/god-and-the-gaze-a-visual-reading-of-lady-gaga/.
8 Gaga interview, *MTV News*, 25 April 2011.
9 Gaga interview, *Skorpion Show*, 23 February 2011.
10 Neil Strauss. 'The Broken Heart and Violent Fantasies of Lady Gaga.' *Rolling Stone*, 8 July 2010.
11 Kumari. Yoü.
12 Gray. *Performance*, 7.
13 Heather Saul. 'Lady Gaga Answers Religious Blogger Over Claims about Catholic Celebrities.' *Independent*, 11 May 2016. www.independent.co.uk/news/people/lady-gaga-answers-religious-blogger-over-claims-about-catholic-celebrities-a7024376.html.
14 *Crux*. 'Lady Gaga's Mass Pics and Posts on Faith Stir Catholic Reaction,' 11 May 2016. https://cruxnow.com/church/2016/05/11/lady-gagas-mass-pics-and-posts-on-faith-stir-catholic-reaction/.
15 Instagram. ladygaga. www.instagram.com/p/BFO1b9rpFFC/?hl=en.
16 Guthrie Graves-Fitzsimmons. 'The Provocative Faith of Lady Gaga.' *The Washington Post*, 5 February 2017. www.washingtonpost.com/news/acts-of-faith/wp/2017/02/05/the-gospel-according-to-lady-gaga/?utm_term=.183c1365d5f1.
17 *Vigilant Citizen*. '"God is a Woman" by Ariana Grande: The Esoteric Meaning.' 30 July 2018. https://vigilantcitizen.com/musicbusiness/god-is-woman-by-ariana-grande-the-esoteric-meaning/.

18　Alexis Okeowo. 'The Provocateur Behind Beyoncé, Rihanna, and Issa Rae.' *The New Yorker*, 26 February 2017. www.newyorker.com/magazine/2017/03/06/the-provocateur-behind-beyonce-rihanna-and-issa-rae.

19　Okeowo. Provocateur.

20　Okeowo. Provocateur.

21　Inna Arzumanova. 'The Culture Industry and Beyoncé's Proprietary Blackness.' *Celebrity Studies,* 7, no. 3 (July 2016): 421–424.

22　Aisha Durham. '"Check On It": Beyoncé, Southern Booty, and Black Femininities in Music Video.' *Feminist Media Studies*, 12, no. 1 (2011): 35–49.

23　Durham. Check, 41.

24　*Musings of a Renegade Futurist.* 'Black Secret Technology: Beyoncé's Formation.' 7 February 2016. https://netarthud.wordpress.com/2016/02/07/black-secret-technology-beyonces-formation/.

25　Omise'eke Natasha Tinsley. 'Beyoncé's "Lemonade" Is Black Woman Magic.' *Time*, 25 April 2016. http://time.com/4306316/beyonce-lemonade-black-woman-magic/.

26　Vincent Miller. *Consuming Religion: Christian Faith and Practice in a Consumer Culture.* (London Bloomsbury, 2004).

27　Candice Benbow. 'Beyoncé's "Lemonade" and Black Christian Women's Spirituality.' *Religion and Politics*, 28 June 2016. https://religionandpolitics.org/2016/06/28/beyonces-lemonade-and-black-christian-womens-spirituality/.

28　Benbow. Beyoncé's.

Chapter 8

Celebrity death

The death of a famous individual generates a range of media-related ritual activities. When a celebrity dies the news becomes a flash flood of messages across a range of media platforms. Social media enables an immediate engagement through sharing, likes and comments. Images appear on feeds and memories are evoked. Within a few moments famous friends and colleagues begin to 'pay tribute.' On television news the Twitter comments of those who were close to the celebrity are read out and set alongside hastily put together phone and Internet-generated interviews. Friends speak from their own homes, or where they are working on location. In this initial phase of media ritual mourning, the attention is primarily on summing up the life and contribution of the celebrity, who has so recently departed. Death becomes a point of closure on the self, a moment where it is possible to say what he or she meant to the world of comedy or music or theatre or sport or film or fashion. With most celebrities this brief account of a life flashes past in our news feed, and then attention quickly moves elsewhere. Their face perhaps appears in the, 'those we have lost,' section of an awards show, where they are again briefly remembered, along with others we may, or may not, have heard of. Celebrity death seamlessly woven into media coverage is the norm, but every so often a loss occurs that becomes a major cultural moment. Broadcast schedules are interrupted. Coverage on the Internet goes viral, and people start to gather on the streets in places that are significantly related to the celebrity who has died. It is on these occasions that the coverage in all forms of media becomes a deluge. The remembrance of a life becomes connected to a more visceral emotion concerning the self. In these public acts of mourning the death of the celebrity is articulated with a charged processing of what their life 'meant' as it intersected with what they mean to their fans. The death of a celebrity is a moment when Celebrity Worship is intensified and focused.

Sales and celebrity death

Celebrity Worship is always linked to products, even in death. Celebrities are primarily a vehicle to sell things, and death is a significant moment in the commercial cycle. Steve Jones points out that in the music business, it has become something of a truism that death is, 'a great career move.'[1] The rapper Tupac's posthumous album, 'Don Killuminati: The Seven Day Theory,' which was released in 1997, broke records for the number that were sold. In 2002, Elvis Presley was again topping the charts, with a multimillion selling record 'ELV1S/30 #1 HITS.'[2] When Kurt Cobain's suicide was reported he was immediately linked to what has been labelled the dead rock star club, which includes: Keith Moon, Janis Joplin, Jimi Hendrix and John Lennon. The difference with Cobain, as Jones points out, was that in contrast to these others, he had committed suicide.[3] This fact did not prevent conspiracy theorists from speculating that his death was staged by the record company, who had heard that Cobain was about to quit the music business, and they saw the potential to lift the slowing sales of Nirvana albums.[4]

Making the most of a celebrity death is a complex business, with a range of opportunities that can bring significant income streams. At the centre of these economic realities lies the ownership of the celebrity image. Other forms of copyright and royalties are generally protected with a legally defined period, e. g. death plus 50 years. This is, however, not the case when it comes to the brand or image of a celebrity. For living celebrities, the legal situation is protected. While a celebrity is alive no one can profit through trading in the reproduction of a name, portrait, or picture of that person, without first receiving written consent. Once someone has died, however, the rights that are linked to the reproduction of an image or a name, cease to exist. This means that relatives and managers need to quickly act to generate a distinct commodity out of the celebrity's image that can then be protected and, as a result, it can lead to the generation of revenue.[5] In 2018, the Forbes list for the top earning dead celebrities was topped by Michael Jackson, who earned $400 million. The second highest earner was Elvis Presley at $40 million. Presley continues to sell over one million albums each year, but the main income comes from tickets to Graceland, his home in Memphis.[6]

Presley's posthumous pop career is managed by Elvis Presley Enterprises Inc. The company manages Graceland, and it asserts the right to ownership of Elvis's name, voice, face and signature. Elvis's Graceland estate and its contents are owned by his daughter, Lisa Marie Presley, but it is managed through Elvis Presley Enterprises by its chief executive, Jack Soden. The company seeks 'to bring Elvis into the twenty-first century.'[7] Alongside managing Graceland, and the rights associated with merchandising and music publishing, the business seeks to generate new projects such as films, music recordings and stage shows, as well as developing Elvis's profile on the Internet. In 2019, the 'Elvis Lives' concert tour came to the UK. The show was billed as a 'Graceland approved tribute show.' It featured a live band and three Elvis impersonators. Alongside the live acts, there was also archive video footage of Elvis. Christie Marcy, who attended the show in Salt Lake City in 2017, noted that the Elvis impersonators corresponded to periods in The King's career. There was a young Elvis, a movie star Elvis and a Las Vegas Elvis. This last Elvis, Marcy called, 'Fat Elvis.' The reviewer was, however, most taken with the reaction of the fans. Each Elvis (including Fat Elvis), was in turn given a gift of a teddy bear by a member of the audience, and several elderly women threw panties onto the stage. Marcy identifies with the reaction of the crowd, who appeared to react in ways that recalled their past relationship to the singer. As she says,

> I knew that the three men onstage were not the real Elvis Presley. I'm pretty sure all the women in the house knew that, too. But that didn't stop them from feeling like teenagers again when he took the stage. When we're talking about value per dollar – that's unbeatable.[8]

Camille Paglia likens the purchase of merchandise and memorabilia that is associated with dead celebrities, to the Roman Catholic cult of the saints. 'Cobain is a martyr to the god of rock in some way. Buying his merchandise is like buying the relics of the saint.'[9] For those close to Nirvana the opportunities that came with Cobain's death were definitely a consideration, both in the immediate aftermath of his suicide, and in the long term. *Billboard* reported an almost immediate rise in the sales of the band's existing albums, and were quickly speculating on how the record company might move to capitalise on the upsurge in interest generated by Cobain's death, by putting out previously unreleased material. In the UK, *Melody Maker* reported on the rise in sales of the band's albums. Tower Records in London's Piccadilly began to play the album 'Nevermind,' and a member of staff in the shop expressed something of the irony in the commercialisation of Cobain's suicide. 'I know, it's really awful. Somebody dies and you try to make money out of it. But it's not just a sell-out thing. It is kind of like a tribute as well.'[10]

Summing up the self

Obituaries and funeral tributes are a regular feature of the rituals that are associated with death. Each generates particular forms of representation that function as a kind of closure. The sociologist Tony Walter describes how funerals in the UK are becoming more personalised and orientated towards an appreciation of the life of the person who has died. A new category of funeral celebrant has started to emerge. These celebrants offer innovative forms of ritual that are more personalised and individual than traditional Christian liturgies. The result is funeral services that seek to celebrate a life. This shift towards the identity and meaning of the person who has died in funeral rituals also affects formal Christian services. In a church context, Walter argues, clergy are increasingly required to negotiate a space for more personal forms of tribute alongside the formal theological frameworks of the liturgy and sermon.[11] The shift, towards mourning as a celebration of a life, mirrors the wider changes in religion that are oriented towards a self-spirituality.[12]

For fans, celebrity death represents a moment for taking stock, or summing up a life. The complicating factor is that the person who has died is someone who is known, and yet also not known. Known through media representation, and yet not known 'personally.' Funerals and memorialisation can therefore become a moment where something of the private person becomes evident. In 2015, the funeral of the British singer and TV personality, Cilla Black, took place in her home city of Liverpool. Cilla came to fame in the 1960s, as a teenage singing star with close links to the Beatles. Her single, 'Anyone who had a heart,' was the biggest selling single by a UK woman artist in the 1960s. After several UK hits, she became host of her own Saturday evening variety and music-based television shows, and in 1985 she became the much-loved host of the dating show 'Blind Date.' If a date went particularly well, Cilla would famously ask the couple, 'Should I buy a hat?' in anticipation of a wedding. Her death was unexpected and sudden, coming after a fall and a subsequent stroke in her villa in Spain. She was 72. Following her death, a greatest hits compilation went to number one in the UK charts. Her funeral was held in St Mary's Roman Catholic Church in Woolton, Liverpool, and it was broadcast live on the BBC. In the TV commentary it was explained that the tributes would take place before the formal Roman Catholic liturgy was started. This allowed space for a highly personal, and at times slightly irreverent personal tone to be adopted in the tributes that were given by her show business friends and her son, Robert Willis. Speaking after the funeral her other son, Ben Willis, acknowledged the affection that his mother was held in by the British public. He said, my mother was 'always young at heart. I think this was one of the reasons so many people loved her dearly. She loved being a star. She lived to entertain and to make people happy. But she also valued her privacy greatly.'[13] In his tribute, Sir Cliff Richard, who was a close friend, said that Cilla was, 'our greatest TV presenter probably of all time.'[14] A frequent theme of the tributes and the news coverage, was both the affection that she was held in, and her ordinariness. Her humble beginnings in Liverpool were emphasised, and her manner with people. 'She treated everyone just as she saw them, no matter their background.'[15] Cilla, and her husband Bobby, were described as two working-class kids from Liverpool who made the impossible possible. Jimmy Tarbuck, in his tribute, called her 'Liverpool's Cinderella.' Others spoke of her as the nation's favourite big sister, the country's favourite auntie and the girl next door.

In the newspaper coverage of Cilla Black's funeral, there are significant themes that form part of the regular rituals of celebrity mourning. The themes that are ritually repeated in the tributes and in the news reporting, convey a sense of why people care about this person, in other words the funeral addresses the affective power of a celebrity such as Cilla. A key theme seen at Cilla's funeral is the emphasis that is placed on authenticity. Cilla is seen as being authentic, because of her working-class roots, and her origins in Liverpool. Cilla is Cinderella, the girl who was not invited to the ball, but the one who through magic becomes the nation's sweetheart. She was a friend of celebrities but above all she was linked to the Beatles from the very beginning in Liverpool. This is a level of magic celebrity connection that few can claim. At the same time, the talent that Cilla brought to bear, particularly through her television presenting, but also in her early success in the music business, is emphasised. Friends claimed that Cilla was one of the very best presenters on TV that we have ever seen. Thousands lined the streets of Liverpool to watch her coffin pass; in fact the service was delayed in order to allow people to get their moment to pay their respects as the hearse went by. Yet, despite the fact that she was known as 'our Cilla,' there was also the recognition that she was someone who guarded her privacy. She was in part mysterious. Some of the pleasure in the tributes that were paid to Cilla lay in what was revealed about her private life. The entertainer Paul O'Grady, who is also from Liverpool, became a close friend after the death of Cilla's husband, Bobby. O'Grady spoke about introducing Cilla to the gay nightclub scene in New York, and about the time when they were both locked out of her house in Barbados and were caught by neighbours trying to climb through a window.[16]

The ritualised themes that are seen in the reporting of the funeral of Cilla Black, are also evident in the media coverage of the death of David Bowie the following year. Bowie died on the 11 January 2016, from cancer. He had kept his illness secret, only revealing it to a few of his close friends and collaborators. Two days before his death, he released his last album, 'Blackstar'. Writing in the *Daily Telegraph*, McCormack commented that, 'like a great magician vanishing amidst his last illusion, Bowie's final act appears as masterfully and mysteriously staged as everything else in his extraordinary career.'[17] Bowie's career had been characterised by the generation of a series of characters, or persona, starting with his breakthrough, Ziggy Stardust. Each of his characters had been taken up and then killed off by the singer as his music evolved. At the same time, he was famously reclusive, and in his later years refused to give any interviews, or even to promote his own albums. In 2013, he released his first album after more than a decade of silence. The release of 'Next Day' was simply announced on his webpages, with no tour, or media interviews. The musicians on the album, and those producing the art work, were required to keep the project and their involvement in it, secret until after it had been released. The elusive and ever-shifting nature of Bowie's performance of himself, was both part of his attraction to his fans, but also a challenge when it came to his death. Quite simply the dilemma was, which Bowie was being mourned?

For the media, summing up the 'meaning' of David Bowie, at the time of his death, was a complex enterprise. Jack Black argues that in the immediate aftermath the newspapers engaged in a process of 'reification.'[18] The reification of celebrity, Black says, renders individuals as 'social objects.' This fixing of the meaning of the famous individual arises as the meanings associated with the celebrity are objectified in media representation, and then consumed by audiences.[19] Fundamental to this process is a desire to seek the 'authentic celebrity.' Authenticity often emerges in celebrity discourse as a consideration of the natural and unschooled talent that an individual possesses.[20] The tributes to Cilla Black follow this pattern. The desire to affirm the essential giftedness of a famous person is, however, held in tension with the realisation that fame is manufactured, and it is a part of a commercial negotiation. Black found that media accounts of David Bowie, following his death, emphasised the 'authentic Bowie,' as simply a boy from Brixton, London, who is a genuine person and a nice guy. At the same time, it was clear that the artist was also seen as a kind of genius, and something of an icon. He was spoken of as 'one of the greatest performers in history.'[21] Yet in the same breath reporters would stress how normal he was. This conveyed the message that in some way, Bowie had never lost a connection with his background and his upbringing. His approachability, however, was contrasted with a distance that many experienced when they met Bowie. As one interviewer noted, 'Bowie was always hyper-aware of how he was coming across. I've never felt so strongly when interviewing someone that what I was getting was an acted-out projection.' Despite this observation, the interviewer is clear that what he was observing wasn't fake, or cynical in any way. Bowie, despite the artifice and construction, was experienced as being true to himself.[22] The balance between a range of performed characters and the evident down-to-earth South London 'mate,' that those who spent any time with him spoke about, was one of the central conundrums of the artist. This was expressed by the journalist, Dempsey, 'What struck me both times I met him was how disturbingly normal he was off-stage. He was a chameleon; onstage he was an eccentric, at times even avant-garde, performer but off-stage he was a down-to-earth Brixton boy who was thoughtful, gracious and generous with his time.'[23] Bowie's penultimate album 'The Next Day,' in many ways was interpreted as Bowie himself asking these questions concerning his own history and identity. Here, uncovering the 'real Bowie', as Black puts it, became part of the artistic process. Part of the issue was the extent to which Bowie's musical characters became the means for self-reinvention and exploration through onstage performance and representation.

Bowie's multiple persona, and indeed musical influences and styles, meant that he had a fan base that was large and diverse. For the newspapers covering his death, this led to the assertion that Bowie was internationally and universally appreciated. According to the *Daily Record*, 'Everyone has a Bowie song in their heads, and everyone can feel cool because of Bowie's amazing creative legacy.'[24] For many commentators, Bowie's death was framed within the reactions of previous generations to the death of figures such as: John Lennon, President Kennedy and Elvis Presley. Black argues that these kinds of connections serve to reify the celebrity in relation to wider national and political events. As the *Irish Times* put it:

If you were 16 in 1969 – you saw the Russian tanks rolling into Prague, you saw the first landing on the moon, you heard David Bowie singing 'Space Oddity' – that haunting, tragicomic figure of Major Tom, floating around in his capsule, far above the world. It was only later that you realised how it described not only a man strung out on drugs but a more general kind of isolation and loneliness. He was describing the time we were in.

The objectifying of Bowie in relation to wider political and cultural events is an indication of the affective dimensions of the reactions to his death. With his death there is a sense of the death of times past. The self of the celebrity is therefore fixed in relation to individual and social memories. This aspect of the mourning of Bowie arises from the kinds of relationships that fans developed over time in relation to his music and this 'iconic' image.' While Bowie himself remained something of a mystery, one journalist spoke about the way that he had created a space that 'helped us discover ourselves.'[25] Black argues that the multiple persona of David Bowie provided a stable reference point for fans that supported them in generating their own identities. Alongside the themes of authenticity and identity, Black identified a significant aspect of the newspaper coverage that he surveyed, emphasised the immortality of Bowie. The singer, it was said, would never fade, he would always be seen as current and in fashion. Immortality, however, comes through a selective preservation in the media of aspects of the artist's life and performance.[26] This fixing of the record is a significant part of the process of reification that follows a celebrity death.

Processing emotional connections

The death of a celebrity becomes a moment for a ritualised assessment of the meaning of a star. Meaning, however, extends beyond the attempt to reify the characteristics or achievements of the celebrity, into the personal and the affective. Celebrity death generates an emotional response in fans and the wider public, because the person meant something to them. Making sense of this emotional attachment is complex, partly because the celebrity is generally only known through processes of mediation. Sean Redmond reflects on his own relationship to David Bowie in response to the release of the single 'Where are we now?' in 2013. In the song, Bowie revisits his previous persona, and he explicitly asks his fans to make a similar journey. Redmond recalls how, as a teenager growing up in what he terms a 'grim 1980s milieu,' the album 'Diamond Dogs,' 'struck a powerful chord for him.' The intimate, and yet mysterious and strange, character of David Bowie, provided an emotional attachment, which he names as an, 'identification with difference.'[27] In an autoethnographic moment, Redmond writes about the time when he was watching the video for the song, 'Where are we now?' 'Within seconds of hearing the first vibrato chords of this wistful song, and of seeing the memorial images of the Berlin in which Bowie did some of his finest work, I find myself in a flood of tears.' The video, he says, acts as a memory or a structure of feeling, 'that has thrown up all sorts of nostalgic impressions, affects, and ultimately taken me right back to a heightened moment of personalised time, of enchanted plenitude, as this question begins to fall from my wet lips …'[28]

The relationships that fans develop with celebrities vary in intensity. Courbet and Fouquet-Courbet researched the response of fans to the death of Michael Jackson.[29] The reaction of these fans often was characterised by shock and disbelief. Emma who was 23 at the time said, 'I didn't realise what had happened. I stood in a state of shock, in front of my television screen. I didn't know what to do and it was a big drama for me.'[30] A major feature of this first reaction was the role that significant intermediary figures played in relation to the fans' reactions. These 'attachment figures' included parents, siblings, lovers and friends. The interviewees spoke about the death of Michael Jackson in relation to events or moments in their life that were linked to these attachment figures, who were in their micro-social worlds. A memory of, for instance, a birthday party where Michael Jackson's music played a part, and how this moment was shared with their significant individuals was frequently mentioned. As Paul aged 32 put it,

> I immediately thought of my brother with whom I held great parties and where we danced like MJ, we were teenagers. What made me sad was that I was never going to relive what I had lived with my brother when we made his choreographies. My brother is important for me.[31]

The loss of the celebrity was frequently linked with a sense of loss about their own past. It was often said that something of their identity and memory had died along with Michael Jackson. As Ryan said, 'I said to myself, 'It's not possible. Part of my childhood is being stolen …'[32] Many of those interviewed, when they first heard the news, attempted to contact their attachment figure to talk about Jackson's death. They also reported that they were prompted to try to speak to their attachment figure because they were worried that this connection had also been lost to them. In some cases, the attachment figure had died, and this led to additional feelings of loss. One of those interviewed shared how it was her mother who had introduced her to the music of Michael Jackson. Her mother had died two years previously, and hearing Michael Jackson's music brought back her memories and grief for her mother. Hearing the music made her think of her mother and it made her cry.

The relationship formed between fans and a dead celebrity can also operate as an identity marker. Courbert and Fouquet-Courbert found that fans often spoke about Michael Jackson as a 'part of them.'[33] This emotional connection that individual fans spoke about is contrasted with others who spoke about a social connection. For these people, the relationship to Michael Jackson operated in the context of a fan group and shared experiences. For the first type of fans, mourning became a complex negotiation of their sense of self. The feeling that in some ways something about themselves had died with Michael Jackson, required a period for processing what had taken place. On social media, this group might post individual messages, such as 'I miss you.'[34] Those fans who regarded themselves as part of a group, processed their grief in a different way. In many cases, the group of Michael Jackson fans that they were a part of continued to exist even after his death. This enabled the sharing of memories and feelings between these fans. The fan group gave a sense of security and connection that helped individuals to process the death of the singer.

The processing of grief, and the complexities of emotional attachment to celebrities, is explored by Scott Radford and Peter Bloch in their study of online grieving. On the 18 February 2001, the NASCAR (National Association of Stock Car Auto Racing) driver, Dale Earnhardt Sr, was killed in a crash at the Daytona race track. At the time of his death, Dale Earnhardt was regarded as the best racer of his generation.[35] Following the fatal crash, fans used a series of online discussion groups to post messages to share their sense of loss. The messages demonstrated aspects of the stages of denial, anger, bargaining, depression and acceptance described by Kubler-Ross and Kessler as the grieving process. Statements of fans such as 'Why him and not me,' were quite typical. One fan posted, 'I know part of me died Sunday afternoon in the 4th turn at Daytona. I wish I could have traded places with Dale. I would give anything to bring him back.'[36] A number of fans spoke about problems with sleep, crying and loneliness. As the grieving process developed many of those posting on the sites began to share stories of their pilgrimages to places where significant victories took place, or when they had brief encounters with Earnhardt. Radford and Bloch describe this as 'introjection,' a process whereby individuals can, 'relive and re-interpret past interactions with the deceased and reinforce relevant memories.'[37] Some fans experienced a disconnection, between their regular day-to-day lives and their sense of loss. One fan spoke about the disbelief and lack of sympathy with his feelings of loss that he experienced among his colleagues at work. The online message groups became a place where he felt that his attachment to Earnhardt was understood and he could find a community, with whom it was possible to share and process his feelings.[38] Another significant coping mechanism involved the purchase of consumer goods that were seen as being particularly meaningful. Radford and Bloch call this 'incorporation'. The dead driver had been connected to a large range of commercial merchandising contracts. Some of the fans measured their grief by speaking about the quantity of these endorsed goods that they had acquired. Some started their posts on the fan sites by saying that they were wearing Earnhardt-branded clothing, or sitting in front of signed photographs, or replica model racing cars. The products acted as a point of connection and intimacy, as well as authenticity, within the group.

Fans of the stock car driver Dale Earnhardt experienced an intense period of grief, but the researchers also noticed that this period of loss was relatively short-lived. Fans appeared to pass through the stages of grief in a remarkably short period.[39] This is in contrast to those who developed a strong attachment to Elvis Presley. Among Elvis fans, according to Erica Doss, memorialisation has become a ritualised and elaborate social activity.[40] Elvis is quite distinct in the levels of devotion that he continues to inspire among fans. During what is known as Elvis week, an annual event held in Memphis, the city fills with tens of thousands of fans. These crowds, says Doss, display, 'a kind of emotional intensity and reverence that intimates Elvis's popular culture canonization.'[41] The connection to Elvis, Doss argues, is unique in American culture, and its roots cannot simply be explained by the efforts of those who seek to continue to generate money from the singer. Elvis represents a complexity of different images that allow for a variety of connections between fans and the star. On the one hand, there is the young Elvis who was rebellious, linking musical sensibilities from black music, to a white working-class persona. This Elvis is the blue-collar kid, who grew up in poverty, and yet made it good. Then there is Elvis the soldier, who served in the military, and Elvis the B movie teen idol, who appeared in countless romantic Hollywood films. Elvis also represents family values, with his marriage to Priscilla in 1967, and the birth of their daughter, Lisa Marie Presley. Added to this, is the Elvis who was a devoted Christian, who sang gospel songs with his band before he went on stage, and Elvis the philanthropist, who would impulsively give away lavish gifts to strangers he met. Then there was Elvis the rhinestone-clad Las Vegas superstar, who morphs into the pill popping, bloated figure of pain and suffering that he was at his death. The multiple images associated with Elvis represent a complex array of personal characteristics that facilitate a range of different kinds of attachment and identification for fans. Elvis's image, says Doss, 'was and remains, ambiguous and contradictory, solid but unstable.'[42] Since the 1950s, it has been clear that Elvis has been continually made and remade to facilitate individual and corporate interests. It is this process that has led to Elvis's iconic status for his fans in popular culture. The ritualised behaviour of fans at Elvis week in Memphis arises from the complex range of different meanings that fans generate around the dead singer.

Celebrity death, rituals and funerals

The death of a celebrity is a time when audiences seek to make sense of their emotional connection with the person who has died. The process of working through the attachments that are there, between individuals and groups of fans, and the famous person who has died is facilitated by the appropriation of a range of different ritual practices of memorialisation. It was the death of Princess Diana in August 1997 that brought many of these practices into a new kind of social formation. Famously, the then Prime Minister, Tony Blair, in the immediate aftermath of Diana's death, struck the right note by speaking of her as, 'the People's Princess,' a term he had borrowed from Julie Burchill.[43] In her interview with Martin Bashir, where she revealed the tensions within her marriage to Prince Charles, Diana was asked if she thought she might ever be Queen. Her response was to say, 'I'd like to be a queen in people's hearts, but I don't see myself being Queen of this country.'

The public mourning that took place in London, over the two-week period following the car crash in Paris, was unexpected, but it formed part of a much wider pattern of response to such tragedies. Douglas Davies lists a number of events that were similar in the public response. These include the death of Princess Charlotte and her baby in 1817, the sinking of the Titanic in 1912, the assassination of John F. Kennedy in 1963, and the Hillsborough soccer stadium deaths in 1989.[44] 'The Diana Event,' as Davies calls it, should be seen as part of a continuity in public mourning, but it was also particular and distinct both in the scale of the response and in the way that this was expressed. The media played a central role in generating an atmosphere of national shock and mourning. The BBC and other TV channels switched to a wall-to-wall news coverage. This media flooding of the airways quickly led to a public response focused on Kensington Palace but extending to sites across the country. Thousands of flowers and tributes were brought to these places of mourning, and local authorities opened their doors for people to sign books of remembrance. The creation of places of mourning led to these becoming public shrines of grief. These shrines represented a democratised form of religious practice that created an articulation between religious or religious-like practices and Celebrity Culture. These included lighting candles, saying prayers, the use of the image of Diana as a kind of icon or sacred object. This is mixed with wreath laying, and other forms of funerary activity that are part of the social act of mourning. This link between the religious and Celebrity Culture continued into the service that was held in Westminster Abbey, where the formal rituals of the Anglican Church sat alongside Elton John's song 'Goodbye England's Rose.' The song is a reworking of the artist's hit 'Candle in the Wind.' The lyrics of the original song, which were written by Elton John's writing partner, Bernie Taupin, spoke about the death of Marilyn Munroe, and the tragedy of her life. In the reworked version, new verses were added that made an explicit reference to Diana, but the chorus remained the same as in the original. This therefore set up a link between the death of Diana and the celebrity narrative of Marilyn Munroe. The merging of celebrity discourse with the sacred is further illustrated by the wave of applause that broke out among those waiting outside the Abbey in the streets when the song ended and at other points during the service. The rituals of the pop concert becoming merged with the formal rituals of the Church of England.

A similar merging of religious ritual and Celebrity Worship is seen in the creation of shrines, and ways that fans gather in informal ways to mark the death of a celebrity. In 2009, with the sudden death of Michael Jackson, fans quickly gathered outside the UCLA Medical Center, where he was being treated and outside his home. They brought flowers, lit candles and played his songs on their handheld devices.[45] These actions served to create informal sacred sites through the use of material objects associated with mourning. In this constructed environment, the fans were able to generate a common feeling, sharing in the event and supporting each other. In the immediate aftermath of Jackson's death, Gary Laderman commented on the spiritual connection and religious practices associated with mourning. 'People draw from that spiritual connection with celebrities like Jackson notions of identity, a sense of the sacred, the potential for transformation, a set of moral values, the sense of possibility of transcendence or overcoming the limitations of life.'[46] These comments were set within the complex environment that followed the revelations of the court case accusing Jackson of child abuse, and previous allegations that had been settled out of court. The contested nature of Jackson, and the complex relationships that fans formed with him, were all on display in the immediate aftermath of his death. The informal gathering and ritualised forms of mourning, functioned as a means to process this complexity. For Laderman, the events around Jackson's death were not unprecedented. He compared them to the outpouring of public grief that took place in 1926 when the Hollywood screen idol, Rudolph Valentino, died suddenly while in hospital. Valentino, Laderman argues, 'was one of the earliest entertainers to inspire both religious devotion among star-struck followers and profit-driven fervour to give those followers as many intimate details of his life as possible.'[47] When news of Valentino's death broke, tens of thousands of fans surrounded the funeral home where he was staying. They wanted to be close to him, if possible, to touch his body and maybe take something away with them. Eventually the body of the star was made available for fans to pay their respects. They did so in their thousands, with it being estimated that seventy-four people per minute walked past his embalmed corpse. There were reports of frenzied fans fainting or kissing the coffin as they passed by. For Laderman, these events signal a new kind of religious devotion that is a kind of religion where the practices and rituals around the 'sacred' celebrity can often be of more significance and widespread than formal religion.[48]

Celebrity Worship and celebrity death

The death of a celebrity represents a moment of summing up a life. Through media rituals and fan behaviours what emerges are the deep currents of Celebrity Worship. Through death what is processed is a life of a significant individual, but this takes place in relation to more personal forms of remembrance. The celebrity is linked to what they mean to the audience and to places, people and particular experiences. In the death of a celebrity what is ultimately revealed is the extent to which Celebrity Worship is primarily concerned with the self. A celebrity may be dead but it is what he or she means to me that really counts and that is why they are mourned.

Notes

1 Steve Jones. 'Better Off Dead: Or Making it the Hard Way.' In *Afterlife as After Image: Understanding Posthumous Celebrity*. Edited by Steve Jones and Joli Henson. (New York: Peter Lang, 2005), 3.
2 Erica Doss. 'Elvis Forever.' In *Afterlife as After Image: Understanding Posthumous Celebrity*. Edited by Steve Jones and Joli Henson. (New York: Peter Lang, 2005), 61–80.
3 Jones. Better, 13.
4 Jones. Better, 3.
5 Jones. Better, 7.
6 Zack O'Malley Greenburg. 'The Highest-Paid Dead Celebrities of 2018.' *Forbes List*, 31 October 2018. www.forbes.com/sites/zackomalleygreenburg/2018/10/31/the-highest-paid-dead-celebrities-of-2018/.
7 Doss. Elvis.
8 Christie Marcy. 'Concert Review: Elvis Lives at Eccles.' *Salt Lake Magazine*, 19 February 2017. www.saltlakemagazine.com/concert-review-elvis-lives-eccles/.
9 Jones. Better, 7.
10 Jones. Better, 8.
11 Tony Walter. 'Judgement, Myth and Hope in Life-centred Funerals.' *Theology*, 119, no. 4. (2016): 253–260.
12 Paul Heelas. *The New Age Movement*. (Oxford: Blackwell, 1996), 18.
13 Leanne Bayley. 'Cilla Black's Funeral: Friends and Family Pay Respects.' *Glamour Magazine*, 20 August 2015. www.glamourmagazine.co.uk/article/cilla-black-has-died-aged-72-celebrity-tributes.
14 Hugo Gye and Gemma Mullin. 'Has Cliff Ever Sung a Song That Meant More to Him? Tearful Singer Belts Out Emotional Farewell to His Friend.' *MailOnline*, 20 August 2015. www.dailymail.co.uk/news/article-3204595/Cilla-Black-funeral-takes-places-Liverpool.html.
15 Gye and Mullin. Has Cliff.
16 Gye and Mullin. Has Cliff.
17 Jack Black. 'The Reification of Celebrity: Global Newspaper Coverage of the Death of David Bowie.' *International Review of Sociology*, 27, no. 1 (2017): 202.
18 Black. Reification.
19 Black. Reification, 205.
20 Black. Reification, 206.
21 Black. Reification, 209.
22 Black. Reification, 210.
23 Black. Reification, 211.
24 Black. Reification, 213.
25 Black. Reification, 215.
26 Black. Reification, 217.
27 Sean Redmond. 'Who am I now? Remembering the Enchanted Dogs of David Bowie' *Celebrity Studies*, 4, no. 3. (2013): 380–383.
28 Redmond. Who.
29 Didier Courbet and Marie-Pierre Fouquet-Courbet. 'When a Celebrity Dies … Social Identity, Uses of Social Media, and the Mourning Process Among Fans: The Case of Michael Jackson.' *Celebrity Studies*, 5, no. 3 (2014): 275–290.
30 Courbet and Fouquet-Courbet. When.
31 Courbet and Fouquet-Courbet. When.
32 Courbet and Fouquet-Courbet. When.
33 Courbet and Fouquet-Courbet. When.
34 Courbet and Fouquet-Courbet. When.

35 Scott K. Radford and Peter H. Bloch. 'Grief, Commiseration, and Consumption Following the Death of a Celebrity.' *Journal of Consumer Culture,* 12, no. 2 (2012): 142.
36 Radford and Bloch. Grief, 146.
37 Radford and Bloch. Grief, 147.
38 Radford and Bloch. Grief, 148.
39 Radford and Bloch. Grief, 151.
40 Doss. Elvis.
41 Doss. Elvis, 63.
42 Doss. Elvis, 65.
43 Douglas Davies. 'The Week of Mourning.' In *Mourning Diana.* Edited by Tony Walter. (New York: Berg, 1999), 3–18.
44 Davies. The Week.
45 Mark Coleman. 'Michael Jackson is Dead: Fans Mourn Outside Hospital.' *The Daily Telegraph,* 26 June 2009. www.telegraph.co.uk/culture/music/michael-jackson/5645517/Michael-Jackson-is-dead-fans-mourn-outside-hospital.html.
46 Gary Laderman. *Sacred Matters: Celebrity Worship, Sexual Ecstacies, The Living Dead and Other Signs of Religious Life in the United States.* (New York: The New York Press, 2009).
47 Laderman. *Sacred,* 66.
48 Gary Laderman. 'Michael Jackson's Death: Does Fame Trump Faith.' *Beliefnet.com.* www.beliefnet.com/faiths/2009/michael-jacksons-death-funerals-faith-and-fame.aspx.

Chapter 9

Evangelical Celebrity Culture

Celebrity Worship has become a significant force in the development of contemporary Christianity. This is particularly the case among American evangelical Christians, who have generated their own kinds of celebrification through their use of media. Embracing Celebrity Culture has had profound effects on these churches. The process of celebrification within churches comes about as communities have sought to use media to spread their message. Using media in this way inevitably requires a human presence, to both facilitate communication, but also to generate an emotional connection. These individuals, who feature in evangelical culture, are transformed by the action of the media and as a result they are 'celebritised.' Christian celebrities range from the pastors of mega-churches, to those celebrated for their missionary endeavours, to evangelists, and more recently worship leaders; there are also celebrities who have used their fame gained elsewhere as a means to promote their Christian faith. While the intention may have been to spread the message through the use of media the resulting celebrification might have wholly unintended consequences, and some of these can be negative and counterproductive to the original purpose and intention of the churches that adopt these processes.

Rob Bell and a Christian media storm

In 2011, Rob Bell, the pastor of the Michigan-based Mars Hill Bible Church, published *Love Wins: A Book About Heaven, Hell and the Fate of Every Person Who Ever Lived*.[1] The book unleashed an unprecedented media backlash that engulfed the evangelical world, not just in the United States, but around the world. The controversy was covered in the mainstream media, with Bell being featured on the cover of *Time* magazine.[2] When the book was leaked ahead of publication the evangelical preacher, John Piper, tweeted, 'Farewell Rob Bell.'[3] The central idea in *Love Wins* was far from new, or indeed, theologically shocking. The idea of hell and eternal damnation had been questioned by scholars, preachers and theologians many times before. What made Bell's suggestion – that hell might not exist, or perhaps more accurately that we do not really know about the afterlife – significant, was his status as an internationally recognised preacher. In other words, it was not exactly what was said that was catching the headlines, but who was saying it. The ferocious backlash that the book provoked among evangelical Christians was attributed by John Meacher, writing in *Time* magazine, to the acknowledged influence that Bell was able to command within the evangelical world. The source of Bell's influence and hence significance came primarily from his media profile.

Rob Bell founded Mars Hill when he was 28. By the time he was 30, he had, says Meacher, become a celebrity in the evangelical world. In 2007, *Time* magazine ran an article on Bell with the title, 'The Hipper Than Thou Pastor.'[4] In the article, he was described as a 'rockstar preacher' within the evangelical movement.[5] His Mars Hill church, at its peak, numbered 10,000 members, and with the publication of his first book 'Velvet Elvis,' Bell became a regular on the evangelical conference speaking circuit. These activities, in themselves, were not what lay at the root of his popularity. In 2001, Bell started to film a series of short videos exploring the Christian faith. The videos were marketed under the title NOOMA, and they were produced locally by a small Christian media company. The name NOOMA, was taken from the Greek word for spirit, *pneuma*. Each video was shot on location with Bell shown walking down the street, or strolling through a forest speaking about faith, in an accessible but realistic downbeat style. The NOOMA videos each featured tracks from contemporary Christian artists, and, in 2005, a compilation album was released with these tracks featured. Twenty-nine of these videos were released over a seven-year period, between 2002 and 2009. The films looked and felt more like a video for a band, such as Coldplay or Radiohead, than a theological description of faith. In 2005, the films were picked up by the Christian publishing house, Zondervan, in what was almost the equivalent of an indie band signing to a major record label. The NOOMA videos went a significant way towards establishing Bell as a distinctive and important voice in the evangelical world. For a generation of young Christians, these videos represented a new take on a conservative faith. John Pavlovitz describes the following that Bell had achieved, 'He had a rabid army of fellow believers who hung on every word he uttered, who lapped up every morsel he tossed them, who cheered him on like a local kid making the Bigs. For a while, it was a Christian Bubble love fest.'[6]

The controversy that swept across the evangelical world with the release of *Love Wins* needs to be set against the backdrop of the profile the Bell had generated through this media presence. What Bell said was seen as dangerous, not simply because he was an evangelical who was questioning his faith, but because of his following. The reaction was primarily coming, then, not so much because of the ideas, but because of the perceived danger that these ideas represented from someone who had become a huge celebrity on the Christian scene. This 'power' and influence was birthed by growing a remarkable Church, and through the evident abilities that Bell had as a communicator, but it is the reproduction of his image and persona through the media processes of celebrification that brought about the transformation of a local preacher into a global religious leader. In other words, what is evident is that the authority and the power of a religious leader is somehow amplified or transformed into more than the message, and more than the person, through the action of the media. The Bell phenomenon forms part of an enduring pattern within American religious life where evangelical Christians have sought to make use of the media to spread the message since the revivals of the eighteenth century.

Celebrity and the rise of evangelical Christianity

American Christianity, says Nathan Hatch, has been decisively shaped by a democratic and populist orientation.[7] 'Religious populism, reflecting the passions of ordinary people and the charisma of democratic movement builders, remains the oldest and deepest of impulses in American life.'[8] Central to these dynamics in religious life, have been a series of remarkable individuals, who have been, in large part, the architects of evangelicalism. These individuals, Hatch argues, derived their authority not from education, or their position within major denominations, but from 'the democratic art of persuasion.'[9] The significance of these leaders derives from the dispersed nature of their followers, and the networks of activities that they have been able to birth.[10] Hatch sees the generation of these networks and institutions as being of more enduring significance than the fame achieved by individual preachers. What this perhaps underestimates, is the extent to which religious celebrity enables the growth of evangelicalism. It is the emotional connection that the celebrity preachers were able to generate that brought about the connection to their followers. This connection is amplified and made more effective through the use of media, such as the radio or the television, and more recently social media and the Internet. The institutions enable individuals to generate fame and hence, for Hatch, they are of more enduring significance, but this underplays the way that religious celebrity is the affective driving force behind evangelicalism.

The use of media to promote the gospel has been one of the mainstays of evangelicalism in the United States. Harry Stout describes the eighteenth century preacher, John Whitefield, as the prototype for all evangelical evangelists. With the rise of a consumer culture, Whitefield shaped his ministry towards a mass audience by adopting methods associated with the new dynamics of the marketplace to promote his message. Whitefield employed a publicist and a business manager, who would travel with him, and go ahead to towns to develop links with the local newspapers, and use publicity to generate an audience for his preaching. He also used the print media to publish his sermons and his journal, thereby generating a method of keeping a connection to his audience when he was travelling elsewhere. Whitefield preached more than 18,000 times, and his sermons became events that were characterised by drama, such that Stout can describe his preaching as a form of entertainment. The crowds that came to his sermons could not be contained inside any of the buildings or churches, and so Whitefield would preach in the open air. His method was quite literally to take the Christian message into the market place. For Stout, these activities, however, are a part of a much wider reshaping of American society around consumerism and market forces. Whitefield's use of media meant that he realigned evangelical religion, as part of this new environment, and as a result, he transcended denominational restrictions and boundaries. The gospel message, presented as media-based entertainment, transformed religious life but at the heart of it was the personality of George Whitefield. Stout describes him as the first 'religious celebrity.' This status is not simply a function of his popularity, it also comes from how he used media to gain this position in people's imaginations.[11]

The orientation towards the use of media within evangelicalism enabled significant figures within the movement to generate a form of authenticity that bypassed more established forms of authority. Figures such as Billy Sunday (1862 to 1935), who was originally a professional baseball player with the Chicago White Stockings: Sunday came to faith while he was in Chicago, and at the request of the YMCA, he started his life as a Christian minister. This association with the YMCA allowed Sunday to develop an evangelistic ministry that was independent of any formal denominational or Church affiliation. Sunday, like Whitefield, benefited from paying close attention to developing an organisation that raised money and marketed his various campaigns. When the local churches could not accommodate the crowds that came to hear him, Sunday started to use a large circus tent in which to hold his meetings. It was here that many thousands 'hit the sawdust trail' and gave their lives to Christ. Billy Sunday was not without his critics. His style of preaching was very unorthodox and at times verging on the profane.[12] He regularly expressed a disdain for the liberal Christian elites. 'The Lord save us,' he is reported to have said, 'from off-handed, flabby-cheeked, brittle-boned, weak-kneed, thin-skinned, pliable, plastic spineless, effeminate, ossified, three-carat Christianity.'[13] Sunday developed the habit of preaching to women only meetings, where men were banned. For the audiences of the day this brought a sense of drama and danger to these meetings. Sunday's style was to warn of moral failings through the use of explicit and suggestive illustration. Women, particularly mothers, he argued, must know about the details of what it is to sin in order to protect their daughters. At one of these women only meetings, he ended his message with a poem. 'Little girl you look so small,/ Don't you wear no clothes at all?/ Don't you wear no che-mise shirt?/ Don't you wear no party skirt?/ Don't you wear no underclothes/ But your corset and your hose?'[14]

Women, in particular, reacted to Sunday's celebrity status by storming his meetings and filling every available seat that they could find. It was reported at one meeting that some of these women had to be led away by the local fire-fighters.[15] His wife, Helen Sunday, recounted in her tribute to her husband after his death that there were 'insistent women,' who hammered so loudly on doors and yelled so vigorously that there were occasions when Billy could not be heard when he was preaching.[16] Bendroth argues that Sunday's effect on women brought a level of entertainment and eroticism to the practice of evangelical preaching. Women, it seemed, were attracted to the rough form of muscular Christianity that Sunday represented.[17] The preacher traded on his former life as an athlete. When he had completed his sermon, he had an aide wrap a fur coat around his shoulders, and he would be led to an adjacent room, where his personal trainer would rub him down. In an environment reminiscent of a professional boxer, Sunday would receive prominent guests as he was being tended to in these ways.[18] What is also clear, is that the celebrity status of Sunday, engendered the kind of fan behaviour that was later only associated with pop stars, such as Elvis or the Beatles. At his crusade in Boston, nurses in hospital uniforms were stationed around the auditorium prepared to tend to any women who fainted during the service.[19] This combination of the use of media publicity, and innovation in the organisation of evangelistic meetings, was repeated by large numbers of evangelists in the United States in the early part of the twentieth century. Possibly the most successful of these was the Pentecostal preacher, Aimee Semple McPherson.

McPherson combined the evangelistic methods of Whitefield and Billy Sunday, with the Pentecostal practices of speaking in tongues and healing. She relied upon the organisational abilities and financial acumen of her mother, Mildred Kennedy, and together they travelled across America in her 'full gospel car.'[20] In 1917, she launched her own magazine *The Bridal Call*. Like Billy Sunday and Whitefield, McPherson's preaching was dramatic and popular in style, drawing in thousands to her meetings. According to Matthew Avery Sutton, McPherson was the 'first religious celebrity of the mass media era.' The status of McPherson as a religious celebrity is echoed by David Edwin Harrell. In 1924, McPherson remarked that with the advent of radio, it had become possible to, 'stand in the pulpit, and speaking in a normal voice, reach hundreds of thousands of listeners,' and carrying on, 'the winged feet of the winds, the story of hope, the words of joy, of comfort, of salvation.'[21] She utilised the full range of available media at the time, including print, radio and film to promote her message.

This ability to make use of media alongside her 'dazzling religious theatrics and a penchant for publicity' made her 'one of the most famous personalities of the interwar years.' At the time, many questioned the rise of figures, such as McPherson, who appeared to be simply engaged in promoting themselves, rather than the Christian religion. Entertainment-based, highly promoted, celebrity driven, evangelicalism was much debated and criticised. In 1926, McPherson mysteriously disappeared, while swimming on Santa Monica beach. Her mother, and her son, assumed that she had been swept away to sea and drowned. Five weeks after she had disappeared, and as her funeral was being planned, the preacher reappeared in Mexico, claiming that she had been kidnapped. Newspaper coverage accused her of lying about the kidnap, and the story was widely repeated that McPherson had eloped with a married man,

Kenneth Ormiston, who the reporters claimed was her lover. McPherson always denied these stories, and in a subsequent trial, it was found that they were false. Stories of sexual encounters and illicit affairs, however, continued to spread, and she was criticised for her style of dress and her Hollywood lifestyle. The newspapers were filled with stories and speculation concerning what had happened to her. Speculation about McPherson continued after her death, with some newspapers running stories saying that she had been buried with a phone, so she could call for help when she was resurrected. Others claimed that she had been murdered by Roman Catholics, who had poisoned her with a slow-working chemical.[22] When she died, her body was laid in state in Los Angeles, and around forty-five thousand people waited in line, into the early hours of the morning, to file past her body.[23]

The connection between American religion and the use of media has been a continuing characteristic of evangelical culture. The use of radio by preachers in the 1920s enabled them to develop popular ministries that had no connection to formal Church structures or institutions. Media, in particular radio, and then following that, television, became a significant extension of their activities beyond the confines of Church buildings and congregations. Charles Fuller, whose programme, 'Old-Fashioned Revival Hour,' came to represent the increasing popularity of conservative evangelical preaching. In 1940, Fuller's weekly radio audience was estimated at 20 million people. According to *Newsweek*, 'Between the death of Billy Sunday in 1935 and the rise of Billy Graham fourteen years later, Americans who sought that same kind of old-time religion turned to an evangelist named Charles Edward Fuller.' The rise of what became known as the 'electronic Church,' led to a new kind of celebrity Christian preacher, who could attract a vast audience, and generate revenues that were far beyond anything seen within formal Church structures. The reach and power of media, therefore, led to a transformation of American Christianity. At the heart of these changes there was the Christian celebrity. These were people who had been transformed by processes of mediation and whose lives had become the subject for media attention and speculation.

Mega-churches, celebrity pastors and social media

The contemporary mega-church phenomenon, seen in Rob Bell's religious activities, has its roots in the evangelical culture developed by figures such as Billy Sunday, Aimee Semple McPherson and Charles Fuller. A mega-church has been defined as a congregation that has over 2,000 members.[24] Celebrity preachers in the United States have found ways to attract huge congregations, and built their Churches by adopting marketing strategies and approaches to religion as a commodity that have been specifically adapted to digital technology and social media. Jessica Johnson argues that it is the technology utilised by celebrity pastors that lies behind the rise of the mega-church movement.[25] Those who attend these churches are participants in an evangelical industry that, 'thrives on elevating megachurch pastors to media elite status.'[26] The generation of a mega-church is often linked to an individual minister, who is generally male and usually young. The labour involved in creating this kind of Church, says Johnson, does not come from one person alone. The mega-church model relies upon the collective work of hundreds of individuals, who not only give money, but build 'social capital' in the community, by promoting the ministry of the pastor and the activities of the Church. The members of the Church legitimise the position of the pastor by buying his books, sharing his podcasts, liking his Facebook status updates and re-tweeting his tweets. The success of the mega-church, therefore, rests on the extent to which members of the congregation do not simply attend meetings and services, but also take part in the 'marketing prerogative, that is linked to the collective effort of members, whose evangelical identity is constituted by said labor and sacrifice.'[27] Mega-churches are, in effect, corporations that operate on market principles, rather than upon the directions, or theological frameworks, generated by denominations. Evangelicalism should, therefore, be regarded as kind of 'industrial complex' that has developed specific media practices that are designed to facilitate the rise of an elite class of celebrity pastor. In effect, the evangelical world has developed its own self-sustaining productive processes that maintain the status of a select group of individuals, who people the round of conferences and promote their books and ministries. This industrial complex functions in ways that are distinct from, and in part exclude, those who are ministers in smaller or medium-sized Churches, who are largely absent from events that only feature 'best-selling' evangelical authors.[28]

The Christian publishing market has been estimated as being worth around $7 billion a year.[29] The link to the mega-churches has been a significant element in this highly lucrative commercial marketplace. Publishers pitch book deals at mega-church pastors because they know that, even if the sales are limited to the members of their Church, the book will be a commercial success, and that even with these in-house sales, this may then be enough to launch a book into a wider consciousness, with the all important, 'best seller' tag on its cover. Johnson illustrates this process by an examination of the ministry of Mark Driscoll, and the eventual scandal that arose from the marketing campaign surrounding the publication of his book, *Real Marriage*.[30] Driscoll rose to prominence as the cofounder of Mars Hill Church in Seattle, that was started in 1996. By the time that it was eventually dissolved as a Church in 2014, it had spread to fifteen different facilities, in five cities in the US, and at its height there were around 13,000 people attending regularly. Mars Hill had satellite campuses in Albuquerque, New Mexico, Portland, Oregon and Orange County, California, as well as the main Church in Seattle. From the start, Driscoll was a preacher who courted controversy, preaching, for instance, a sermon on biblical oral sex. Donald Miller described him as, 'Mark the cussing pastor,' in his book *Blue Like Jazz*.[31] Driscoll was also accused, in 2000, of tweeting under a pseudonym a series of tweets that described women as, by the design of God, the 'home' for a man's penis.[32] Despite these controversial aspects of his ministry, many were drawn to his brand of muscular Christianity that reasserted the headship of men over women, and drew heavily on Puritan and Calvinist theology. In Seattle, 4,000 people a week were attending his Church in 2007, and his international reputation was being built by a savvy use of digital technology. Podcasts of Driscoll's sermons were being widely consumed around the world, and he regularly topped the podcast download charts.[33]

Driscoll's fall from celebrity preacher status was almost as rapid as his rise. In 2014, a story was taken up by the press, concerning the misuse of funds from Mars Hill Church, in order to manipulate sales figures, with the intention that *Real Marriage* would be listed on the *New York Times* Best Seller list. It was alleged that almost $250,000 was misappropriated and used to buy copies of the publication, in a way that would ensure that the book was indeed a best seller. These were funds that were earmarked by the Church for overseas Church Planting.[34] Driscoll was said to have been seen in the parking lot of a major Christian conference, handing out copies of his book for free. He was eventually asked to leave by the organisers of the event.[35] This was not the first time that Driscoll had been enmeshed in a controversy around his writing. In 2013, he was accused of plagiarism by the radio host Janet Mefferd. When this story became news, a series of other allegations of plagiarism began to surface. The Christian publishing business was rocked by this scandal; some publishers defended Driscoll, while others were publicly critical of his work. The story shifted towards 'mistakes' that might have been made by 'ghostwriters,' who were working on Driscoll's books. Janet Mefferd's radio station was eventually forced to take down the recordings of the show from their website. Speaking after the event, the producer of the radio show, Ingrid Schlueter, is reported to have said, 'there is an evangelical celebrity machine that is more powerful than anyone realizes. You may not go up against the machine. That is all.'[36] Schlueter effectively accused what she called 'the evangelical industrial complex,' of acting in ways that protected its commercial interests, rather being concerned with the truth of the story.[37] These various controversies, in themselves, did not lead to Driscoll's demise. What eventually led to him resigning his position at Mars Hill, were accusations of bullying and mismanagement. In 2014, a number of the senior leaders from Mars Hill started to post stories concerning the leadership style that Driscoll adopted. They accused him of being cut-throat and autocratic, prone to anger, and personal hubris. Kyle Firstenberg, who had been at the church, almost from its beginnings, made his problems with Driscoll's leadership style clear.

> The reputation Driscoll got for being the cussing pastor simply because he used harsh language from the pulpit was nothing compared to the swearing and abusive language he used daily with staff. When people asked me how I liked working at Mars Hill, I would simply say, 'It is a great church

to attend, but I wouldn't recommend working here.' It was well known with the staff that what was preached on Sunday was not lived out Monday morning with the staff.[38]

The pressure of these revelations eventually led to Driscoll standing down as minister of Mars Hill Church in 2014, and within a very short while, the Churches he had founded disbanded their association with each other. The demise of Driscoll also hit the headlines and caused ripples throughout the evangelical world. Like Rob Bell, Mark Driscoll was a celebrity preacher because of his use of the media, and it was this status that made the subsequent revelations and his eventual resignation from the Church he founded, headline news.

Worship leaders and celebrity

Within evangelical culture a new kind of celebrity has emerged in the last thirty years. This is the worship leader, a cross between a rock star and the Church organist. The worship leader has burst onto the celebrity evangelical world, with the rise in contemporary worship music. Contemporary worship music has its roots in early forms of Pentecostalism, but it originates, in its current form, in the Jesus Movement of the 1970s.[39] The Jesus Movement saw large numbers of young people convert to Christianity, many of whom had previously been part of the hippie subculture in the US.[40] While the Christianity that these young people began to embrace, was evangelical, and mainly Pentecostal in practice, they did not leave behind their mode of subcultural dress or their musical taste. What developed was a merger of youth orientated style, and conservative charismatic Christianity. The result was a flowering of what became known as, 'Jesus Music,' and with this came a realignment of the Christian cultural industries, towards a youth-based kind of music. The new hippie style of Christianity was soon fed by a network of record companies, publishing houses, festivals and, of course, musicians and artists.[41] In the United States, the musical genre of Contemporary Christian Music (CCM) was born, and increasingly important to this growing area of media-based evangelical Christian culture, was the development of new styles of worship. Nathan Meyrick traced the origins of this new form of praise and worship that developed from the Jesus Movement in the 1960s, to Calvary Chapel in Costa Mesa, California.[42] The new cultural formation that was forged in California imported into charismatic Christianity, not simply a different kind of music, or a subcultural youth-orientated style, but it also brought the sensibilities and cultural logic of the popular music industry. The logic of the music business created Christian music stars, who released albums and toured the world. Fan cultures and patterns of consumption and identity formation, which were originally formed in the secular pop music world, became a part of the new Christian subculture.[43]

In the US, with its larger consumer-based Christian market, Contemporary Christian Music was prioritised over Praise and Worship Music.[44] In the UK, however, there was a much smaller market and musicians inspired by the Jesus Movement developed their own forms of CCM. These artists were motivated to use their music as a form of evangelism. The problem was that it very quickly became clear that they could not support themselves simply by writing and performing. In the 1980s, British artists, such as Graham Kendrick pioneered a shift from CCM towards worship music, where a combination of album sales, and the support of Christian networks and Churches, offered a viable economic basis for a fulltime ministry. Central to these developments was the support of publishing companies, such as Kingsway Music, and the development of Christian events and festivals, such as New Wine and Spring Harvest, and the generation of a distinctive new source of income through the development of what has become Christian Copyright Licensing International.[45] These factors combined, enabled the UK to evolve a worship culture that fused the processes of production and distribution associated with the mainstream popular music, with what Rob Warner has termed 'entrepreneurial evangelicalism.'[46] Led by worship leaders, such as Martin Smith and his band Delirious, Tim Hughes and Matt Redman, the move into worship by young Christian musicians in the UK, led to what Monique Ingalls calls, the British Invasion of the US, in the 1990s. This new style of Praise and Worship music from the UK, brought about significant changes in the American scene. The British invasion led to Nashville-based CCM-orientated companies founding Worship Music divisions. Within a few short years, worship music became the fastest growing area within Christian popular music with unit sales doubling in volume between 1997 and 2002.[47] The success of the British worship artists was very quickly replicated by US-based musicians. Worship leaders started to become highly profitable within the US CCM genre. An artist such as Michael W. Smith, for example, was able to reinvent himself as a 'worship leader.' This says Meyrick, enabled him to re-ignite his career. Smith's album 'Worship,' which was released in 2001, was certified a year later as Platinum by the Recording Industry Association of America, and incredibly eight years later it had continued to sell and was certified as being double multi-platinum.[48] The effect of these developments on local Churches was a shift in the style of music that was being played during worship. This change, at a local level, was driven by celebrity. The songs that were becoming popular in congregations carried with them a close link between the music and the individuals who both wrote and performed the songs, the Celebrity Worship leader.

The celebrification of the evangelical Christian worship leader, has come about through a convergence of factors within the subculture. Nathan Myrick identifies three central elements that combined to bring about the changes in the worship style of American Churches. The first is the way that Churches have moved towards the use of media as a means to market a specifically Christian lifestyle. The second is the commodification of religious artefacts and objects, e.g. worship songs and recordings, as key religious identifiers, and thirdly the role that celebrity has played in offering an 'authentication' for a particular style of religious music consumerism.[49] US-based Christian music companies recognised a commercial opportunity in the worship music that was emerging from the UK. In signing artists, like Matt Redman and Martin Smith, however, a key driver, argues Myrick, was a perceived double authenticity that these British artists brought to the genre and it was this that American record executives and Churches bought into. These new worship leaders were seen as being authentic, firstly because of their apparent faithfulness to their belief, as it was experienced by those who shared in worship with them. Key to this sense of faithfulness, says Ingalls, was the role of 'gesture' in leading, that was interpreted as a genuine commitment to a style of worship.[50] These gestures did not simply give credence to the act of worship, they also focused attention on the worship leader themselves as the source and guarantor of authenticity. Closely linked to the notion of gesture in leading worship, was the fact that these musicians composed their own songs. They were seen as the 'real deal,' because these songs were their own heartfelt expression of faith.

The authenticity of the Celebrity Worship leader, however, was not limited to their personal beliefs. The new wave of Christian musician was expected to be rooted in the life of the local Church. This generally meant that the worship leader should be employed, and regularly active, leading worship in a congregation. Meyrick argues, that this connection to a local Church community, legitimated both the worship leader and the songs that they produced, as genuine, and a part of the ongoing spiritual experience of a group of worshiping Christians. The songs then, were distinct from entertainment, or the usual products of the Christian music industry.[51] These were artefacts that had a provenance in real spiritual experiences of actual communities. Fundamental to these processes of authentication was a concern to ensure that the worship leader was not seen primarily as an entertainer, or a performer. They were to be regarded as something distinct, a worship leader. The link to the local Church, resulted in a linked phenomenon where senior pastors and megachurches began to realise, that if they were to benefit from the new developments in worship, then they would need to include a prominent worship leader on their ministerial staff. The worship leader quickly became an essential component in a successful ministry. This phenomenon can be seen in the UK, where Mike Pilavachi launched the Soul Survivor Festival with the support of a young Matt Redman. Matt's songs, as much as Mike's preaching, became one of the distinctive features of Soul Survivor. A similar dynamic is seen in the US, where the worship leader Chris Tomlin, partnered with Louie Giglio to launch the Passion Festivals and Passion City Church.

The Christian Celebrity Worship leader is manufactured by a process of production that is based around the use of technology and an aesthetic that has been taken from the staging of large-scale rock concerts. Contemporary worship relies on sophisticated technology, not simply in terms of musical equipment and sound reproduction; technology extends to the sophisticated use of visual displays and staging. Worship events use live images of the worship leader to focus attention on the act of worship. Most events will be professionally lit, and the stages will be dressed to project a feel, and to create an image for the event. Visual projection for worship is more complex than that for a regular rock concert even, however, because lyrics as well as images of the band must be combined. These technological dynamics lie at the heart of what Myrick calls, the 'celebrity model' of worship. The playlist of the Celebrity Worship leader will include original compositions, but it will also reproduce the 'hits' of the worship scene. The most-played songs are recorded in the Christian Copyright Licensing International (CCLI) charts, and a selection from these most sung songs will generally form a part of the repertoire of most mainstream worship leaders. This generates a self-referential environment, where the celebrity status of worship leaders is effectively reinforced through the use of their songs, at both large events, and in smaller Churches. Linked to this use of songs is the way that the Christian worship scene has increasingly made use of streaming and YouTube to distribute their songs. These forms of technology mean that the songs, and the sophisticated production packages that they are marketed through, are easily accessible to local Churches. With this facility, however, there is also the continued focus on the worship leader as the one who conveys this material.[52] The Celebrity Worship leader is therefore, both constructed by this mediation, and distributed by it.

The authenticity of worship leaders carries within it a tension and contradiction. On the one hand, the concern within the Christian worship scene has been to create a distance between the worship leader as a performer, or as some kind of rock star. A range of strategies have been adopted, as part of the construction of the role of the worship leader, to facilitate a sensibility that locates them as in some way 'ordinary.' The idea that leading worship is a performance, or a 'gig', has been discouraged. At the same time, the ways in which the worship songs are promoted and presented, militate against this sensibility. The notion of authenticity, described by Meyrick, carries this tension within it. The worship leader is presented as a spiritual leader who is 'authentic' by being located in a community, but this construction itself creates a form of celebrity that rests on a perceived genuine spirituality.

Branding and the celebrity church

Alongside the rise of the celebrity preacher and the Celebrity Worship leader, there has been a parallel development of the Church itself as a celebrity. Central to this process has been the strong emphasis that has been placed on generating a distinctive brand, as part of a strategy for Church growth. One of the largest mega-church brands is Hillsong Church, that originated in the suburbs of Sydney, Australia. Originally founded in 1983, with 45 people attending it has grown to over 25,000 members in Sydney alone. In addition to this, Hillsong have a number of campus locations on five continents.[53] Contemporary worship music has been central to the identity of Hillsong to such an extent that the Church and the musical products that carry its name, have become almost synonymous. What Hillsong represents is a shift away from an evangelical strategy, where advertising and media was primarily regarded a means to disseminate a message, towards embracing the Church as a brand. Central to the notion of branding is the realisation that the Church should have a distinctive 'personality.'[54] Examples of branded Churches include: Holy Trinity Brompton in London with its Alpha Course, and Saddleback Church, led by Rick Warren, that has promoted the 'Purpose Driven Church' books and materials. These Churches have a brand identity, that is carried by media-generated commodities. The products have enabled the Churches to become more than a local congregation. They have global reach that is created through the marketing of distinctive forms of evangelical Christian communication. It is the use of media to communicate with a diffused global audience that characterises mega-churches as distinctive, rather than a particular theology or message.[55] Branding is the means by which these products develop an emotional connection with a wider audience. The brand operates as a personality that invites affective engagement from those who are drawn towards the products, and through processes of identification and the formation of group identities, related to the products and the events at which they are promoted, a connection is forged between the brand and evangelical Christians around the world. This process leads to a new form of evangelical celebrity: the celebrity Church.

The global reach of Hillsong has been facilitated by its widespread use of communication technologies. The Church was originally called 'Hills Christian Life Centre,' but in 2001 it changed its name to Hillsong Church. The name was originally used to refer to the worship music that the Church produced, distributed, and marketed under the label, Hillsongs, through the business linked to the Church, Hillsong Music Association. The shift in the name of the Church came about, because in everyday interactions, people began to refer to the Church as, Hillsong Church. According to Brian Houston, what lay behind this was that 'the name Hillsong actually became famous ... around the world.'[56] Central to the change in name was the intention that the focus should not be on celebrity individuals, but on the Church as the central personality or brand. Effectively the Church was to be the celebrity.

The evolution of the Church as a brand, has been traced by Tanya Riches and Tom Wagner, through the worship music, and the linked products and marketing that were released by Hillsong, between 1985 and 2012. Riches and Wagner identify five phases in the development of Hillsong. In the first phase the worship in the Church was led by Geoff Bullock, who released the first recording, a cassette tape, 'Spirit and Truth' in 1988. The second phase, from 1995 to 1997, was initiated under the leadership of the worship pastor, Darlene Zschech. Darlene remained with the Church until 2007. In phase two, links were made with a US-based music publishing company and record label. In

1993, Zschech released her song, 'Shout to the Lord,' and this became a huge hit in the US. As a result, Hillsong and Zschech were suddenly famous. At this time, Brian Houston claimed that, 'Shout to the Lord,' was sung by 35 million people every week.[57] In 1998, the Church's youth band 'United' released an album of original songs. Under guidance of Zschech, the band and their songs became closely allied to the identity of the Church. An example of this, cited by Riches and Wagner, is that the logo of Hillsong Church appeared, for the first time, on the cover artwork of United's releases. Phase four, reflected the international reach of Hillsong, with their London Church releasing worship albums. In 2008, the final phase, saw a consolidation, with London releases being closed down, and 'Hillsong LIVE' being marketed, as the expression of the worship of the global congregation, and 'United' being the label for touring worship events. Hillsong Music Association, at this point signed a deal with Sony EMI, that launched them firmly onto the global scene. The phases identified by Riches and Wagner, correspond to a gradual shift in the way that Hillsong marketed itself through its music.[58] These changes are evident in the cover artwork of Hillsong LIVE albums over the five phases of the development of the Church.

The early albums that emerge from Hillsong are characterised by a series of landscape photographs. The images feature the photography of Australian artist, Ken Duncan. Each of these images emphasise the 'Australianness' of the product, with pictures of Sydney Harbour Bridge, and other recognisable landscapes from the country. In the second and third phases, the images on the worship albums shift towards key individuals, both song leaders and musicians. The most frequent individual that is featured, at this stage, is Darlene Zschech. In some of these images, Darlene is seen singing, but there are also images of the Australian landscape that are used as part of the montage. In 2002, the cover art starts to include images of the congregation worshipping, and the Hillsong logo is also part of the representation. In phase four, with the release of the Hillsong LIVE franchise in 2006, the depiction of the congregation worshipping becomes more prominent, along with a number of worship leaders, featured on the album. By the final phase, the branding of Hillsong has become fully integrated in all of the products released by the Church. Images on the cover art showcase the global nature of the congregations. Riches and Wagner describe this as, a moment when the Church is represented as a, 'tribal community of discourse.' Individual worship performers are replaced by more collective and congregational imagery. It is 'the church that is visually presented as the artist.'[59]

Celebritisation and evangelical Christianity

The history of contemporary forms of evangelical Christianity has been decisively shaped by the use of media. Motivated by the desire to find ways to share faith with as many people as possible, successive generations have harnessed the media to their cause. The use of media has, however, not been without its problems. The use of media effectively catapulted preachers, worship leaders and eventually churches, into a level of fame that both enabled communication but also led to recurring scandals and negative media coverage. The dynamic of the rise and fall within Celebrity Culture more generally was often played out in the evangelical subculture. Adopting the forms of communication that different media platforms and technologies have made available has led to success in terms of numbers and economic benefit, but it has also reshaped how authority and leadership functions in these churches. Media profile has given individuals a platform and a position that arises from their abilities to perform to the camera and project themselves through social media. These processes sideline more traditional structures of authority and allow individuals to build their own Churches and organisations without reference to denominations. Similarly, the faithfulness of congregational members becomes increasingly associated with the products that are generated by these Churches and celebrity individuals. These are powerful forces and it is clear that Churches such as Hillsong seek to manoeuvre in this new and dynamic space, in ways that make use of forms of communication while trying to follow a theological vision.

Notes

1 Rob Bell. *Love Wins: A Book About Heaven, Hell and the Fate of Every Person Who Ever Lived.* (New York: Harper Collins, 2011).
2 Jon Meacham. 'Pastor Rob Bell: What if Hell Doesn't Exist?' *Time,* 4 April 2011.
3 Meacham. Pastor.
4 David Van Biema. 'The Hipper-Than-Thou Pastor.' *Time,* 6 December 2007.
5 Van Biema. The Hipper.
6 John Pavlovitz. 'What the Continued Crucifying of Rob Bell Says about Modern Christianity.' https://johnpavlovitz.com/2014/12/10/the-continued-crucifying-of-rob-bell-and-what-it-says-about-the-state-of-modern-christianity/.
7 Nathan Hatch. *The Democratisation of American Christianity.* (New Haven, CT: Yale University Press, 1989).
8 Hatch. *The Democratisation,* 5.
9 Hatch. *The Democratisation,* 211.
10 Hatch. *The Democratisation,* 211.
11 Harry Stout. *The Divine Dramatist: George Whitefield and the Rise of Modern Evangelicalism.* (Grand Rapids, MN: Eerdmans, 1991).
12 *Christianity Today.* 'Billy Sunday Salty Evangelist.' www.christianitytoday.com/history/people/evangelistsandapologists/billy-sunday.html.
13 Margaret Bendroth. 'Why Women Loved Billy Sunday: Urban Revivalism and Popular Entertainment in Early Twentieth-Century American Culture.' *Religion and American Culture: A Journal of Interpretation,* 14, no. 2 (Summer 2004): 251.
14 Bendroth. Why, 255.
15 Bendroth. Why, 255.
16 Bendroth. Why, 252.
17 Bendroth. Why, 253.
18 Bendroth. Why, 257.
19 Bendroth. Why, 260.

20 Healing and Revival. 'The Foursquare Gospel.' https://healingandrevival.com/BioASMcPherson.htm.

21 David Edwin Harrell. 'Oral Roberts Media Pioneer.' In *Communication and Change in American Religious History*. Edited by Leonard Sweet. (Grand Rapids, MN: Eerdmans, 1993), 320.

22 Matthew Avery Sutton. *Aimee Semple McPherson and the Resurrection of Christian America*. (Cambridge: Cambridge University Press, 2007), 269.

23 Sutton. *Aimee*, 270.

24 Scott Thumma, Dave Travis and Rick Warren. *Beyond Megachurch Myths: What We Can Learn from America's Largest Churches*. (New York: John Wiley and Sons, 2007).

25 Jessica Johnson. 'Megachurches, Celebrity Pastors, and the Evangelical Industrial Complex.' In *Religion and Popular Culture in America*. Edited by Forbes Bruce and Jeffrey Mahan. (Oakland, CA: University of California Press, 2017, 3rd Edition), 160.

26 Johnson. Megachurches, 160.

27 Johnson. Megachurches, 162.

28 Johnson. Megachurches, 163.

29 Johnson. Megachurches, 164.

30 Mark Driscoll. *Real Marriage: The Truth about Sex, Friendship, and Life Together*. (Nashville, TN: Thomas Nelson, 2012).

31 Donald Miller. *Blue Like Jazz: Non-Religious Thoughts on Christian Spirituality*. (Nashville, TN: Thomas Nelson, 2003).

32 Sarah Bailey. 'Controversial Preacher Mark Driscoll Stripped from Hillsong Conference Line-up.' *The Washington Post*, 2 June 2015.

33 *Premier Christianity*. 'The Rise and Fall of Mark Driscoll.' www.premierchristianity.com/Past-Issues/2014/December-2014/The-rise-and-fall-of-Mark-Driscoll.

34 *Premier Christianity*. Rise.

35 Ruth Graham. 'The Evangelical Celebrity Machine.' *Slate* 11 December 2013. https://slate.com/human-interest/2013/12/mark-driscoll-plagiarism-accusations-janet-mefferd-accused-the-seattle-pastor-on-air-and-then-backed-down-what-happened.html.

36 Alex Murashko. 'Mark Driscoll Remains Silent as Circle of Plagiarism Accusation Now Includes Questions on Ghostwriting; John Piper Chimes in on Twitter.' *The Christian Post*, 12 December 2013. www.christianpost.com/news/mark-driscoll-remains-silent-as-circle-of-plagiarism-accusations-now-includes-questions-on-ghostwriting-john-piper-chimes-in-on-twitter.html.

37 Graham. The Evangelical.

38 Valerie Tarico. 'Christian Right Mega-Church Minister Faces Mega-Mutiny for Alleged Abusive Behaviour.' *Salon*, 3 April, 2014. www.salon.com/control/2014/04/03/christian_right_mega_church_minister_faces_mega_muntiny_for_abusive_behavior_partner/.

39 Swee Hong Lim and Ruth Lester. *Lovin' on Jesus: A Concise History of Contemporary Worship*. (Nashville, TN: Abingdon Press, 2017).

40 Steven Tipton. *Getting Saved from the Sixties*. (Berkeley, CA: University of California Press, 1982).

41 Pete Ward. *Selling Worship*. (Milton Keynes: Paternoster, 2005).

42 Nathan Myrick. 'Double Authenticity: Celebrity, Consumption, and the Christian Worship Music Industry.' *The Hymn*, 69, no. 2 (2018) 22.

43 Ward. *Selling*.

44 Monique Ingalls, 'Contemporary Worship Music.' In *Continuum Encyclopedia of Popular Music of the World*, Volume 8. (London: Continuum, 2012).

45 Ward. *Selling*. Ingalls. Contemporary, 149.

46 Robert Warner. *Reinventing English Evangelicalism 1966–2001.* (Milton Keynes: Paternoster, 2007).
47 Ingalls. Contemporary, 150.
48 Myrick. Double, 24.
49 Nathan Myrick. 'Celebrity Model of Music Ministry: Characteristics and Consideration.' *The Hymn,* 69, no. 3. (2018).
50 Myrick. Celebrity, 24.
51 Myrick. Celebrity, 24.
52 Myrick. Celebrity, 26.
53 Tanya Riches and Tom Wagner. 'The evolution of Hillsong Music: From Australian Pentecostal Congregation into Global Brand.' *Australian Journal of Communication,* 39, no. 1 (2012): 21.
54 Riches and Wagner. The evolution, 19.
55 Riches and Wagner. The evolution, 20.
56 Riches and Wagner. The evolution, 21.
57 Riches and Wagner. The evolution, 23.
58 Riches and Wagner. The evolution, 23.
59 Riches and Wagner. The evolution, 30.

Bibliography

1 John 4:18 *New Revised Standard Version* (NRSV)

Abdin, Crystal. *Internet Celebrity: Understanding Fame Online.* Bingley: Emerald Publishing, 2018.

Adorno, Theodore. *The Culture Industry.* London: Routledge, 1991.

Alberoni, Francesco. 'The powerless elite: theory and sociological research on the phenomenon of the stars.' In *The Celebrity Culture Reader.* Edited by David Marshall, 108–123. London: Routledge, 2006.

Arnold, Matthew. *Culture and Anarchy.* Cambridge: Cambridge University Press, 1869.

Artlyst. 'George Michael Wham Graffiti Poster.' 14 September 2010. www.artlyst.com/news/george-michael-sentenced-latest-wham-graffiti-photo/.

Arzumanova, Inna. 'The Culture Industry and Beyoncé's Proprietary Blackness.' *Celebrity Studies* 7(3) July 2016: 421–424.

Bailey, Sarah. 'Controversial Preacher Mark Driscoll Stripped from Hillsong Conference Line-up.' *The Washington Post,* 2 June 2015.

Barron, Lee. *Celebrity Cultures.* London: Sage, 2014.

Barthes, Roland. *Mythologies.* London: Paladin Books, 1957 (English Translation 1972).

Bayley, Leanne. 'Cilla Black's Funeral: Friends and Family Pay Respects.' In *Glamour Magazine,* 20 August 2015. www.glamourmagazine.co.uk/article/cilla-black-has-died-aged-72-celebrity-tributes.

BBC News. 'Iran: Happy Video Dancers Sentenced to 91 Lashes and Jail.' 19 September 2014. www.bbc.co.uk/news/world-middle-east-29272732.

BBC News. 'David Cameron 'I won't serve third term' (EXCLUSIVE).' 23 March 2015. www.youtube.com/watch?v=rG0T2UqDqO8.

BBC News. 'Worshipping Celebrities Brings Success.' Last updated 13 August 2013. http://news.bbc.co.uk/1/hi/health/3147343.stm.

Beaudoin, Tom. *Virtual Faith: The Irreverent Spirituality of Generation X.* San Francisco, CA: Jossey Bass, 1998.

Bell, Rob. *Love Wins: A Book About Heaven, Hell and the Fate of Every Person Who Ever Lived.* New York: Harper Collins, 2011.

Benbow, Candice. 'Beyonce's "Lemonade" and Black Christian Women's Spirituality.' *Religion and Politics,* 28 June 2016. https://religionandpolitics.org/2016/06/28/beyonces-lemonade-and-black-christian-womens-spirituality/.

Bendroth, Margaret. 'Why Women Loved Billy Sunday: Urban Revivalism and Popular Entertainment in Early Twentieth-Century American Culture.' *Religion and American Culture: A Journal of Interpretation* 14(2) (Summer 2004): 251–271.

Berger, Peter and Luckmann, Thomas. *The Social Construction of Reality.* London: Penguin, 1966.

Bernstein, Jacob. 'Stand Back: Sandra Bernhard Speaks Her Mind.' *Women's Wear Daily,* 4 June 2009. https://wwd.com/eye/people/stand-back-sandra-bernhard-speaks-her-mind-2156863/.

Biressi, Anita and Nunn, Heather. *Reality TV: Realism and Revelation.* London: Wallflower Press, 2005.

Black, Jack. 'The Reification of Celebrity: Global Newspaper Coverage of the Death of David Bowie.' *International Review of Sociology* 27(1) 2017: 202–224.

Boorstein, Daniel. From Hero to Celebrity: The Human Pseudo Event. In *The Celebrity Culture Reader.* Edited by David Marshall, 72–79. London: Routledge, 2006.

Bourdieu, Pierre. *Distinction: A Social Critique of the Judgement of Taste.* London: Routledge, 1984.

Boyd, Malcolm. *Christ and Celebrity Gods.* Greenwich, CT: Seabury Press, 1958.

Braudy, Leo. The longing of Alexander. In *The Celebrity Culture Reader.* Edited by David Marshall, 35–54. London: Routledge, 2006.

Brockington, Dan. 'Towards an International Understanding of the Power of Celebrity Persuasions: A Review and a Research Agenda.' *Journal of Celebrity Studies* 6(4) (2015): 486–504.

Brunsdon, Charlotte. 'Feminism, Post Feminism, Martha and Nigella.' *Cinema Journal* 44 (2) (Winter 2005): 110–116.

Calderwood, Imogen. '88% of People Who Saw *Blue Planet II* Have Now Changed Their Lifestyle.' *Global Citizen,* 1 November 2018. www.globalcitizen.org/en/content/88-blue-planet-2-changed-david-attenborough/.

Campbell, Heidi. *When Religion Meets New Media.* London: Routledge, 2010.

Carroll, Helen. 'How Noel Edmonds, 69, got Tarzan's body for the I'm a Celebrity Jungle – Using Electromagnetic Mats, Japanese Workouts and … a Glass of Champagne a Day.' *Daily Mail,* 27 November 2018.

Cashmore, Ellis. *Celebrity/Culture.* London: Routledge, 2006.

CBS News 'Celebrity Plastic Surgery Disasters.' www.cbsnews.com/pictures/celebrity-plastic-surgery-disasters/8/.

Christianity Today. 'Billy Sunday Salty Evangelist.' www.christianitytoday.com/history/people/evangelistsandapologists/billy-sunday.html.

Cockcroft, Lucy. 'Cult of Celebrity is "Harming Children."' *The Telegraph,* 14 March 2008. www.telegraph.co.uk/news/uknews/1581658/Cult-of-celebrity-is-harming-children.html.

Coleman, Mark. 'Michael Jackson is Dead: Fans Mourn Outside Hospital.' *The Daily Telegraph,* 26 June 2009. www.telegraph.co.uk/culture/music/michael-jackson/5645517/Michael-Jackson-is-dead-fans-mourn-outside-hospital.html.

Cosmopolitan. 'The Nation is Obsessed with Kate Middleton's Amazing Style.' 6 March 2019. www.cosmopolitan.com/uk/fashion/celebrity/g3517/kate-middletons-outfits-style-fashion/.

Courbet, Didier and Fouquet-Courbet, Marie-Pierre. 'When a Celebrity Dies … Social Identity, Uses of Social Media, and the Mourning Process Among Fans: The Case of Michael Jackson.' *Celebrity Studies* 5(3) (2014): 275–290.

Crux. 'Lady Gaga's Mass Pics and Posts on Faith Stir Catholic Reaction.' 11 May 2016. https://cruxnow.com/church/2016/05/11/lady-gagas-mass-pics-and-posts-on-faith-stir-catholic-reaction/.

Davie, William R., King, C. Richard and Leonard, David J. 'A Media Look at Tiger Woods – Two Views.' *Journal of Sports Media* 5(2) (Fall 2010): 107–116.

Davies, Douglas. The week of mourning. In *Mourning Diana*. Edited by Tony Walter, 3–18. New York: Berg, 1999.

Davies, Ioan. *Cultural Studies and Beyond Fragments of Empire*. London: Routledge, 1995.

Day, Abby and Lee, Lois. 'Making Sense of Surveys and Censuses: Issues in Religious Self-Identification.' *Religion* 44(3) (2014): 345–356.

DeCordova, Richard. The discourse on acting. In *The Celebrity Culture Reader*. Edited by David Marshall, 91–107. London: Routledge, 2006.

Doss, Erica. Elvis forever. In *Afterlife as After Image: Understanding Posthumous Celebrity*. Edited by Steve Jones and Joli Henson, 61–80. New York: Peter Lang, 2005.

Driscoll, Mark. *Real Marriage: The Truth about Sex, Friendship, and Life Together*. Nashville, TN: Thomas Nelson, 2012.

du Gay, Paul, Hall, Stuart, Janes, Linda, Mackay, Hugh and Negus, Keith eds. *Doing Cultural Studies: The Story of the Sony Walkman*. London: Sage, 2013.

Durham, Aisha. '"Check On It": Beyonce, Southern Booty, and Black Femininities in Music Video.' *Feminist Media Studies* 12(1) (2011): 35–49.

Dyer, Richard. *Heavenly Bodies: Film Stars and Society*. London: Routledge, 1986.

Edwards, Katie. 'How Beyonce's Virgin Mary Imagery Challenges Racist, Religious and Sexual Stereotypes.' *The Washington Post*, 14 July 2017. www.washingtonpost.com/news/acts-of-faith/wp/2017/07/14/how-beyonces-virgin-mary-imagery-challenges-racist-religious-and-sexual-stereotypes/?utm_term=.40219f3afbfa.

Elliott, Anthony. 'I Want to Look like That: Cosmetic Surgery and Celebrity Culture.' *Cultural Sociology* 5(4) (2011): 463–477.

Elliott, Anthony, and Lemert, Charles. *The New Individualism: The Emotional Costs of Globalization*. London: Routledge, 2006.

Ellison, Jenny. Not Jane Fonda: aerobics for fat women only. In *The Fat Studies Reader*. Edited by Esther Rothblum and Sondra Solova, 312–319. New York: New York University Press, 2009.

Feasey, Rebecca. Get a famous body: star styles and celebrity gossip in *Heat* magazine. In *Framing Celebrity: New Directions in Celebrity Culture*. Edited by Su Holmes and Sean Redmond, 177–194. London: Routledge, 2006.

Fletcher, Robert. 'Blinded by the Stars? Celebrity, Fantasy, and Desire in Neoliberal Environmental Governance.' *Journal of Celebrity Studies* 6(4) (2015): 457–470.

Forbes, Bruce and Mahan, Jeffrey (eds). *Religion and Popular Culture in America*. Berkeley, CA: University of California Press, 2017 (3rd edn).

Freitas, Donna. *The Happiness Effect: How Social Media is Driving a Generation to Appear Perfect at Any Cost*. Oxford: Oxford University Press, 2017.

Frith, Mark. *The Celeb Diaries: The Sensational Story of the Celebrity Decade*. London: Ebury Press, 2008.

Frow, John. 'Is Elvis God? Cult, Culture, Questions of Method.' *International Journal of Cultural Studies* 1(2) (1998): 197–210.

Gaga interview, MTV News, 25 April 2011.

Gaga interview, Skorpion Show, 23 February 2011.

Gamson, Joshua. *Claims to Fame: Celebrity in Contemporary America*. Berkeley, CA: University of California Press, 1994.

Gamson, Joshua. 'The Unwatched Life Is Not Worth Living: The Elevation of the Ordinary in Celebrity Culture.' *Theories and Methodologies* 126(4) (2011): 1061–1069.

Giddens, Anthony. *Modernity and Self Identity*. Cambridge: Polity Press, 1991.

Graham, Ruth. 'The Evangelical Celebrity Machine.' *Slate*, 11 December 2013. https://slate.com/human-interest/2013/12/mark-driscoll-plagiarism-accusations-janet-m
efferd-accused-the-seattle-pastor-on-air-and-then-backed-down-what-happened.html.

Graves-Fitzsimmons, Guthrie. 'The Provocative Faith of Lady Gaga.' *The Washington Post*, 5 February 2017. www.washingtonpost.com/news/acts-of-faith/wp/2017/02/05/the-gospel-according-to-lady-gaga/?utm_term=.183c1365d5f1.

Gray, Richard, ed. *The Performance Identities of Lady Gaga: Critical Essays*. Jefferson, NC: McFarland, 2012.

Gye, Hugo and Mullin, Gemma. 'Has Cliff Ever Sung a Song That Meant More to Him? Tearful Singer Belts Out Emotional Farewell to His Friend.' *MailOnline*, 20 August 2015. www.dailymail.co.uk/news/article-3204595/Cilla-Black-funeral-takes-places-Liverpool.html.

Halberstam, Jack. *Gaga Feminism: Sex, Gender and the End of Normal*. Boston, MA: Beacon Press, 2012.

Hall, Stuart. Encoding/decoding. In *Culture, Media, Language: Working Papers in Cultural Studies, 1972–79*. Edited by Stuart Hall, Dorothy Hobson, Andrew Lowe, and Paul Willis, 128–138. London: Hutchinson, 1973.

Hall, Stuart. On postmodernism and articulation: an interview with Stuart Hall. In *Stuart Hall: Critical Dialogues in Cultural Studies*. Edited by David Morley and Chen Kuan-Hsing, 131–150. London: Routledge, 1996.

Harrell, David Edwin. Oral Roberts: Religious Media Pioneer. In *Communication and Change in American Religious History*. Edited by Leonard Sweet, 320–334. Grand Rapids, MN: Eerdmans, 1993.

Harvey, David. *The Condition of Postmodernity*. Oxford: Blackwell, 1989.

Hatch, Nathan. *The Democratisation of American Christianity*. New Haven, CT: Yale University Press, 1989.

Havitz, Mark, and Dimanche, Frederick. 'Leisure Involvement Revisited: Conceptual Conundrums and Measurement Advances.' *Journal of Leisure Research* 29(3) (1997): 245–278.

Hawkes, Rebecca and Saunders, Tristram Fane. 'Ariana Grande One Love Manchester Concert: Fans Shower Ariana with Praise after Moving, Joyous Night.' *The Telegraph*, 5 June 2017. www.telegraph.co.uk/music/what-to-listen-to/ariana-grande-one-love-manchester-concert-live/.

Healing and Revival. 'The Foursquare Gospel.' https://healingandrevival.com/BioASMcPherson.htm.

Heelas, Paul. *The New Age Movement*. Oxford: Blackwell, 1996.

Heelas, Paul and Woodhead, Linda. *Spiritual Revolution: Why Religion is Giving Way to Spirituality*. Oxford: Blackwell, 2005.

Hjarvard, Stig. 'The Mediatisation of Religion: A Theory of the Media as Agents of Religious Change.' *Northern Lights* 6 (2008).

Hjarvard, Stig. 'The Mediatization of Religion: Theorising Religion, Media and Social Change.' *Culture and Religion* 12(2) (2011): 119–135.

Hjarvard, Stig. *The Mediatization of Culture and Society*. London: Routledge, 2013.

Hjarvard, Stig. 'Mediatization and the Changing Authority of Religion: Media Culture and Society.' *Media, Culture and Society* 38(1) (2016): 8–17.

Hollows, Joanne. 'Feeling Like a Domestic Goddess: Postfeminism and Cooking.' *European Journal of Cultural Studies* 6(2) (2003): 179–202.

Holmes, Su and Redmond, Sean. 'A Journal in Celebrity Studies.' *Celebrity Studies* 1(1) (2010): 1–10.

Hoover, Stuart. *Religion in the Media Age*. London: Routledge, 2006.

Hoover, Stuart and Lundby, Knut, eds. *Rethinking Media Religion and Culture*. London: Sage, 1997.

Horton, Donald and Wohl, Richard R. 'Mass communication and Para-social Interaction: Observations on Intimacy at a Distance.' *Psychiatry: Interpersonal and Biological Processes* 19(3) (1956): 215–229.

Howells, Richard. 'Heroes, Saints and Celebrities: The Photograph as Holy Relic.' *Celebrity Studies* 2(2) (2011): 112–130.

Huss, Boaz. 'The New Age of Kabbalah: Contemporary Kabbalah, the New Age and Postmodern Spirituality.' *Journal of Modern Jewish Studies* 6(2) (2007): 107–125.

Hutchings, Timothy. *Creating Church Online: Ritual, Community and New Media*. London: Routledge, 2017.

Hutton, Jen. 'God and the "Gaze": A Visual Reading of Lady Gaga.' In *Chicago Art Magazine*, 2 July 2010. http://chicagoartmagazine.com/2010/07/god-and-the-'ga ze'-a-visual-reading-of-lady-gaga/.

Ingalls, Monique. Contemporary worship music. In *Continuum Encyclopedia of Popular Music of the World Volume 8*. Edited by David Horn and John Shepherd, 147–152. London: Continuum, 2012.

Ingalls, Monique. Transnational Connections, Musical Meaning, and the 1990s 'British Invasion' of North American Evangelical Worship Music. In *The Oxford Handbook of Music and World Christianities*. Edited by Jonathan Dueck and Suzei Ana Reilly. Oxford: Oxford University Press, 2016.

Instagram. ladygaga. www.instagram.com/p/BFO1b9rpFFC/?hl=en.

Jenkins, Henry. *Convergence Culture: Where Old and New Media Collide*. New York: New York University Press, 2006.

Johnson, Jessica. Megachurches, celebrity pastors, and the evangelical industrial complex. In *Religion and Popular Culture in America*. Edited by Bruce Forbes and Jeffrey Mahan, 159–176. Oakland, CA: University of California Press, 2017 (3rd edn).

Johnson, Lorie. 'Music Superstar Katy Perry Denounces Her Devoutedly Christian Upbringing.' CBN News, 20 April 2017. www1.cbn.com/cbnnews/entertainment/2017/april/music-superstar-katy-perry-denounces-her-devoutly-christian-upbringing.

Jones, Steve. Better off dead: or making it the hard way. In *Afterlife as After Image: Understanding Posthumous Celebrity*. Edited by Steve Jones and Joli Henson, 3–16. New York: Peter Lang, 2005.

Katee, Annita. 'Kylie Jenner Gets Pulses Racing as She Flashes Her Flat Midriff During Valentine's Day Makeup Tutorial.' *Daily Mail*, 31 January 2019.

Khamisa, Susie, Ang, Lawrence and Welling, Raymond. 'Self-branding, "Micro-celebrity" and the Rise of Social Media Influencers.' *Celebrity Studies* 8(2) (2017): 191–208.

Klopp, Jacques. 'Britain's Party Leaders Throw Kitchen Sink at the Election.' *Business Insider*, 1 May 2015.

Kumari, Ashanka. '"Yoü and I": Identity and the Performance of Self in Lady Gaga and Beyoncé.' *Journal of Popular Culture* 49(2) (2016): 403–416.

Laderman, Gary. *Sacred Matters: Celebrity Worship, Sexual Ecstasies, The Living Dead, and Other Signs of Religious Life in the United States.* New York: The New Press, 2009.

Laderman, Gary. 'Michael Jackson's Death: Does Fame Trump Faith.' Beliefnet www. beliefnet.com/faiths/2009/michael-jacksons-death-funerals-faith-and-fame.aspx.

Langer, John. 'Television's "Personality System".' *Media Society and Culture* 4 (1981): 351–365.

Leavis, Frank R. Mass civilisation and minority culture. In *Cultural Theory and Popular Culture: A Reader.* Edited by John Storey, 12–21. Hemel Hempstead: Harvester Wheatsheaf, 1994.

Lee, Lois. 'Secular or Nonreligious? Investigating and Interpreting Generic 'Not Religious' Categories and Populations.' *Religion* 44 (2014): 466–482.

Lim, Swee Hong and Lester, Ruth. *Lovin' on Jesus: A Concise History of Contemporary Worship.* Nashville, TN: Abingdon Press, 2017.

Lofton, Kathryn. *Consuming Religion.* Chicago, IL: University of Chicago Press, 2017.

Lofton, Kathryn. *Oprah The Gospel of an Icon.* Berkeley, CA: University of California Press, 2011.

Lynch, Gordon, ed. *Between Sacred and Profane: Researching Religion and Popular Culture.* London: I.B. Tauris, 2007.

MacKenzie, Donald and Wajcman, Judy. *The Social Shaping of Technology.* Buckingham, UK: Open University Press, 1999.

Mahan, Jeffrey. *Media Religion and Culture: An Introduction.* London: Routledge, 2014.

Maltby, John, Houran, James and McCutcheon, Lynn. 'A Clinical Interpretation of Attitudes and Behaviors Associated with Celebrity Worship.' *The Journal of Nervous and Mental Disease* 191(1) (2003): 25–29.

Mansfield, Louise. '"Sexercise": Working Out Heterosexuality in Jane Fonda's Fitness Books.' *Leisure Studies* 30(2) (2011): 237–255.

Marcy, Christie. 'Concert Review: Elvis Lives at Eccles.' *Salt Lake Magazine*, 19 February 2017. www.saltlakemagazine.com/concert-review-elvis-lives-eccles/.

Marshall, David. New media – new self. In *The Celebrity Culture Reader.* Edited by David Marshall, 634–644. London: Routledge, 2006.

Marshall, David. 'The Promotion and Presentation of Self: Celebrity as Marker of Presentational Media.' *Celebrity Studies* 1(1) (2010): 35–48.

Marthe, Emily. 'Why Celebrities Stopped Following Kabbalah.' *Vice*, 21 May 2017. www.vice.com/en_us/article/mbqvmy/why-celebrities-stopped-following-kabbalah.

Marwick, Alice E. 'Instafame: Luxury Selfies in the Attention Economy.' *Public Culture* 27(75) (2015): 137–160.

Mason, Ann and Meyers, Marian. 'Living with Martha Stewart Media.' *Cinema Journal* 44(2) (Winter 2005): 110–116.

McCutcheon, Lynn. 'Conceptualization and Measurement of Celebrity Worship.' *British Journal of Psychiatry* 93(1) (2002): 67–87.

McGuigan, Jim. *Cultural Populism.* London: Routledge, 1992.

McGuire, Meredith B. *Lived Religion: Faith and Practice in Everyday Life.* Oxford: Oxford University Press, 2008.

McLuhan, Marshall. *Understanding Media: The Extensions of the Self.* London: Routledge, 1964.

Meacham, Jon. 'Pastor Rob Bell: What if Hell Doesn't Exist?' *Time*, 14 April 2011.

Miller, Donald. *Blue Like Jazz: Non-Religious Thoughts on Christian Spirituality.* Nashville, TN: Thomas Nelson, 2003.

Miller, Vincent. *Consuming Religion: Christian Faith and Practice in a Consumer Culture.* London: Bloomsbury, 2004.

Moodie, Clemmie. 'Gary Barlow on Shedding Five Stone – But He Didn't Need a Fad Diet to Do It.' *Mirror*, 30 November 2013. www.mirror.co.uk/3am/celebrity-news/ gary-barlow-shedding-five-stone-2866963.

Morin, Edgar. *The Stars.* Minneapolis: University of Minnesota Press, 1972. (English translation 2005).

Murashko, Alex. 'Mark Driscoll Remains Silent as Circle of Plagiarism Accusation Now Includes Questions on Ghostwriting; John Piper Chimes in on Twitter.' *The Christian Post*, 12 December 2013. www.christianpost.com/news/mark-driscoll-remains-silent-as-cir cle-of-plagiarism-accusations-now-includes-questions-on-ghostwriting-john-piper-chim es-in-on-twitter.html.

Musings of a Renegade Futurist. 'Black Secret Technology: Beyonce's Formation.' 7 February 2016. https://netarthud.wordpress.com/2016/02/07/black-secret-technolo gy-beyonces-formation/.

Myers, Jody. *The Kabbalah Centre and Contemporary Spirituality.* Northridge, CA: California State University, 2008.

Myrick, Nathan. 'Celebrity Model of Music Ministry: Characteristics and Consideration.' *The Hymn* 69(3) (2018a).

Myrick, Nathan. 'Double Authenticity: Celebrity, Consumption, and the Christian Worship Music Industry.' *The Hymn* 69(2) (2018): 21–27.

New York Post. 'Beymaculate Conception.' 2 February 2017. https://nypost.com/cover/ covers-for-february-2-2017/.

NME. 'Coldplay's Chris Martin Declares Religious Belies – Daily Gossip.' 3 June 2008. www.nme.com/news/music/daily-gossip-587-1333314#zj6rr0aMzwwIMzuP.99.

Norman, Matthew. 'David Cameron's Kitchen: A Microcosm of the Hierarchical Society a Tory Victory Would Give Us.' *Independent*, 20 March 2015.

Nunn, Heather and Biressi, Anita. '"A Trust Betrayed": Celebrity and the Work of Emotion.' *Celebrity Studies* 1(1) (2010): 49–64.

Okeowo, Alexis. 'The Provocateur Behind Beyonce, Rihanna, and Issa Rae.' *The New Yorker*, 2 February 2017. www.newyorker.com/magazine/2017/03/06/the-provoca teur-behind-beyonce-rihanna-and-issa-rae.

O'Malley Greenburg, Zack. 'The Highest-Paid Dead Celebrities of 2018.' *Forbes List*, 31 October 2018. www.forbes.com/sites/zackomalleygreenburg/2018/10/31/the- highest-paid-dead-celebrities-of-2018/.

O'Regan, Valerie. 'The Celebrity Influence: Do People Really Care What They Think?' *Celebrity Studies* 5(4) (2014): 469–483.

O'Reilly, Tim. 'What is Web 2.0: Design Patterns and Business Models for the Next Generation of Software.' *Communications and Strategies* 1 (2007): 17–38.

Paglia, Camille. *Sex, Art and American Culture.* New York: Vintage, 1992.

Pavlovitz, John. 'What the Continued Crucifying of Rob Bell Says about Modern Christianity.' https://johnpavlovitz.com/2014/12/10/the-continued-crucifying-of-rob-bell-a nd-what-it-says-about-the-state-of-modern-christianity/.

Pidd, Helen and Halliday, Josh. '"Let's Not Be Afraid": Ariana Grande Returns to Manchester.' *The Guardian*, 5 June 2017.

Postman, Neil. *Amusing Ourselves to Death.* London: Penguin, 1985.

'The Rise and Fall of Mark Driscoll.' *Premier Christianity*, December 2014. www.premier christianity.com/Past-Issues/2014/December-2014/The-rise-and-fall-of-Mark-Driscoll.

Radford, Scott K. and Bloch, Peter H. 'Grief, Commiseration, and Consumption Following the Death of a Celebrity.' *Journal of Consumer Culture* 12(2) (2012): 137–155.

Read, Carly. 'Royally Bizarre: Princess Charlotte's Face "Appears" in Meghan Markle's Knees.' *Express*, 17 January 2019.

Redmond, Sean. 'Who am I now? Remembering the Enchanted Dogs of David Bowie.' *Celebrity Studies* 4(3) (2013): 380–383.

Respers, Lisa. 'Celine Dion on Criticism She's Too Thin: "Leave Me Alone."' *CNN Entertainment*, 31 January 2019.

Richards, Jeffrey, Wilson, Scott and Woodhead, Linda eds. *Diana the Making of a Media Saint*. London: I.B. Tauris, 1999.

Riches, Tanya and Wagner, Tom. 'The Evolution of Hillsong Music: From Australian Pentecostal Congregation into Global Brand.' *Australian Journal of Communication* 39 (1) (2012): 17–36.

Riley-Smith, Ben. 'Ed "Two Kitchens" Miliband: Politicians and the Photos that Inadvertently Come to Define Them.' *Telegraph*, 17 May 2019.

Roberts, Stephen. 'Beyond the Classic: Lady Gaga and Theology in the Wild Public Space.' *International Journal of Public Theology* 11 (2017): 163–187.

Rojek, Chris. *Celebrity*. London: Reaktion Books, 2001.

Roof, Wade Clark. *Spiritual Marketplace: Baby Boomers and the Remaking of American Religion*. Princeton, NJ: Princeton University Press, 1999.

Ryan, Harriet. 'Philip Berg Dies: Controversial Kabbalah Rabbi with Celebrity Followers.' *The Washington Post*, 21 September 2013.

Sastre, Alexandra. 'Hottentot in the Age of Reality TV: Sexuality, Race, and Kim Kardashian's Visible Body.' *Celebrity Studies* 5(1–2) (2013): 123–137.

Saul, Heather. 'Lady Gaga Answers Religious Blogger Over Claims about Catholic Celebrities.' *Independent*, 11 May 2016. www.independent.co.uk/news/people/lady-gaga-answers-religious-blogger-over-claims-about-catholic-celebrities-a7024376.html.

Saunders, Emmeline and Kindon, Frances. 'Troubled Ant McPartlin's Car Crash Revealed to be his Third in Three Weeks.' *The Mirror*, 20 March 2018.

Schofield Clark, Lynn. 'Considering Religion and Mediatisation through a Case Study of *J+K's Bbig Day* (The J K Wedding Entrance Dance): A response to Stig Hjarvard.' *Culture and Religion* 12(2) (2011): 167–184.

Schultze, Quentin J. 'Evangelical Radio and the Rise of the Electronic Church, 1921–1948.' *Journal of Broadcasting & Electronic Media* 32(3) (1988): 289–306.

Sergeant, Philip and Caroline, Tagg, eds. *The Language of Social Media: Identity and Community on the Internet*. Basingstoke: Palgrave, 2014.

Sherwood, Harriet. 'Preaching to the Converted: How Kabbalah Keeps on Growing.' *The Guardian*, 26 October 2015.

Smith, Christian. *Soul Searching: The Religious and Spiritual Lives of American Teenagers*. Oxford: Oxford University Press, 2005.

Stam, Orin. *The Passion of Tiger Woods*. Durham: Duke University Press, 2011.

Stout, Daniel. *Media and Religion: Foundations of an Emerging Field*. London: Routledge, 2012.

Stout, Harry. *The Divine Dramatist: George Whitefield and the Rise of Modern Evangelicalism*. Grand Rapids, MN: Eerdmans, 1991.

Strauss, Neil. 'The Broken Heart and Violent Fantasies of Lady Gaga.' *Rolling Stone*, 8 July 2010.

Sullivan, Danny. 'Kim Kardashian Talks Social Media: Loves Instagram, Twitter is Fun, Facebook for Branding.' *Marketing Land*, 6 February 2013. https://marketingland.com/live-blog-kim-kardashian-talks-social-media-brand-building-more-32738.

Sutton, Matthew Avery. *Aimee Semple McPherson and the Resurrection of Christian America*. Cambridge: Cambridge University Press, 2007.

Swash, Rosie. 'George Michael: Arrested After Crashing Car into Shop.' *The Guardian*, 6 July 2010.

Tarico, Valerie. 'Christian Right Mega-Church Minister Faces Mega-Mutiny for Alleged Abusive Behaviour.' *Salon*, 3 April 2014. www.salon.com/control/2014/04/03/christian_right_mega_church_minister_faces_mega_muntiny_for_abusive_behavior_partner/.

The Kabbalah Centre. 'Karen Berg.' https://kabbalah.com/en/people/karen-berg.

Thumma, Scott, Travis, Dave and Warren, Rick. *Beyond Megachurch Myths: What We Can Learn from America's Largest Churches*. New York: John Wiley and Sons, 2007.

Tiidenberg, Katerin. *Selfies: Why We Love (and Hate) Them*. Bingley: Emerald Publishing, 2018.

Tillich, Paul. *Dynamics of Faith*. New York: Perennial Classics, 1956.

Tinsley, Omise'eke Natasha. 'Beyonce's Lemonade Is Black Woman Magic.' *Time*, 25 April 2016. http://time.com/4306316/beyonce-lemonade-black-woman-magic/.

Tipton, Steven. *Getting Saved from the Sixties*. Berkeley, CA: University of California Press, 1982.

Tolson, Andrew. 'The History of Television Celebrity: A Discursive Approach.' *Celebrity Studies* 6(3) (2015): 341–354.

Tracy, Abigail. 'The Genius of Kim Kardashian.' *Vanity Fair Hive*, 10 June 2016. www.vanityfair.com/news/2016/06/kim-kardashian-kimoji-entrepreneurship.

Turner, Graeme. *British Cultural Studies: An Introduction*. London: Routledge, 2003 (3rd edn).

Turner, Graeme. *Understanding Celebrity*. London: Sage, 2004.

Turner, Graeme, Bonner, Frances and Marshall, David. *Fame Games: The Production of Celebrity in Australia*. Cambridge: Cambridge University Press, 2000.

Van Biema, David. 'The Hipper-Than-Thou Pastor.' *Time*, 6 December 2007.

Vigilant Citizen. '"God is a Woman" by Ariana Grande: The Esoteric Meaning.' 30 July 2018. https://vigilantcitizen.com/musicbusiness/god-is-a-woman-by-ariana-grande-the-esoteric-meaning/.

Walter, Tony. 'Judgement, Myth and Hope in Life-centred Funerals.' *Theology* 119(4) (2016): 253–260.

Ward, Geoff. 'The Passion of Tiger Woods: An Anthropologist Reports on Golf, Race and Celebrity Scandal.' *Sport in Society: Cultures, Commerce, Media, Politics* 17(6) (2014): 855–858.

Ward, Pete. *Selling Worship*. Milton Keynes: Paternoster, 2005.

Ward, Pete. *Gods Behaving Badly: Media, Religion and Celebrity Culture*. Waco, TX: Baylor University Press/SCM Press, 2011.

Warner, Robert. *Reinventing English Evangelicalism 1966–2001*. Milton Keynes: Paternoster, 2007.

Williams, Raymond. The analysis of culture. In *Cultural Theory and Popular Culture: A Reader*. Edited by John Storey. 56–63. Hemel Hempstead: Harvester Wheatsheaf, 1994.

Williams, Raymond. *Keywords: A Vocabulary of Culture and Society*. London: Fontana, 1976.

Williams, Raymond. *Marxism and Literature*. Oxford: Oxford University Press, 1977.

Williams, Raymond. *Culture*. London: Collins, 1981.

Winston, Diane, ed. *Small Screen, Big Picture: Television and Lived Religion*. Waco, TX: Baylor University Press, 2009.

Ynet. 'Madonna: I am Not Jewish, I am an Isrealite.' 23 May 2015. www.ynetnews. com/articles/0,7340,L-4640263,00.html.

YouTube. 'Lenny Henry is reunited with the five orphans he met in 2010.' www.you tube.com/watch?v=851VkU5CbNc.

YouTube. 'Jane Fonda on her Legendary Workout Videos.' www.youtube.com/watch? v=8YEMrzoRsRY.

Zhao, Shanyang, Grasmuck, Sherri and Martin, Jason. 'Identity Construction on Facebook: Digital Empowerment in Anchored Relationships.' *Computers in Human Behavior* 24 (2008): 1816–1836.

Index